MW01293674

"With the background of pas
Dempsey provide Christ follo
and strategy for spiritual form
walk with Christ and grounded in the Word of God. Whether you are just
beginning your Christian walk, leading others to walk with Christ, or weary
in your own walk, this book points us back to the Scriptures to remind us that
he who started a good work in you will carry it on to completion until the day
of Christ Jesus."
— Brian Autry, executive director, Southern Baptist Convention
of Virginia

"As a pastor I am constantly concerned about the spiritual well-being of the
people at Thomas Road Baptist Church. Spiritual growth is an important part
of discipleship, and we need simple but effective approaches to aid and assist
the people we serve. Rod Dempsey and Dave Earley have been helping people
know and follow Jesus for more than three decades. Their simple approach to
spiritual growth—loving God, loving one another, and loving our neighbor with
connected habits and disciplines—will help you and your church follow Jesus."
— Jonathan Falwell, senior pastor, Thomas Road Baptist Church,
Lynchburg, VA

"Rod Dempsey and David Early present a solid approach to spiritual formation. Their emphasis is biblical, balanced, practical, and effective. They challenge us to engage in a life of spiritual development by loving God, loving one
another, and loving our neighbors. Their insights will challenge your thinking,
stir your heart, and bless your soul. Don't miss it!"
— Ed Hindson, founding dean, distinguished professor of religion,
Rawlings School of Divinity, Liberty University

"I have known Rod and Dave for many years. They planted a church together
in Columbus, Ohio, and saw that church grow and multiply new churches
through evangelism, small groups, and solid discipleship. Now they teach at
Liberty University on discipleship and leadership development. They are about
developing healthy disciples, in healthy groups, in healthy churches. Their book
Spiritual Formation Is . . . will help anyone develop habits and disciplines that
will deepen their love for God, love for one another, and love for their neighbor."
— Ed Stetzer, Billy Graham Chair of Church, Mission, and Evangelism,
executive director, Billy Graham Center, Wheaton College

"This book represents decades of study and experience. The wisdom the authors have gleaned, and share here, could result in a quantum leap in your spiritual life. This volume is intensely practical, appropriately candid, thorough, balanced, profound, and yet easily understandable to the hungry hearted. I enthusiastically recommend *Spiritual Formation Is . . .* to all who desire a deep walk with Christ and a fruitful life."

—Harold Vaughan, founder, Christ Life Ministries

Spiritual Formation Is...

DAVE EARLEY AND ROD DEMPSEY

Spiritual Formation Is...

How to Grow in Jesus with Passion and Confidence

B&H
ACADEMIC
NASHVILLE, TENNESSEE

Spiritual Formation Is . . .
Copyright © 2018 by Rod Dempsey and Dave Earley Ministries

Published by B&H Academic
Nashville, Tennessee
All rights reserved.

ISBN: 978-1-4627-7675-7

Dewey Decimal Classification: 248.84
Subject Heading: DISCIPLESHIP \ SPIRITUAL LIFE \ CHRISTIAN LIFE

The web addresses referenced in this book were live and correct at the time of the book's publication but may be subject to change.

Some material in Chapter 16 previously published in *Prayer: The Timeless Secret of High-Impact Leaders*, ©2008, AMG Publishers. Used by Permission.

Cover illustration © ixpert/shutterstock.

Printed in the United States of America

1 2 3 4 5 6 7 8 9 10 VP 23 22 21 20 19 18

Contents

Part 3: The Practices and Disciplines of Spiritual Formation

The Upward Disciplines — Loving God

The Inward Disciplines — Love One Another

The Outward Disciplines — Love Your Neighbor

Introduction

STOP! Press the PAUSE button. Don't read anything further until you consider this suggestion. We ask you to do something different with this book. Begin at the end.

Go to the back of the book (Appendix) and take the assessments. First, take the "Personal Spiritual Growth Assessment." Second, if you want to determine the spiritual health of a group, take the inventory called "Group Spiritual Growth Assessment."

After taking the assessments, you can read the book with renewed insight. You should also have a new commitment to "work out your own salvation with fear and trembling" (Phil 2:12).

Now press the CONTINUE button.

We believe spiritual growth is predicated on spiritual health.

We believe the foundation for spiritual health is obedience to Christ.

We believe a healthy believer will make for a healthier church.

We believe a church filled with vibrant, healthy Christ followers will become a vibrant, healthy church.

We believe spiritual health is the result of obeying the three-directional command of Jesus to: (1) love God; (2) love one another; and (3) love your neighbor.

We believe spiritual formation is a personal, individual obligation. No one else can grow for you. You will notice that we included many of our own personal struggles with spiritual growth throughout this book.

We believe this book will be a blessing to you. We are also excited that as a result of reading and applying it, you will grow in your love for God, love for other believers, and love for your neighbors. As you do, you will be more like Jesus.

Part 1

The Principles of Spiritual Formation

1

The Process of Being Changed to Be Like Jesus

Dave Earley

Maybe you can identify with me. Several years ago I had a problem. As I dealt with a debilitating illness, I realized that not only was my body sick, but my soul needed attention as well.

I was not the person I wanted and needed to be. I found that I was becoming shallow and superficial. My life was way too busy. My heart and soul were too cluttered. My spiritual attention span was getting shorter and shorter. I kept struggling with the same sin issues.

I wanted to be an agent of transformation in the lives of others. But my spiritual tanks were empty, and I felt as though I had nothing to give. I wanted to be more loving, but I battled impatience and irritability with others' imperfections.

I was struggling to hear God's voice clearly. My relationship with God had become dry and stagnant. I had always longed to go deeper with God, but I was losing that desire.

I realized that if I did not do something about it soon, I was headed for trouble.

So I took drastic but practical measures. I created a spiritual growth plan, rearranged my schedule to carve out an hour every night to focus on my personal spiritual growth, and dove into a stringent reading and study plan.

Over the next few years, I worked my way through nearly forty books on spiritual formation. Some came from ancient authors and some from the present. At first I was not totally sure what spiritual formation was, but I knew I needed it. Eventually the pieces began to fit into place. Everything pointed back to one key biblical text on spiritual growth.

> Now the Lord is the Spirit, and where the Spirit of the Lord is, there is freedom. We all, with unveiled faces, are looking as in a mirror at the glory of the Lord and are being *transformed* into the same image from glory to glory; this is from the Lord who is the Spirit. (2 Cor 3:17–18, emphasis added)

Put simply, spiritual formation is the process of being changed to be more like Jesus. Yet as the apostle Paul explains in this passage, there is more to it than that. Expressed more fully, spiritual formation is:

> **an ongoing, gradual process of glorious transformation into the image of Jesus by the Spirit of God that is available to every believer as a result of honestly and intentionally seeking the face of God.**

Let's walk back through 2 Cor 3:17–18 and break down this definition:

> **Spiritual formation is the process of being changed to be more like Jesus.**

The goal of spiritual transformation is becoming more like Jesus. If you are not changing and growing, you are not experiencing spiritual formation. This is a process of change Paul refers to as a glorious transformation.

A Glorious Transformation

Four glorious transformations are seen in Scripture. The transfiguration of Jesus (Matt 17:1–2), the transfiguration of Moses (Exod 34:29–35), the ongoing transformation of the believer (2 Cor 3:17–18), and the ultimate transformation of the believer (1 Cor 15:50–54).

The Transfiguration of Jesus

> After six days Jesus took Peter, James, and his brother John and led them up on a high mountain by themselves. He was *transfigured* in front of them, and his face shone like the sun; his clothes became as white as the light. (Matt 17:1–2, emphasis added)

The Transformation of Moses

In 2 Cor 3:6–18, Paul argues that the new covenant of forgiveness in Christ is vastly superior to the old covenant of the law. The new covenant gives life (v. 6), provides righteousness (v. 7), is permanent (v. 11), brings hope (v. 12), is Christ centered (v. 16), and is empowered by the Spirit (v. 17).

In 2 Corinthians 3, Paul exposed the emptiness of religion without a growing relationship with God. He contrasted living a life of religious law with living a life in the Spirit of God. He spoke of the old covenant's "ministry that brought death" (3:7) and the greater glory of the new covenant.

Then Paul went back to the Old Testament book of Exodus and the initial giving of the law. God is a Spirit, and when he wanted to reveal himself to man visibly, it was by reducing all of his attributes to light, which often was seen as a fire. In this case Paul referred to the transfiguration of Moses as the divine glory manifested on Moses's face when he left the presence of God and brought the Ten Commandments down from Mount Sinai.

> As Moses descended from Mount Sinai—with the two tablets of the testimony in his hands as he descended the mountain—he did not realize that *the skin of his face shone as a result of his speaking with the LORD.* (Exod 34:29, emphasis added)

The glory reflected on Moses's face was so intensely brilliant that looking at him was like looking at the sun. The Israelites couldn't even look at his face. Not surprisingly, a man with such a supernatural glow on his face scared people. So Moses wore a veil in public so as to not blind people.

> When Aaron and all the Israelites saw Moses, *the skin of his face shone!* They were afraid to come near him. . . . But whenever Moses went before the LORD to speak with him, he would remove the veil until he came out. After he came out, he would tell the Israelites what he had been commanded, and the Israelites would see that *Moses's face was radiant.* Then Moses would put the veil over his face again until he went to speak with the LORD. (Exod 34:30–35, emphasis added)

When Moses spent honest time talking with the Lord, it showed all over his face. His face would brilliantly glow with the blinding glory of God.

The glow of God on Moses's face was not a self-generated shine. His glow was actually an *after*glow from being in the presence of God. The radiant glory of God was the source of the original shine, and what lingered on Moses's face was merely a reflection of that. So in a sense Moses was a moon to God's sun. He had no light of his own; he merely reflected that which came from God.

The difference between the new covenant and the old is that under the old covenant, the transformation for Moses was on the outside. But under the new covenant, the transformation begins on the inside. Under the old covenant, the glory on Moses's face was temporary and quickly faded. Under the new covenant, we are given an eternal glory that fades not.

The Transformation of the Believer

> We all, with unveiled faces, are looking as in a mirror at *the glory of the Lord and are being transformed* into the same image from glory to glory. (2 Cor 3:18, emphasis added)

The goal of spiritual formation is the glorious transformation of the believer. Moses is the only one under the old covenant who is described as having a glorious transformation. But Paul states that under the new covenant, transformation is available and expected of "all" believers.

My parents truly gave themselves to God the last two decades of their lives. They read the Word, they prayed, they served, they participated in Christian community through their church and small group, they gave generously, and they did it in a fresh, honest, daily manner.

My mom became a prayer warrior as she learned to pray in the presence of God, and it showed. In spite of her many physical pains and limitations, her beautiful blue eyes and amazingly generous spirit radiated the life and love of God to all she met. God's love shone through her and warmed even coldhearted people. Strangers remarked how deeply they were touched by just a few minutes in her presence.

At the end of his life, my dad also had the glow. Even through the last year and a half of his life, when he had terminal cancer throughout the bones in his upper body, he went all in for God. Being around him was like being in sunshine. He spent time with God every morning, and God shone through him the rest of the day. Even though he was in his eighties, he would always be at his Sunday-morning-greeter position outside the church, smiling and waving at every car entering our church parking lot. Even when he was too weak to stand, he would sit to greet people arriving for worship. Guests would comment on the man whose smile made them feel accepted and welcome.

Transformation into the Image of Jesus

Now the Lord is the Spirit, and where the Spirit of the Lord is, there is freedom. We all, with unveiled faces, are looking as in a mirror at the glory of the Lord and are being *transformed into the same image* from glory to glory; this is from the Lord who is the Spirit. (2 Cor 3:17–18, emphasis added)

When we gaze into the face of Jesus and see the glory of the Lord, a process of transformation takes place. The verb *transformed* (*metamorphoo*) describes the amazing change a caterpillar experiences as it becomes a butterfly. An ugly worm all wrapped in itself becomes a beautiful winged creature able to soar away. This aptly describes the transformation made through the gospel as self-centered sinners are changed into glorious, holy overcomers reflecting the glorious love of Jesus.

The ultimate goal of this glorious transformation is that the believer would reflect the image of Jesus. Paul wrote that we are changed "into the same image" (2 Cor 3:18). Later he clarified that the glorious image is the image of Christ. The goal of Paul's ministry was to labor "until *Christ* is formed [*morphoo*] in you" (Gal 4:19, emphasis added).

Paul told the Ephesians that the role of saints was to be equipped for ministry and grow until they all reached a place of maturity "measured by *Christ's* fullness" (Eph 4:11–13, emphasis added). He also told the Romans "that all things work together for the good of those who love God, who are called according to his purpose. For those he foreknew he also predestined *to be conformed to the image of his Son*" (Rom 8:28–29, emphasis added).

Spiritual formation is the process of transformation that occurs as a believer becomes more and more like Jesus. Spiritual formation is not merely doing spiritual disciplines. It is not merely about reading more chapters of the Bible or keeping a better spiritual journal. Those are merely means of helping us gaze into the face of Jesus so we may be transformed to think, act, feel, and look more like him.

That's what happened with Sarah. She came to our ministry in Las Vegas as a twenty-two-year-old college graduate and new wife. Her passion was working with sex-trafficking victims and students. When Sarah smiles, the glow of God is evident in her life. As you get to know her, you are drawn to her infectious love and joy. Her Christlike personality, warm smile, and love caused her to be selected homecoming queen at her large public high school. Sarah radiates the beauty of Jesus.

The goal of spiritual transformation is becoming more like Jesus. But how does this occur? The rest of the passage explains.

Spiritual Formation Is an Ongoing Process— "From Glory to Glory"

> Now the Lord is the Spirit, and where the Spirit of the Lord is, there is freedom. We all, with unveiled faces, are looking as in a mirror at the glory of the Lord and are being transformed into the same image *from glory to glory*; this is from the Lord who is the Spirit. (2 Cor 3:17–18, emphasis added)

The phrase *from glory to glory* describes the gradual nature of spiritual formation. Spiritual formation is an ongoing process of moving from one degree of glory to another. It is growing in the ever-increasing splendor of the image of Jesus.

The apostle Paul wrote half the letters in the New Testament. He and Barnabas were the first intentional new covenant missionary church planters in history. He was a powerfully gifted apostle. He got to see the glories of heaven. Many consider him to be one of the greatest Christians of all time.

Yet, as he approached the end of his life, he was not content with his level of spiritual formation. He did not think he had arrived. He kept pressing on in his pursuit of Christ and commanded that same attitude of us.

> Not that I have already reached the goal or am already perfect, but I make every effort to take hold of it because I also have been taken hold of by Christ Jesus. Brothers and sisters, I do not consider myself to have taken hold of it. But one thing I do: Forgetting what is behind and reaching forward to what is ahead, I pursue as my goal the prize promised by God's heavenly call in Christ Jesus. Therefore, let all of us who are mature think this way. (Phil 3:12–15)

In a similar manner, the apostle Peter begins and ends his second letter by commanding his readers to continue growing in various areas of Christlikeness.

> For this very reason, *make every effort* to supplement your faith with goodness, goodness with knowledge, knowledge with self-control, self-control with endurance, endurance with godliness, godliness with brotherly affection, and brotherly affection with love. (2 Pet 1:5–7, emphasis added)

But *grow* in the grace and knowledge of our Lord and Savior Jesus Christ. To him be the glory both now and to the day of eternity. (2 Pet 3:18, emphasis added)

Spiritual formation does not happen all at once. It happens by degrees as a gradual, ongoing process of becoming more and more like Jesus.

Spiritual Formation Is the Result of Seeking the Face of God— "Looking as in a Mirror"

We all, with unveiled faces, are looking as in a mirror at the glory of the Lord and are being transformed into the same image from glory to glory; this is from the Lord who is the Spirit. (2 Cor 3:18, emphasis added)

You tend to become like the one you behold.

Several years ago the *New York Times* published an article about research suggesting long-married couples begin to look alike. The article begins:

Science is lending support to the old belief that married couples eventually begin to look alike.

Couples who originally bore no particular resemblance to each other when first married had, after 25 years of marriage, come to resemble each other, although the resemblance may be subtle, according to a new research report.

Moreover, the more marital happiness a couple reported, the greater their increase in facial resemblance.[1]

So just as people who have been happily married for twenty-five years begin to look alike, it would stand to reason that as we consistently pursue our relationship with Jesus, over the years we will look more and more like him. As we look into the mirror of God's Word and strive to apply what it shows us about ourselves and our Savior (Jas 1:22–24), we begin to mirror him.

Spiritual formation is more than doing disciplines and keeping rules. Spiritual formation is about a deepening relationship with God that causes us to look more and more like him. It grows as we pursue him.

Spiritual Formation Is Enabled by the Spirit of the Lord

Now the Lord is the Spirit, and where *the Spirit of the Lord* is, there is freedom. We all, with unveiled faces, are looking as in a mirror at the glory of the Lord and are being transformed into the same image from glory to glory; *this is from the Lord who is the Spirit.* (2 Cor 3:17–18, emphasis added)

None of us has the power to transform ourselves into the image of Jesus. The Holy Spirit is the agent of transformation. He changes as we intentionally spend time in the presence of the Lord. We will discuss this further in chapter 9.

Spiritual Formation Is for Every Believer—"We All"

> *We all*, with unveiled faces, are looking as in a mirror at the glory of the Lord and are being transformed into the same image from glory to glory; this is from the Lord who is the Spirit. (2 Cor 3:18, emphasis added)

The Corinthian church was not known for its spiritual maturity. In the first half of 1 Corinthians, Paul rebuked the members for their shortcomings. After a year and a half pastoring them, Paul went on to plant more churches in other places. In his absence things fell apart. Factions developed, sexual morals crumbled, worship got off track.

Yet Paul wrote to these Corinthians that spiritual formation is available for all of us. Spiritual formation is for every believer, not just the spiritually elite, not just the mystical, not just the introverted, not just the highly disciplined, and not just the people who have no problems in their lives. All of us can and must put ourselves in position to receive the grace of God to be changed into the image of Jesus.

Conclusion

Spiritual formation is the process of being changed to be more like Jesus. It is the ongoing, gradual process of glorious transformation into the image of Jesus by the Spirit of God that is available to every believer as a result of honestly and intentionally seeking the face of God. It is the fruit of a relationship with God.

In the rest of this book, we will unpack this definition of spiritual formation in a way that I trust will help you better understand how it works and how to do your part.

First, we will give you some expanded answers to common questions about spiritual formation. Next, we will discuss the essential principles of spiritual growth. Then, we will explain the primary spiritual disciplines necessary to experience spiritual transformation. They are grouped under the headings: loving God, loving one another (i.e., fellow believers), and loving our neighbors (i.e., nonbelievers). Last, we will help you create a workable plan for your ongoing spiritual growth and health.

— Quote to Consider —

"He must increase, but I must decrease."

—John the Baptist, John 3:30

— Questions to Ponder —

1. Do you ever feel like the author, desperately in need of spiritual transformation?
2. What is the goal of spiritual formation?
3. Based on 2 Cor 3:17–18, how would you define *spiritual formation*?
4. What is the difference between spiritual formation and spiritual disciplines?

Note

1. Daniel Goldman, "Long-Married Couples Do Look Alike, Study Finds," *New York Times*, August 11, 1987, accessed January 20, 2017, http://www.nytimes.com/1987/08/11/science/long-married-couples-do-look-alike-study-finds.html.

2

Spiritual Formation Is . . .

Measured by Spiritual Fruit

Dave Earley

M ost of us aren't living the lives God intended for us. The New Testament describes a life few of us consistently experience. I'm certainly not the first to make this observation.

Vance Havner was one man who astutely expounded the situation, arguing, "Most Christians have been subnormal for so long that when they become normal they are thought to be abnormal." He further noted, "What we call revival is simply New Testament Christianity, the saints getting back to normal."[1]

The goal of spiritual formation is to help you live the life God intended. It enables you to live the *normal* Christian life. Maybe you have tried to live a good Christian life and failed. I know I have done that more than I care to admit. I have found that it is impossible to live a good Christian life on my own. But one person lived the life God intended, and he can help us do the same.

Jesus Lived the Life the Father Intended

On two separate occasions the Scriptures record the joyous proclamation of the Father, "This is my beloved Son, with whom I am well-pleased" (Matt 3:17; 17:5). Jesus, the sinless Son of God in human flesh, was the one person who perfectly and thoroughly lived as the Father intended humankind to live on earth. The goal of spiritual formation is to change us into people living as Jesus did, living life as the Father intended.

In the first chapter, we described spiritual formation as "the process of being changed to be more like Jesus." But what exactly does "being changed to be more like Jesus" look like? Jesus taught that it would entail the bearing of spiritual fruit.

Spiritual Fruit

Remember, spiritual formation is a spiritual reality. You can't have *spiritual* formation without the high-level activity of the Holy *Spirit*, including the production of *spiritual fruit* through us.

The night before Jesus was crucified, he used the analogy of a vine and branches to teach about the nature of true discipleship (John 15:1–16).[2] In the analogy, he is the vine, and we are the branches.

> Live in me. Make your home in me just as I do in you. In the same way that a branch can't bear grapes by itself but only by being joined to the vine, you can't bear fruit unless you are joined with me. "I am the Vine, you are the branches. When you're joined with me and I with you, the relation intimate and organic, the harvest is sure to be abundant. Separated, you can't produce a thing. (John 15:4–5 MSG)

> My Father is glorified by this: that you produce much fruit and prove to be my disciples. (John 15:8)

Our ultimate goal in life is, of course, to glorify God. But how is this done? Jesus said God is glorified as we are producing fruit, *and* in producing fruit we prove to be his disciples. In bearing fruit, we live the lives God intended. Bearing spiritual fruit is evidence of spiritual formation.

According to Jesus, the measure of spiritual formation is not the number of seminars attended, workbooks finished, certificates earned, or courses completed. The measure of spiritual formation is fruit. No fruit, no spiritual formation.

At least eight times in John 15, Jesus mentioned the importance of fruit bearing in the life of a disciple. In fact, in his mind, the notion of a sterile branch was completely unacceptable. For the disciple, fruit bearing is so significant that Jesus used hyperbole and stated the branch that failed to produce fruit is removed and cast into the fire. His point is clear: no fruit, no discipleship. No fruit, no spiritual formation.

> Every branch in me that does not produce fruit he removes, and he prunes every branch that produces fruit so that it will produce more fruit. . . . If anyone does not remain in me, he is thrown aside like a branch and he withers. They gather them, throw them into the fire, and they are burned. (John 15:2, 6)

Later in this passage, Jesus teaches that the *purpose* of discipleship is fruit bearing. He states that he appointed disciples *with the express purpose* that they would bear fruit.

I appointed you to go and produce fruit and that your fruit should remain. (John 15:16)

What is spiritual fruit? In nature, fruit is the overflow of abundance of life. When a branch has life flowing through it, fruit is the natural result. When it stops producing fruit, it is evidence that the plant is not healthy, or it may be dead.

In the Christian life, fruit is the overflow of God. When people have God flowing through them (John 7:37–39), spiritual fruit is the natural result. This fruit takes three primary forms.

Christlike Character

As a Christ follower, you are inhabited by the Holy Spirit. The Spirit of Jesus is in you. He is working on you, in you, for you, and through you. He is the primary agent of spiritual transformation (2 Cor 3:18). His presence does not immediately make us perfect, but it does perfect us. It transforms us more and more into the image of Jesus.

But the fruit of the Spirit is love, joy, peace, patience, kindness, goodness, faithfulness, gentleness, and self-control. (Gal 5:22–23)

Obviously *as the life of Jesus streams through the disciple, the personality of Jesus will be formed in the disciple*. The more of Jesus that flows through you, the more like Jesus you will be.

On the positive side, Jesus was honest, righteous, and true. He breathed life into hopeless situations. His life overflowed with amazing love, joy, peace, patience, grace, and mercy. He also was highly spiritually influential. He made the lives of people around him better.

At the same time, Jesus never undermined the production of spiritual fruit. In fact, he never sinned. He never was unrighteously angry. He experienced no guilt or shame. He lived under the canopy of favor from God the Father who looked at him and said, "This is my beloved son, with whom I am well pleased" (Matt 3:17).

Jesus did not lust and was not self-centered or rebellious. He was never bitter. Even though he suffered intense pain, rejection, betrayal, abandonment, and abuse, he did not complain.

Jesus lived above despair and depression. He did not give into fear, worry, or anxiety. He refused to be bitter. He forgave his enemies. He faced the enemy's most vicious attacks courageously.

The Capacity to Fully Receive and Give God's Love

JESUS'S LOVE FULLY RECEIVED

> As the Father has loved me, I have also loved you. Remain in my love. If you keep my commands you will remain in my love, just as I have kept my Father's commands and remain in his love. (John 15:9–10)

John Piper, in commenting on John 15, writes:

> Since the fruit is simply the out-forming of what has passed through the branch from the vine, we should ask, "What is it that we receive from the vine?" Jesus' answer is *love*. Abiding in Jesus means abiding in his love according to verse 9—"As the Father has loved me, so have I loved you. Abide in my love." "Abide in me" is replaced by "Abide in my love," and this shows more specifically what we receive when we are united to the vine, namely, the sap of divine love.[3]

The apostle John, the author of John 15, lived faithfully for God for more than seventy years. He was a beloved pastor and wrote five books of the New Testament: the Gospel of John, 1, 2, and 3 John, and the book of Revelation.

He was a receiver of God's love. In fact he was so full of God's love that it marked his life. Interestingly, John did not refer to himself in his letters as the apostle John or even by his name John. He referred to himself only as the disciple Jesus loved (John 13:23; 19:26; 20:2; 21:20). If you asked John to sign his name, he would write, "Loved by Jesus."

JESUS'S LOVE FULLY GIVEN

> I have told you these things so that my joy may be in you and your joy may be complete. This is my command: Love one another as I have loved you. (John 15:11–12)

What we receive from the vine flows through the branch and leads to fruit. As the love of Jesus flows into our lives, it flows out of our lives to God and others.

But before you can fully give God's love, you must first experience God's love. You must let God's love heal your past, bring meaning to your present, and provide hope for your future.

I pray that he may grant you, according to the riches of his glory, to be strengthened with power in your inner being through his Spirit, and that Christ may dwell in your hearts through faith. I pray that you, being *rooted and firmly established in love*, may be able to comprehend with all the saints what is *the length and width, height and depth of God's love*, and *to know Christ's love* that surpasses knowledge, *so that you may be filled with all the fullness of God*. (Eph 3:16–19, emphasis added)

A person rooted deeply in God's love is a spiritually formed person. As people overflow with God's love, they are a walking revival. They are viral. They are contagious. They are divinely attractive. They are a supernatural magnet. They are spiritually influential. They are living the normal Christian life.

As Ray Stedman states in his book *Body Life*, "The supreme mark of the life of Jesus Christ within the Christian is, of course, *love*. Love that accepts others as they are. Love that is tenderhearted and forgiving. Love that seeks to heal misunderstandings, divisions, and broken relationships."[4]

Connecting Others to Jesus

Just as the fruit of a healthy apple tree is apples and the fruit of a healthy orange tree is oranges, the fruit of a healthy disciple is more disciples. Following his evangelistic conversation with a Samaritan woman in John 4, Jesus gave his disciples a challenge that clearly linked fruit bearing with evangelism and discipleship.

Don't you say, "There are still four more months, and then comes the harvest"? Listen to what I'm telling you: Open your eyes and look at the fields, because they are ready for harvest. The reaper is already receiving pay and gathering fruit for eternal life, so that the sower and reaper can rejoice together. (John 4:35–36)

Jesus had just finished introducing the woman to himself, and the harvest he referenced was one of disciples. The result of their conversation was that she told others and they also believed in him (John 4:39).

People who are living the normal Christian life are so full of God that it powerfully affects others. They are viral. They are infectious. They are carriers. Other people get infected with the love of God and want to live the normal Christian life too.

The Requirement of Fruit Bearing

Remain in me, and I in you. Just as a branch is unable to produce fruit by itself unless it remains on the vine, neither can you unless you remain in me. I am the vine; you are the branches. The one who remains in me and I in him produces much fruit, because you can do nothing without me. (John 15:4–5)

Jesus made his point clear. Just as a branch is merely a dead and useless piece of wood without its connection to the vine, a disciple is destined to barrenness apart from a close connection to him. Without actively pursuing intimacy with Jesus, the disciple has no hope of bearing spiritual fruit.

The vital communion between the disciple and Jesus is of such utmost importance that Jesus mentioned it *ten times* in John 15:4–10! There is no discipleship without fruit bearing, and there is no fruit bearing without abiding in Christ.

Spiritual formation occurs only as we abide in Christ. When we abide in Christ, we cannot help but bear spiritual fruit.

On one hand, Jesus stated it is impossible to live a fruitful life without abiding in him. He stated, "Just as a branch is unable to produce fruit by itself unless it remains on the vine, neither can you unless you remain in me" (John 15:4). He also said, "You can do nothing without me" (John 15:5).

On the other hand, Jesus promised, "The one who remains in me and I in him produces much fruit" (John 15:5). The key to producing fruit is abiding in Christ.

Conclusion

Spiritual formation is not measured by the number of years one has been a Christian, the number of books one has read, the number of Bible verses memorized, or the list of seminars one has attended. It is measured by spiritual fruit.

— Quote to Consider —

"When Jesus put on flesh, He made human existence 'sacred.' Thus, when you are inhabited by Jesus through His Holy Spirit, your life takes on the 'sacred' characteristic as well. This does not mean that you become God or incapable of sinning like Jesus was in His incarnation. However, it does mean that something is qualitatively different about you at the core."

—Adam L. Feldman[5]

— Questions to Ponder —

1. What is the evidence of spiritual formation?
2. What are the three primary expressions of spiritual fruit?
3. What is the requirement for fruit bearing?
4. Which of the three expressions of fruit are you most lacking?

Notes

1. Vance Havner, *Hearts Afire* (Grand Rapids: Revell, 1952), 104.

2. For a similar discussion on this passage and the role of spiritual fruit in discipleship, see Dave Earley and Rod Dempsey, *Disciple Making Is . . . : How to Live the Great Commission with Passion and Confidence* (Nashville: B&H Academic, 2013), chapter 11.

3. John Piper, from sermon given October 1, 1981, at Bethlehem Baptist Church, Minneapolis, MN, accessed October 22, 2011, http://www.desiringgod.org/resource-library/sermons/i-chose-you-to-bear-fruit.

4. Ray Stedman, *Body Life: The Book That Inspired a Return to the Church's Real Meaning and Mission* (Grand Rapids: Discovery House, 1995), 433. Kindle Edition.

5. Adam L. Feldman, *Journaling: Catalyzing Spiritual Growth through Reflection* (Ellicott City, MD: Milltown Publishing, 2013), 8.

3

A Powerful Partnership

Dave Earley

When people are serious about getting physically fit, they hire a personal trainer. A good personal trainer assesses, prescribes, instructs, and encourages. Trainers also provide feedback and accountability in order to help their clients improve their physical fitness. They often use cross training and combine several types of exercises to work various parts of the body for maximum benefit.

In the spiritual life, the Holy Spirit is our resident "personal trainer." He assesses, prescribes, instructs, and encourages us. If we learn to listen, he also provides helpful feedback on our progress.

He uses cross training.

When I speak of *cross training*, I am using that term in a dual sense. First, I am talking about the cross of Christ and the power of the gospel to change us. Spiritual formation is a gospel-centered activity. Our hearts are redeemed and renewed as the story of our life is rewritten by the story of the gospel. Second, when I speak of cross training, I am speaking of the fact that the Holy Spirit uses a variety of means to form us and shape us spiritually, mentally, and emotionally.

A Joint Effort

In the first chapter, we described spiritual formation as *the process of being changed to be more like Jesus.* In this chapter, we learn that *spiritual formation is a joint effort, a powerful partnership.* God does his part and we must do ours.

Paul told the church at Philippi,

> Therefore, my dear friends, just as you have always obeyed, so now, not only in my presence but even more in my absence, work out your own salvation with fear and trembling. For it is God who is working in you both to will and to work according to his good purpose. (Phil 2:12–13)

This passage, written to believers, is not about how to be saved, but how to grow. It does not say "work for" your salvation, because you can't add anything to what Jesus already did! During a physical workout you exercise to develop your body, not to get a body. God gives us the desire and the power to make good choices that please him. That's *his* part. But we also need to do *our* part. We must *work out* the salvation God has put into us. We must make those choices and commitments that please him.

In the next two chapters, we will look at the choices and actions that constitute our means of spiritual formation. In this chapter, we will we discuss the first four means.

Eleven Means of Spiritual Formation

1. **Daily pursuit (Exod 33:7–11)**
2. **Dependent faith (John 15:4–5; 7:37–39)**
3. **Diligent effort (2 Pet 1:3–7)**
4. **Joyful perseverance (Jas 1:2–4; Heb 12:5–8)**
5. Intentional mind renewal (Rom 12:2)
6. Loving God in every circumstance, event, and experience (Rom 8:28–29)
7. Being equipped and doing ministry (Eph 4:11–13)
8. Submission to the Potter (Isa 64:8; Jer 18:6)
9. Positive friendships (Prov 27:17)
10. Learning from good teachers and mentors (Luke 6:40)
11. Choosing to practice spiritual discipline (1 Tim 4:7–9; 1 Cor 9:24–27)

Daily Pursuit

As we saw in chapter 1, at its core spiritual formation is the result of honestly and intentionally seeking the face of God (2 Cor 3:16–18). The example Paul used in 2 Corinthians points back to Moses's tent of meeting.

> Now Moses took a tent and pitched it outside the camp, at a distance from the camp; he called it *the tent of meeting.* Anyone who wanted to consult the LORD would go to the tent of meeting that was outside the camp. . . .

When Moses entered *the tent, the pillar of cloud would come down and remain at the entrance to the tent, and the* LORD *would speak with Moses.* As all the people saw the pillar of cloud remaining at the entrance to the tent, they would stand up, then bow in worship, each one at the door of his tent. *The* LORD *would speak with Moses face to face, just as a man speaks with his friend.* (Exod 33:7, 9–11, emphasis added)

This passage contains three phrases that are especially helpful in our journey into spiritual formation. They speak of the role of place, access, and friendship as foundational for God's transforming work in Moses's life.

A Special Place

Moses had a *place* where he met with God: the tent of meeting. It was away from the hustle of humanity. He went there to shut himself away *from* people so he could shut himself away *with* God.

There is something special about having a particular place to meet God. During my first semester in college, my special place with God was an operating room. Let me explain.

My college was new and had not yet built dormitories. Instead, they rented properties all over town to house students. I happened to be one of a few dozen young men crammed into a tiny ancient hospital building downtown in a rough neighborhood. Its only redeeming virtue was that it was located on a road called Grace Street and it had an operating room, which was the only room not occupied by three or four young men. All that was in it was a desk and a chair. We used it as a prayer room.

When I started college, I was also just starting my journey with God and knew I needed to get close to him. So I locked myself in the operating room at noon every weekday. For the first half hour, I let God speak to me through his Word. I usually read a psalm and wrote in a small notebook what I thought God was saying to me through the psalm. The second half hour I spoke with God.

At first an hour seemed like a long time. After a few days, however, it flew by because *God manifested his presence in that place.* After a few days of getting used to having a daily, sit-down appointment with God, I found myself longing for that time in the operating room each day. I would scramble back from class and dash up the stairs to the operating room in order not to be late for my twelve o'clock appointment with God. Every day God was faithful to meet me and operate on my heart. Each day the Chief Surgeon of Grace Street would use the scalpel of his Word to cut a bit deeper. During that first semester, he cut away from my heart fear, bitterness, lust, selfish ambition, and pride, among other spiritual cancers.

I wish I had the words to convey how amazing it was to meet with God an hour each day. I would love to explain how much it changed and enriched my life. But I can't. I don't have the skill, the time, or the space. But I think you might have an inkling of how transforming it was for me to sit across the desk from my Creator, my Redeemer, my Father, my Counselor, and my Best Friend every day.

The Privilege of Access

The pillar of cloud that greeted Moses in the tent of meeting was the visible manifestation of God's presence. When Moses went into the tent to meet God, God was there to meet him. In Moses's day, few enjoyed this direct, personal, and intimate access to the manifest presence of God. Not so today! We all are invited to "come boldly to the throne of grace" (Heb 4:16 NKJV). God is always willing, ready, and available to meet with us when we make time for him.

We may think God is reluctant to meet with us. We have a mistaken notion that during the time God is meeting with us, he is rolling his eyes, looking at his watch, gazing out the window, and wondering when this encounter will be over so he can move on to other concerns. We think the love he has for us is, at best, a have-to-tolerate-us love. Wrong! God loves us with a head-over-heels, absolutely-crazy-about-us, can't-wait-to-spend-time-with-us, wanting-it-to-last-a-little-longer type of love. Therefore, he gives us privileged access to himself.

The Privilege of Friendship

"The LORD would speak with Moses face to face." Moses employed the *privilege* of friendship with God. He took full advantage of the access afforded him and met with God face to face. Nothing was hidden. It was an honest, open dialogue between friends.

Spiritual formation is about God's presence, not his absence. It is the product of a close relationship. It is primarily about relationship, not disciplines, duties, ritual, or religion.

On the backside of the desert, during his forty years of wandering with the Israelites, Moses developed a familiar friendship with God in that tent of meeting. That is the secret of Moses's inner strength. It was the foundation of his transformation.

Make the commitment to pursue God every day.

Dependent Faith

Remain in me, and I in you. Just as a branch is unable to produce fruit by itself unless it remains on the vine, neither can you unless you *remain in me*. I am the vine; you are the branches. The one who *remains in me* and I in him produces much fruit, because you can do nothing without me. (John 15:4–5, emphasis added)

The branch cannot produce fruit without being connected to the vine. As we discussed in chapter 2, followers of Jesus cannot bear spiritual fruit apart from being connected to Jesus. This connection is a matter of dependent faith.

Everything we try to do ultimately comes to nothing unless it is done as a result of a conscious, abiding dependence upon Jesus (John 15:5).

Jesus stood, and He cried in a loud voice, If any man is thirsty, let him come to Me and drink! He who *believes in Me [who cleaves to and trusts in and relies on Me]* as the Scripture has said, From his innermost being shall *flow [continuously] springs and rivers of living water.* But He was speaking here of the Spirit. (John 7:37–39 AMPC, emphasis added)

The secret of having springs and rivers of living water flowing through your life is daily dependency on the Holy Spirit.

Make the commitment to live in dependency on the Holy Spirit.

Diligent Effort

His divine power has given us everything required for life and godliness through the knowledge of him who called us by his own glory and goodness. By these he has given us very great and precious promises, so that through them you may share in the divine nature, escaping the corruption that is in the world because of evil desire. For this very reason, *make every effort* to supplement your faith with goodness, goodness with knowledge, knowledge with self-control, self-control with endurance, endurance with godliness, godliness with brotherly affection, and brotherly affection with love. (2 Pet 1:3–7, emphasis added)

Peter speaks of God's giving us everything we need for life and godliness. He also speaks of our sharing in the divine nature. This nature is revealed as we are changed into the image of Jesus.

As we noticed from Phil 2:12–13, God has done, is doing, and will do his part in our spiritual formation. It is all available to us. But it is also up to us to do our part. According to Peter, our part is to *"make every effort to supplement"* our faith. We must be diligent to grow to become more like Jesus.

Peter listed eight character qualities, starting with faith and ending with love. He assumed his readers, members of the scattered church, already had saving faith. He stressed that the goal is for believers to live lives of love. In between he noted six other qualities. I do not think they are sequential, and in many ways they overlap. I think Peter was simply making the point that after starting out in faith we must not stop. In order to grow in Christlikeness, we need to put forth intentional effort to grow in Christian character. We will discuss this is more detail in chapter 11.

Make the commitment to add to your faith.

Joyful Perseverance

Consider it a great joy, my brothers and sisters, whenever you experience various trials, because you know that the testing of your faith produces endurance. And let endurance have its full effect, so that you may be mature and complete, lacking nothing. (Jas 1:2–4)

The book of James was written by a son of Joseph and Mary. Joseph and Mary had children after Jesus was born; James was the eldest. He is described in the Bible as someone who initially thought Jesus was crazy (Mark 3:21). He became a follower of Jesus *after* he saw Jesus risen from the dead (Matt 13:55–58; Mark 6:3; John 7:3–5; Acts 1:14; 1 Cor 9:5; Gal 1:19). Seeing a formerly dead man walk and talk has a way of convincing skeptics.

James later became the head pastor of the church of Jerusalem (Acts 15:11–21). This church included tens of thousands of people until they experienced severe deprivation and persecution. Then many of them were forced to flee. Soon they were spread all over the world (Acts 8:1–4).

Living as refugees, James's scattered flock faced persecution from the pagans, from the Jews, and from the Romans. Their lives were extremely difficult. Many were separated from family and friends. Most could get only the lowliest jobs.

To these persecuted people James wrote his pastoral letter, the book of James. In it he gives the goal of spiritual formation as maturity and completeness in Christ. He also gives an important means of spiritual formation: joyful perseverance through the difficulties and pain. The idea is that if we go through hard times without quitting, we can come out more like Jesus on the other side.

James is convinced that persevering through problems leads to spiritual maturity; he states that our responsibility is not merely to grit our teeth and press on. No. We must "consider it a great joy" when we "experience various trials" (Jas 1:2).

As we dig more deeply into this text, we see that James was writing to Christians: "My brothers and sisters." He is not commanding us to *feel* something but commanding us to do something: "Consider it a great joy"!

Note that he does not say *if* you face trials, but *whenever* you face trials. Trials are inevitable.

The word translated "experience" pictures being completely surrounded or swallowed up by trials. The word used for "many" is *piokilois,* which means "diverse, varied, and manifold."

Knowing or *because you know* is in grammatical agreement with the command to "*consider it a great joy*" and introduces the knowledge needed to choose to evaluate trials as a basis for rejoicing. You can consider trials all joy *because* you know something. "Knowing" describes "a knowledge gained from personal experience." James is saying, "This is nothing new; you have seen this in other areas of life, and you'll find it to be true in this area of life also."

Endurance means to "abide under." It is an active word that means when we get hit with trials, we do not passively stand there and fold our hands but actively forge on ahead. Enduring is given as a command: *Do not interrupt the chain of results.* This word reminds us that it is our *continual duty* to let perseverance finish its work. In other words, *do not quit, but persevere. Hang in there. Keep going!*

The end result of enduring trials with joy is spiritual maturity and Christ-likeness "*so that you may be mature and complete, lacking nothing.*" Joyful perseverance through painful problems forms us spiritually in all areas of life.

Make the commitment to respond to trials with joyful endurance.

— Quote to Consider —

"Nothing shapes your life more than the commitments you choose to make. Your commitments can develop you or they can destroy you, but either way, they will define you. Tell me what you are committed to, and I'll tell you what you will be in twenty years. We become whatever we are committed to."

—RICK WARREN[1]

∼ Questions to Ponder ∼

1. Which, if any, of these means of growth surprised you?
2. Which of these means of growth are you currently practicing?
3. Which do you need to add to your cross training regimen?

Note

1. Rick Warren, *The Purpose-Driven Life* (Grand Rapids: Zondervan, 2002), 180.

4

Doing Your Part

Dave Earley

In the previous chapter, we began to discuss how spiritual formation is a partnership (Phil 2:12–13). God does his part by "working in you both to will and to work according to his good purpose." Our part is to make the effort to do "his good purpose."

As we have seen, there are several means of spiritual formation. In the previous chapter, we introduced the first four. In this chapter, we will describe several more.

Eleven Means of Spiritual Formation

1. Daily pursuit (Exod 33:7–11)
2. Dependent faith (John 15:4–5; 7:37–39)
3. Diligent effort (2 Pet 1:3–7)
4. Joyful perseverance (Jas 1:2–4; Heb 12:5–8)
5. **Intentional mind renewal (Rom 12:2)**
6. **Loving God in every circumstance, event, and experience (Rom 8:28–29)**
7. **Being equipped and doing ministry (Eph 4:11–13)**
8. **Submission to the Potter (Isa 64:8; Jer 18:6)**
9. **Positive friendships (Prov 27:17)**
10. **Learning from good teachers and mentors (Luke 6:40)**
11. **Choosing to practice spiritual discipline (1 Tim 4:7–9; 1 Cor 9:24–27)**

Intentional Mind Renewal

Charles Swindoll, in his book *The Tale of the Tardy Oxcart*, tells of the radical transformation of a life through the power of God's Word. In 1787, the *Bounty*, a British ship, set sail. After a difficult journey, she arrived in the South Seas ten months later. After six months, the ship was to return back to England. But the sailors rebelled. They refused to leave the paradise-like setting and the beautiful hospitality of the native girls. Eventually all but nine of the mutinous sailors were captured and punished. But those nine eventually moved to another, more remote island. There they distilled whiskey and lived debauched and riotous lives. Soon murder and disease spread until only one man and a few women and children were left.

Desperate for direction, Alexander Smith found a Bible among his possessions. He began to read it. He was so impressed by what he read that he taught it to the women and children. Twenty years later, the remote island was discovered by another English ship. What was found was a virtual utopia where people lived in decency, harmony, prosperity, and peace. There was no crime, disease, immorality, insanity, or illiteracy. When asked how this was accomplished, Smith's only answer was "The Bible."[1]

The powerful spiritual transformation of the population of a small island happened as a result of intentional mind renewal in the Word of God. The apostle Paul commented on the power of intentional mind renewal to bring about spiritual transformation.

> Do not be conformed to this age, but be transformed by the renewing of your mind, so that you may discern what is the good, pleasing, and perfect will of God. (Rom 12:2)

Of course, one of the Holy Spirit's favorite tools for transformation is his Word. The Word of God grows us in many ways. It is food for our growth (1 Pet 2:20). It is bread for our souls (Matt 4:4). It is the *Holy* Spirit's instrument to make us *holy* (John 17:17) and clean (John 15:3). It is the basis of our discipleship (John 8:31) and the means of liberating our souls (John 8:32). It is the apparatus the Lord uses to teach us, correct us, and equip us for service (2 Tim 3:16).

Notice that merely *having* the Word does not transforms us. It is having our minds *renewed* by the Word (Rom 12:2). *Ingesting* the Word causes us to grow (1 Pet 2:2; Matt 4:4). *Experiencing* the truth of the Word sets us free (John 8:32).

Cognitive Behavior Therapy (CBT) is a popular method of helping people resolve troublesome feelings and behaviors. During the course of treatment, people learn how to identify and change destructive or disturbing thought patterns that have a negative influence on behavior and emotions. An overly simplified description is:

Change the thoughts, change the feelings.
Change the feelings, change the behaviors.

Changing our thoughts to think more biblically will positively impact our feelings. This will ultimately result in the transformation of our behaviors. I call it Cognitive *Bible* Therapy.

In chapter 13, we will go into much more detail about the spiritual discipline of Bible intake. Until then, make it your goal to live in the Word, read it, study it, memorize it, meditate on it, teach it, and apply it.

Loving God in Every Circumstance, Event, and Experience

Most of us know Rom 8:28 well, but we should consider it in light of the next verse.

We know that all things work together for the good of those who love God, who are called according to his purpose. For those he foreknew he also predestined to be conformed to the image of his Son, so that he would be the firstborn among many brothers and sisters. (Rom 8:28–29)

These verses tell us that God's ultimate goal for everything that happens to us is that we might "be conformed to the image of his Son." In other words, God wants to use every circumstance, event, and experience in our lives as part of our spiritual formation. It is amazing to think that every event in life, good or bad, is orchestrated by God and can make us more like Jesus if we allow it to do so.

Note that our part is loving God and living as those called according to his purpose. Our challenge and responsibility is to love God in spite of and in the midst of whatever we face. If good things happen to us, we must keep loving God and not make the mistake of forgetting him. On the other hand, if bad happens to us, we must love the Lord anyway.

Being Equipped and Doing Ministry

And he himself gave some to be apostles, some prophets, some evangelists, some pastors and teachers, equipping the saints for the work of ministry, to build up the body of Christ, until we all reach unity in the faith and in the knowledge of God's Son, growing into maturity with a stature measured by Christ's fullness. (Eph 4:11–13)

Paul told the Ephesian church that God had given them gifted individuals with the express purpose of training them, the church members, to do the work of the ministry. This would result in the growth of the body of Christ.

Churches are weak when the clergy does the ministry and the laity merely receives it. God's plan is for gifted leaders to equip *others* to do the ministry.

I have been a pastor for more than thirty years and a professor for more than ten. My observation is that spiritual growth happens better when someone is serving in a ministry rather than merely sitting in a classroom. People grow more as a result of a seven-day mission trip where they are serving than seven months of merely sitting in a church service watching.

Several years ago, I led a home Bible study for spiritual seekers. Eventually they all were saved, but I realized none of them was serving. So I taught on the value of serving for several weeks. Then I told them I was shutting down the group until they all had a place of service. Steve was the last guy to get plugged into a ministry. An engineer who had never previously attended a church, he decided to serve in our Wednesday evening children's club called AWANA (Approved Workmen Are Not Ashamed). In the club, the kids played games, heard a Bible lesson, and memorized Scripture.

A month after Steve began to serve, I saw him and asked how he was doing. "Great!" he said a little too excitedly. "I have grown more in the last few weeks serving than I did when I was just sitting in your group. These kids are challenging me, and I love it!"

My first six years as a follower of Jesus, I grew largely because I got heavily involved in ministry. I served poor kids, led a Bible study at my high school, and served as chaplain of my wrestling team. I taught Sunday school and Jr. Church. I shared Evangelism Explosion gospel presentations and preached on the streets in England. I did door-to-door evangelism in New York City. I was a traveling youth evangelist, then served as a youth pastor and led a choir. I also led worship. I led college prayer/discipleship groups and helped lead a Child Evangelism Fellowship after-school Good News Club. I led a home Bible study and then served as interim pastor of a small church.

We grow when we are serving, not merely sitting. We grow through giving out and not just by taking in. The life of Christ *in* us was designed to flow *through* us as we minister to others.

Submission to the Potter

The book of Jeremiah is a collection of Jeremiah's prophecies that are probably grouped more by subject than chronology. It is filled with imagery and spiritual object lessons. One of my favorites is this one in chapter 18. It is the image of the potter and the clay.

> This is the word that came to Jeremiah from the LORD: "Go down at once to the potter's house; there I will reveal my words to you." So I went down to the potter's house, and there he was, working away at the wheel. But the jar that he was making from the clay became flawed in the potter's hand, so he made it into another jar, as it seemed right for him to do. The word of the LORD came to me: "House of Israel, can I not treat you as this potter treats his clay?"—this is the LORD's declaration. "Just like clay in the potter's hand, so are you in my hand, house of Israel." (Jer 18:1–6)

When I was a young art student, one day my art teacher brought a potter's wheel into class. It was a large, round, flat wheel that spun around and was powered by a small motor. Then she showed us how to make pots using the clay and the wheel.

If I close my eyes, I can still smell the fresh clay. I can feel the soft, smooth, wet mud in my hands. I can feel it spinning and gently rising under the pressure I put on it. I can see the ugly, shapeless clay slowly taking shape as I molded it.

When you form clay on a potter's wheel, you may have two major problems with the clay. First, if it gets too dry, it is no longer pliable. That's why the potter is always feeding it more water. Second, no matter how good the potter is, if the clay is not centered, the pot is doomed. It will never become beautiful. It ends up a lopsided mess. And the potter must start over.

In the passage quoted above (Jer 18:1–6), for an unknown reason the clay was marred in the potter's hands. It either got dry or off center. The potter could not work with it anymore. So he had to start all over. Valuable time was lost, and possibly the size of the pot was reduced.

From this passage several truths are evident. First, God is the potter. We are the clay. Life is the wheel. Second, God is in the process of molding us to be what he wants us to be. When it comes to our spiritual formation, a third truth is also evident: as living clay, we can and must play our part in the process. We must submit to the will of the potter. As the Lord asks in the passage above, "Can I not do with you as this potter does?" God, the Potter, has the right to do anything he wants with us. Our responsibility is to cooperate with and surrender to his will.

Positive Friendships

Iron sharpens iron, and one person sharpens another. (Prov 27:17)

The Spirit uses other people to sharpen us. The people we choose to be around will determine to a great degree the kind of people we will be. Maybe their example challenges us to reach higher. Maybe it is their insights. It could be their rebuke. It might be their attitude.

When I was a young Christian, I had a friend named Roy. He was a contagious Christian and a huge catalyst to my spiritual growth. Every time I was around him, I was motivated to live for God. He was always talking about the Christian book he was reading, or the new Christian music he was listening to, or the person he was loving to Christ. He prodded me out of bed on Saturdays to go minister to poor children. He dragged me to prayer meetings and Bible studies several nights a week. He challenged me when my dating life was out of line.

I would have not grown nearly as much without Roy in my life. He sharpened me. Spiritual formation is accentuated by being around growing people who challenge us to grow. Spiritual formation happens in relationships.

Learning from Good Teachers and Mentors

A disciple is not above his teacher, but everyone who is fully trained will be like his teacher. (Luke 6:40)

Jesus reminded his disciples of a common first-century truth about rabbis and their students: The goal of the mentor is to reproduce his life in his students. The goal of students is to model the life of their mentor.

When I was a new Christian, I had a youth pastor named Lee. He was a marvelous teacher, and from him I learned the basics of the Christian life. He plugged me into ministries. He coached my spiritual journey. He let me do ministry alongside him. Much of my spiritual DNA came from his passion for evangelism and disciple making.

Beyond that, I enjoyed playing sports with him. I also cherished the times when we just hung out at his house or he took us waterskiing. When I was with him, I watched him like a hawk. I wanted to learn and grow. He was my model.

Humanly speaking, I would not have grown as rapidly as I did without Lee in my life. His teaching and mentoring made the difference.

Choosing to Practice Spiritual Discipline

Train [discipline; go in the gym and sweat] yourself in godliness. For the training of the body has limited benefit, but godliness is beneficial in every way, since it holds promise for the present life and also for the life to come. This saying is trustworthy and deserves full acceptance. For this reason we labor and strive, because we have put our hope in the living God, who is the Savior of all people, especially of those who believe. (1 Tim 4:7–10)

Paul told Timothy, you must *train, discipline yourself in godliness.* Godliness is the overall goal of someone who is becoming more like Jesus. It is the result of spiritual discipline. The word for "train yourself" in the original language is *gym-naz-o,* where we get our word *gymnasium.* It comes from a root word that means "naked" and literally means "go into the gym, strip down, and sweat." We will discuss this means of spiritual growth in chapter 10.

— Quote to Consider —

"We all travel through life experiencing events and circumstances that shape us. How we interpret them determines how God forms and transforms our inner person."

— BILL HULL[2]

— Questions to Ponder —

1. Which, if any, of these means of growth surprised you?
2. Which of these means of growth are you currently experiencing?
3. Which do you need to either be more committed to or add to your training routine?

Notes

1. Charles R. Swindoll, *The Tale of the Tardy Oxcart* (Waco, TX: Word, 1998), 50–51.

2. Bill Hull, *The Complete Book of Discipleship* (Colorado Springs: NavPress, 2006), 191.

Part 2

The Philosophy of Spiritual Formation

5 Spiritual Formation Has Strong Historical Roots

Rod Dempsey

On May 25, 1969, I was standing on the shore of a creek beside the little church my family attended in southern West Virginia. The pastor was standing in the middle of the creek where he had just baptized my twin sister and two others who had recently prayed to receive Christ. Now they were making their profession public. They were confessing to the world that Jesus was Lord of their lives.

I stood there as a nine-year-old boy, and something happened in the core of my being. My heart started to beat quickly. My eyes sharpened their focus. My ears started to hear what the pastor was saying. Suddenly the words the pastor was speaking came alive to me. He was asking, "Is there anyone else who would come forward this beautiful morning and believe in Jesus and follow him in baptism?" As soon as he spoke those words, I knew that there was at least one other person who needed to come forward that morning and follow Christ, and that person was me! I turned to my friend and asked him to hold my Sunday school material, and he promptly said, "No way." I quickly placed the material on the shore of the creek, and I answered the call of the Spirit to come to Jesus. I went forward and was baptized; soon thereafter ten other people responded to the Spirit's call to come and follow Jesus. My spiritual formation journey was just beginning.

That little country church was and is like many other churches in our land. It had a good and godly pastor who loved the Lord, loved people, and preached the gospel. The gospel moved through the community, and many people were being saved. The church needed to build a bigger building in the community, and people were excited to attend. The church proclaimed the good news of the gospel every service. However—and I am careful at this point to say "however"—the church was not able to translate decisions for Christ into disciples of Christ. Outside of Sunday school, there was no organized plan for spiritual formation. Obedience to Christ was called for, but no plan was given for how to obey Christ consistently. No follow-up after a public profession. No personal mentoring.

Failing to have a plan for developing followers of Jesus is not a new phenomenon. A 2015 report released by the Navigators claims only 1 percent of church leaders say "today's churches are doing very well at discipling new and young believers."[1] As a result, many of the people who make professions for Jesus are not able to "put off" the old man and "put on" the new man. This leads many professed followers of Jesus to turn back to their former manner of life and injure not only the testimony of the gospel but also their own spiritual life. In my own life, I struggled for years with desiring to follow Christ but not being able to "walk worthy of the Lord" (Col 1:10). The spirit was willing but the flesh was weak. My spiritual formation was up and down but mostly down. Unfortunately, many followers of Jesus have a similar experience, and unfortunately again, the church of Jesus throughout history has been up and down as it relates to spiritual formation.

THE THREE HISTORICAL STAGES OF SPIRITUAL FORMATION IN THE CHURCH

The First Period

For the sake of understanding spiritual formation in church history, there are three broad eras of the church. The first period is from the day of Pentecost in Acts 2 to two Roman emperors' pronouncement in AD 313 that Christianity would be a legal religion in the empire.[2] In this first era of church history, we observe some of the earliest forms of spiritual formation. It began on the Day of Pentecost, when Peter preached the good news of the gospel and thousands professed Jesus as Lord and followed him in baptism, and the church began to develop certain habits.

> They devoted themselves to the apostles' teaching, to the fellowship, to the breaking of bread, and to prayer.
>
> Everyone was filled with awe, and many wonders and signs were being performed through the apostles. Now all the believers were together and held all things in common. They sold their possessions and property and distributed the proceeds to all, as any had need. Every day they devoted themselves to meeting together in the temple, and broke bread from house to house. They ate their food with joyful and sincere hearts, praising God and enjoying the favor of all the people. Every day the Lord added to their number those who were being saved. (Acts 2:42–47)

This period was marked by love for God (apostles' teaching), love among believers (fellowship, breaking of bread . . . the believers were together and had unity), and love for their fellowman (they sold their property and gave to *anyone* who had need, and they were enjoying the favor of *all* the people). The early church still had the great commandment and the new commandment ringing in their ears. They were determined to follow the central teaching of Jesus, and they did this in the context of intense persecution and poverty. Rodney Stark, who writes extensively about this stage in church history, argues, "In the midst of the squalor, misery, illness, and anonymity of ancient cities, Christianity provided an island of mercy and security."[3]

One result of being spiritually formed (loving God with all their heart) was serving the poor and needy. According to Stark,

> In 251 the bishop of Rome wrote a letter to the bishop of Antioch in which he mentioned that the Roman congregation was supporting fifteen hundred widows and distressed persons. This was not unusual. In about the year 98 CE, Ignatius, bishop of Antioch, advised Polycarp, the bishop of Smyrna, to be sure to provide special support for widows. As Paul Johnson suggests, "The Christians . . . ran a miniature welfare state in an empire which for the most part lacked social services."[4]

We see an early example of this sacrificial serving in Acts 6:1, where the church at Jerusalem had to come up with a plan to serve the Hellenistic Jews because "their widows were being overlooked in the daily distribution [of food]." The early Christians believed in and took seriously the words of Jesus:

> Love the Lord your God with all your heart, with all your soul, and with all your mind. This is the greatest and most important command. The

second is like it: Love your neighbor as yourself. All the Law and the Prophets depend on these two commands. (Matt 22:37–40)

Jesus summarized the entire teaching of the law in just two commands. Later, in the upper room, Jesus instructed his disciples that, in addition to loving God and loving their neighbors, they also needed to "love one another" (John 13:35). Jesus told his followers he wanted them to band together in communities (Matt 16:18: "I will [future tense] build my church") and be involved in aggressively loving God (upward), aggressively loving one another (inward), and aggressively loving their neighbors (outward).

Spiritual formation in the first few centuries was marked by simple obedience to the great commandment, to love God and love our neighbor, and the new commandment to love one another. This simple belief and practice served the church well. The church grew rapidly as it employed this simple and reproducible model of spiritual formation. So rapidly, in fact, that Acts 6:7 reports, "So the word of God spread, the disciples in Jerusalem increased greatly in number, and a large group of priests became obedient to the faith." Simple and reproducible concepts can multiply quickly.

As the church spread and went about loving God, loving one another, and loving neighbors, the result was that Christians excelled in the ministry of mercy. As Stark noted:

> Christianity taught that mercy is one of the primary virtues—that a merciful God requires humans to be merciful. Moreover, the corollary that because God loves humanity, Christians may not please God unless they love one another was even more incompatible with pagan convictions. But the truly revolutionary principle was that Christian love and charity must extend beyond the boundaries of family and even those of faith, to all in need.[5]

The Father's love for us prompted him to send Jesus to show mercy to the people he created. To be spiritually formed in the first era of the church age was to follow the simple commands of Jesus to love God, love our brothers and sisters in Christ (Acts 2:42–47), and love all the people God created. Such love and mercy prompted Christ to come and serve humankind by taking their punishment, the ultimate act of mercy (Phil 2:1–10). Spiritually formed people in the early church were Spirit-filled people as well. Gilchrist Lawson wrote, "The early Christian writers, both the Greek and Roman Fathers of the Church, testify to the fact that in the second century and later, it was customary to pray for Christians to be filled with the Spirit, just as they were prayed for in Bible times."[6] Spirit-filled believers were following Christ's example of loving God preeminently and loving one another personally. As a result, they would take the form of servants and become the visible hands and feet of Jesus to a desperately needy world.

The Second Period

The second period is a much longer era and covered roughly AD 313 to 1517. This era started, as previously mentioned, with a joint decree by the two Roman emperors Constantine and Licinius. Known as the Edict of Milan, this decree stated that the church would no longer be persecuted by the Roman government, and property and land that had been seized by the government would be restored to the church. The edict yielded a union between church and state, by which the Roman emperor exercised significant control over the church. Gilchrist Lawson argues, "The simple New Testament form of church government" grew into "a great ecclesiastical hierarchy seeking to usurp power over both the souls and bodies of men."[7] One unintended consequence was that this period saw a separation of the clergy (who were elevated to nobility status) from the laity (who came to be regarded as something like spiritual peasants). This long era in church history and spiritual formation was marked by hierarchical rule at the church/state level and poverty and illiteracy among the masses. Many term this period the "dark ages" in part because the church seemingly lost its way.

Spiritual formation during this period took a variety of forms. Mystics sought direct, supernatural encounters with God. The monastic movement emerged as a way for some particularly committed believers to express their commitment to holiness. Formal theological study advanced in the High Middle Ages with the advent of Scholasticism. And perhaps most notably for our purposes, the laity came to rely on clergy members as mediators between God and humans. Churches during this time also emphasized architecture to communicate the transcendence of God, and, because most people could not read and books were reserved for the ruling classes, spiritual formation of the masses was severely limited.

The Third Period

The third period began in 1517, when Martin Luther nailed his Ninety-Five Theses to the door of the Castle Church in Wittenberg, Germany. Many Christian leaders during this period influenced spiritual formation or, more accurately, spiritual transformation. The turning point, however, was the Protestant Reformation's recovery of the gospel of salvation by faith in Jesus alone, its restoration of Scripture's primacy as a rule of faith and practice, and its emphasis on the priesthood of every believer. The Reformation was a rich era in church history, which saw figures like Luther, Ulrich Zwingli, John Calvin, and Menno Simons. They emphasized the need for each individual believer to develop a vibrant, personal relationship with God, strengthened by practice of the spiritual disciplines. In the centuries following the Reformation, many of its Protestant heirs continued to emphasize personal spiritual formation. Among those noteworthy in this regard were seventeenth-century German Pietists like Philipp Jakob Spener, the Moravians, Puritans like Richard Baxter, First Great Awakening revivalists like John Wesley and George Whitefield, Second Great Awakening revivalists like Francis Asbury and Charles Finney, and later revivalists like D. L. Moody. These figures and others sought to return the church as a whole and its individual members to spiritual vibrancy.

This stage continues to the present and consists of multiple streams. Most of those streams share a basic understanding of how a church should operate and foster spiritual formation. They agree that each believer needs to pursue an ever-deepening personal relationship with God, aided by personal Bible reading, prayer, and intake of biblical preaching. Debates on spiritual formation center largely on which secondary means best advance the believer's relationship with Christ. Neil Cole summarizes:

> From Baptist to Brethren, from Mennonite to Methodist, the changes in the system [of church life] are relatively untouched over the centuries. Music or no music? Pipe organ or electric guitar? Whether seeing tall ceilings with stained-glass windows, or meeting in a box building without windows, the actual system of church has gone relatively unchanged. You have the priests or pastors, the Sunday service with singing and a sermon, the weekly offering, the pulpit with pews, and the church building.[8]

This means spiritual formation within the church has remained relatively unchanged since the Reformation.

Yet within this rich Protestant heritage, there is need for further reformation when it comes to spiritual formation. Personal mentorship within the membership of local churches seems to have been greatly neglected in recent years. On this point Dallas Willard remarked, "I know of no current denomination or local congregation that has a concrete plan and practice for teaching people to do 'all things whatsoever I (Jesus) have commanded you.'"[9] For spiritual formation to be revived at the local church level, believers must be taught to obey the commands of Jesus, and the commands of Jesus can be summarized as loving God, loving one another, and loving our neighbors. The church that makes progress toward spiritually forming its members will become healthy and revived.

⟞ Quote to Consider ⟝

*"Pastors need to redefine success. The popular model
of success involves the ABCs—attendance, buildings,
and cash. Instead of counting Christians, we need
to weigh them. We weigh them by focusing on the
most important kind of growth—love, joy, peace,
longsuffering, gentleness, goodness, kindness, and so on—
fruit in keeping with the gospel and the kingdom."*

—DALLAS WILLARD[10]

⟞ Questions to Ponder ⟝

1. What are the three major divisions in church history?
2. How did Constantine negatively impact church history?
3. What did Dallas Willard say about the current state of spiritual formation in local churches?

Notes

1. "New Research on the State of Discipleship," Barna, December 1, 2015, *Barna.org*, accessed December 28, 2017, https://www.barna.com/research/new -research-on-the-state-of-discipleship.

2. David F. Wright, "313 The Edict of Milan," *Christianity Today*, accessed February 19, 2018, http://www.christianitytoday.com/history/issues/issue-28/313-edict -of-milan.html.

3. Rodney Stark, *The Triumph of Christianity: How the Jesus Movement Became the World's Largest Religion* (New York: HarperCollins, 2012), 112. Kindle Edition.

4. Stark, 113.

5. Stark, 112–13.

6. J. Gilchrist Lawson, *Deeper Experiences of Famous Christians* (1911; reprt., San Francisco: Jawbone, 2017), 538–40. Kindle Edition.

7. Lawson, 660–61.

8. Neil Cole, *Church 3.0: Upgrades for the Future of the Church* (New York: Jossey-Bass Leadership Network Series, 2010), 7. Kindle Edition.

9. Dallas Willard, "Spiritual Formation and the Warfare between the Flesh and the Human Spirit," dwillard.org, accessed February 19, 2018, http://www.dwillard.org /articles/artview.asp?artID=81.

10. Dallas Willard, "The Apprentices," accessed March 16, 2018, http://www .dwillard.org/articles/individual/apprentices-the.

6 Spiritual Formation Affects the Whole Person

Rod Dempsey

In the fall of 1978, I was a struggling sophomore in college and a struggling follower of Jesus. In fact, it would have been more accurate to say I was not following God's will; I was following my will. My decisions determined my direction. I wanted to go to the college I wanted. I wanted to be with my friends. I wanted to join a fraternity. I wanted . . . I wanted. I was the epitome of self-rule, and I was the perfect picture of a miserable person. Everything I did or everything I attempted was a failure. My foolish pride prevented me from surrendering to the redeeming and restoring Christ. I was one measly and puny secret-agent Christian.

One night some nice people knocked on my dorm room door. They were from Campus Crusade, and they began to share the good news of the gospel with me. About halfway through their presentation, I stopped them and informed them that, even though it may not look like it, I was one of them. Later that night, alone in my room, I looked at the ceiling and prayed. I asked God for mercy and for help. I prayed, "Lord if you let me get home from this semester without severely disciplining me, I will give my life to you."

The semester ended and I went home for break. When I got home, I had mixed feelings. I wanted to follow Christ, but I did not have the power to say yes to God and no to the world, the flesh, and the devil. If you looked up *double-minded* in the dictionary, I believe my picture may have been there. My friends were still influencing me. My will was still paramount. The lust of the flesh, the lust of the eyes, and the pride of life were still drawing me away from the simplicity of obeying and following Christ. I will not say that I forgot about my "foxhole" prayer, but I certainly was not working out my "salvation with fear and trembling" (Phil 2:12). My internal struggle and turmoil continued. I can relate to the apostle Paul's description of his internal struggle:

> For I do not understand what I am doing, because I do not practice what I want to do, but I do what I hate. Now if I do what I do not want to do, I agree with the law that it is good. So now I am no longer the one doing it, but it is sin living in me. For I know that nothing good lives in me, that is, in my flesh. For the desire to do what is good is with me, but there is no ability to do it. For I do not do the good that I want to do, but I practice the evil that I do not want to do. Now if I do what I do not want, I am no longer the one that does it, but it is the sin that lives in me. So I discover this law: When I want to do what is good, evil is present with me. (Rom 7:15–21)

The battle in my mind, will, and emotions waged throughout the break. The war continued until my mother asked me to attend the New Year's Eve service with the family at our church. Even then I told her I had made plans to go out to ring in the new year with my friends. Still my plans and still my friends. As the time drew near either to go out with my friends to a party or to gather with believers, I found myself getting ready to go to church. It was as if the Lord had me in a tractor beam, and I was being drawn to the door of the church. When the time came in the service to light a candle signifying commitment to the Lord in the coming year, I finally surrendered everything to him. With tears streaming down my face and with halting voice, I made a public profession that night that "I was tired of running and I would go anywhere and do anything the Lord asked me to do."

I did not know it, but I experienced a Rom 12:1–2 moment:

> Therefore, brothers and sisters, in view of the mercies of God, I urge you to present your bodies as a living sacrifice, holy and pleasing to God; this is your true worship. Do not be conformed to this age, but be transformed by the renewing of your mind, so that you may discern what is the good, pleasing, and perfect will of God.

Christ redeemed me at salvation, and now I made a presentation of my body to the Lord. My decision to follow Christ meant I would separate from worldly temptations.

The next Sunday a deacon came up to me after the morning service and asked me a question that I will never forget. He asked, "Did you really mean what you said the other night?" I was a little bit taken aback, but I said yes. I was tired of being a secret-agent follower of Jesus. He informed me that I should take some steps and attend a Christian college where I could get started right in my newfound commitment to Christ. Long story short: within a couple of weeks I had transferred away from an environment where I was struggling to walk in a manner worthy of the Lord, and I was enrolled in an environment where I was encouraged to grow in my walk with Christ. My journey of "working out my salvation with fear and trembling" was finally beginning. I had surrendered my will and presented my body. Now I had to learn the progressive and daily habits that would enable me to grow in my love for God—spiritual formation.

When you look at the various injunctions in Scripture to love the Lord, you encounter several different phrases that express virtually the same thing. We are exhorted to love God with our total being. Sometimes we are commanded to love God with our hearts and minds. Other times it is heart and soul. Jesus instructed us to love God with all of our heart, soul, mind, and strength. Paul instructs us to love God with our spirit, soul, and body. Notice these passages:

- Moses's instruction at the giving of the law: "Imprint these words of mine on your *hearts and minds*, bind them as a sign on your hands, and let them be a symbol on your foreheads" (Deut 11:18, emphasis added).
- Moses's explanation of how we should love God: "Do not listen to that prophet's words or to that dreamer. For the LORD your God is testing you to know whether you love the LORD your God with all your *heart* and all your *soul*" (Deut 13:3, emphasis added).
- Moses's counsel that we can find God: "But from there, you will search for the LORD your God, and you will find him when you seek him with all your *heart* and all your *soul*" (Deut 4:29, emphasis added).
- David's exhortation to Israel: "Now determine in your *mind and heart* to seek the LORD your God. Get started building the LORD God's sanctuary so that you may bring the ark of the LORD's covenant and the holy articles of God to the temple that is to be built for the name of the LORD" (1 Chr 22:19, emphasis added).
- Solomon's dedication of the temple: "And when they come to their senses in the land where they were deported and repent and petition you in their captors' land: 'We have sinned and done wrong; we have been wicked,' and when they return to you with all their *heart* and all their *soul*" (1 Kgs 8:47–48, emphasis added).
- Solomon's instruction in Proverbs: "Guard your *heart* above all else, for it is the source of life" (Prov 4:23, emphasis added).

- Jesus's command: "Love the Lord your God with all your *heart*, with all your *soul*, and with all your *mind*" (Matt 22:37, emphasis added). In Mark 12:30 (emphasis added) the phrase goes this way: "Love the Lord your God with all your *heart*, with all your *soul*, with all your *mind*, and with all your *strength*."
- Paul's admonition to the church at Rome: "Therefore, brothers and sisters, in view of the mercies of God, I urge you to present your *bodies* as a living sacrifice, holy and pleasing to God; this is your true worship. Do not be conformed to this age, but be transformed by the renewing of your *mind*, so that you may discern what is the good, pleasing, and perfect will of God" (Rom 12:1–2, emphasis added).
- Paul's instruction to the church at Thessalonica: "Now may the God of peace himself sanctify you completely. And may your whole *spirit, soul, and body* be kept sound and blameless at the coming of our Lord Jesus Christ" (1 Thess 5:23, emphasis added).
- And from the book of Hebrews: "For the word of God is living and effective and sharper than any double-edged sword, penetrating as

QUADRANTS FOR LOVING GOD

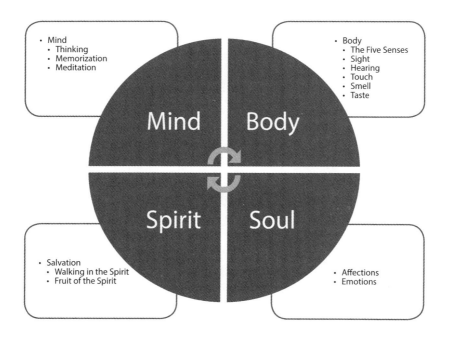

far as the separation of *soul and spirit, joints and marrow.* It is able to judge the thoughts and intentions of the *heart*" (Heb 4:12, emphasis added).

So the question is this: How are we expected to love God? Do we love God with our minds? Do we love God with our hearts? Do we love God with our souls? Do we love God with our strength and might? Do we love God with our bodies? Do we love God with our spirits? The answer to this is obviously: we are to love God totally with all of our mind, soul, body, spirit, and to the full capacity of our strength. A summary of all these different ideas is to love the Lord with all your heart. If someone says they love you with all their heart, they are saying they love you with all of their being. They love you with their mind, their will, their emotions, their finances, their bodies, even down to their soul. Let's explore some ways we are to love God.

Mind

We should love God with the mind he has given us. That means we should read and meditate on wholesome things. Paul told the Philippian church: "Finally brothers and sisters, whatever is true, whatever is honorable, whatever is just, whatever is pure, whatever is lovely, whatever is commendable—if there is any moral excellence and if there is anything praiseworthy—dwell [think] on these things" (Phil 4:8). Colossians 3:2 may be the clearest teaching on this subject: "Set your minds on things above, not on earthly things." This is clear. In the process of spiritual formation, we should be reading, studying, memorizing, and meditating on things that will strengthen our spiritual lives. Also, we should not be spending copious amounts of time and energy absorbing the world's philosophy and value system. We are being transformed by the renewing of our minds.

If we are not systematically renewing our minds, we will too easily fall prey to the world's values and priorities. We should set our minds on what is above, *not* on what is on the earth. There is a positive and there is a negative. Positive: *think on things above*; negative: *not on what is on the earth*. In a given week what do you think about the most? Money? Stuff? Food? A person? Health? In my rebellion against God's rule and reign over my life, my mind was totally focused on what I wanted. The temporal affairs of this life had my attention. Following Christ means realigning your thinking away from the things of the earth and focusing on eternal values. Whatever occupies your attention has your heart.

Body

The apostle Paul helps us understand what happened when we believed the gospel and surrendered to Christ. He informed the Corinthian church: "Don't you know that your body is a temple of the Holy Spirit who is in you, whom you have from God? You are not your own, for you were bought at a price. *So glorify God with your body*" (1 Cor 6:19–20, emphasis added). When we accept Christ, we surrender *everything* to him. There is no conditional surrender as it relates to the King of kings and Lord of lords. This is the same truth Paul explained to the church at Rome:

> Therefore do not let sin reign in your mortal body, so that you obey its desires. And do not offer any parts of it to sin as weapons for unrighteousness. But as those who are alive from the dead, offer yourselves to God, and *all the parts of yourselves* to God as weapons for righteousness. (Rom 6:12–13, emphasis added)

This passage tells us not to let sin reign in our mortal bodies and to "offer all the parts of yourselves to God." All the parts of our bodies to Christ! Our eyes. Our hands. Our feet. Our ears. Our tongues. Can you imagine going a whole day with your eyes seeing only what Christ wanted you to see? Going a whole day only serving people with your hands? A whole day only following in the footsteps of Jesus? A whole day listening only to the things that would please Jesus? A whole day speaking only the words Christ would want you to speak? You may say that is impossible, and you would be correct *if* it were left up to you to perform those actions in your own power. This is where the power of God's Holy Spirit can give us the daily victories we desire *if* we are consistently feeding the Spirit and starving our sinful nature.

The spiritual disciplines of hearing, reading, studying, memorizing, and meditating on God's Word empower his Spirit to have greater control over us, enabling us to use our bodies in ways that glorify God. When I rebel against God, I notice that my fallen nature begins to have the upper hand, and I begin to follow my sinful desires. If someone offends me, I want to use my tongue to strike back. God's Word tells us that we should listen to psalms and hymns and sing spiritual songs. What does my sinful flesh tell me to do? My flesh desires to listen to words and music that are not glorifying to Christ. What does my sinful nature want to watch on television or in the movies? You get the drift. Your sinful flesh is a beast, and it seeks to find avenues to go against God's plan. Without daily and continual Spirit control, it will lead you to use your body in ways that do not honor Christ.

Spirit

When we present to God our bodies and we love God with our minds, the Spirit of God leads and guides us in our daily walk with Christ. Again Paul writes to the churches of Galatia:

> I say then, walk by the Spirit and you will certainly not carry out the desire of the flesh. For the flesh desires what is against the Spirit, and the Spirit desires what is against the flesh; these are opposed to each other, so that you don't do what you want. But if you are led by the Spirit, you are not under the law. (Gal 5:16–18)

If we are led by the Spirit, we will *not* carry out the desire of the flesh. Our mind, our will, our emotions, our physical appetites will be under the Holy Spirit's control, and we will more consistently say yes to God and no to the flesh. However, when our minds are controlled by the things of this world and our sinful appetites, the flesh will have the upper hand. Walking in the Spirit is the result of our conscious decision to surrender control of our lives to Christ and then to "work out our salvation with fear and trembling" (Phil 2:12). We work out our salvation by daily investing in habits and disciplines that will feed the Spirit and starve the flesh.

Paul says in Col 1:28–29, "We proclaim him, warning and teaching everyone with all wisdom, so that we may present everyone mature in Christ. I labor for this, striving with his strength that works powerfully in me." In the original language, "mature" in verse 28 means "complete" or "lacking nothing." That means every area of a person's life should be examined and thoughtfully surrendered to the rule and reign of Christ.

Soul

All the aspects of a human being are to be transformed and conformed to the rule and reign of Christ. At salvation, the spirit is renewed/restored. From there, the body needs constant renewal. In addition, your soul (mind, will, emotions) needs to be renewed/restored on a continual basis. As we examine every area of our inner self, we intentionally submit every area to the rule and reign of Christ. We do this by practicing good habits (rehabituation) that feed the Spirit and breaking any habits that feed the flesh (dehabituation). As this process operates, we begin to experience "walking in the Spirit," and the Spirit leads us to greater levels of Christlikeness. Our love for Christ grows deeper as our love for the things of this world fades. We love Christ with every fiber of our being as we make choices to prioritize that love.

— Quote to Consider —

"Spiritual formation doesn't happen in a program at the church. It happens by living your life. We really need to stay away from creating programs as our goal. Programs have their place, but they must be subordinated to the spiritual life. You just start doing these simple practices and teaching the gospel of the kingdom."

—DALLAS WILLARD[1]

— Questions to Ponder —

1. Name the top three things in your life that you love.
2. How do you know you love them?
3. How can you love Christ more deeply?

Note

1. Dallas Willard, "The Apprentices," accessed March 16, 2018, http://www .dwillard.org/articles/individual/apprentices-the.

7 Spiritual Formation Impacts the Community of Believers

Rod Dempsey

I started playing basketball in the second grade. By the time I was in the sixth grade, I was traveling to tournaments. I played throughout high school and even played one year in college. Later in college, I played on an intramural team. After college I got married, had children, and worked two jobs, but I still found time to play. On and on I played until my midfifties. At that point, injuries started to mount, and I could sense my body was wearing out. First, my knee started swelling. Then inflammation in my back forced me to take some time off. Finally, one spring day, I was playing, and as I was running, it felt like I had a flat tire. I remember walking off the court and saying to myself, "I don't believe I will ever play basketball again."

I went to my family doctor, and he did a few simple range-of-motion tests. After the assessment, he said he thought I had "avascular necrosis" in my hip joint. I mentioned to him that the diagnosis had an unwelcoming sound. He simply replied, "I believe you don't have blood flowing to your hip joint, and you probably need to have hip replacement surgery." I went to a specialist and the X-rays were conclusive. The cartilage in my left hip was worn out. In just a few months, I went from playing basketball two to three days a week to having great difficulty walking just a few steps. My body was not functioning the way it was designed to, and it was not able to accomplish the simplest of tasks. It was and is a frustrating experience for your body not to function the way it was designed. A few simple tests to determine the diagnosis was all that was needed to determine that my body had a serious problem. This physical condition needed to be corrected. If it was not corrected, I would be limping for the rest of my earthly existence. Not only would I be hobbled by this physical limitation, but it would also be noticeable to anyone I met. My body was not functioning according to God's design. Now keep in mind, this was the result when *one* part of my body was not functioning according to God's design. What happens when 60, 70, 80 percent of the members of the body of Christ are not functioning? Spiritual formation is about equipping and developing all parts of the body of Christ to be healthy and do what they have been gifted to do. Being leads to doing.

What Are the Vital Signs?

I believe we can measure the health of Christ's body much in the same way a physician measures the health of a human body. For example, when you go to a doctor for your annual exam, one of the first tests is a basic recording of certain baseline measurements. The doctor wants to know what your vital signs are. How much do you weigh? How tall are you? What is your body temperature? What is your resting heart rate? What is your blood pressure? Do you have any allergies? Do you smoke? Are you on any medication? Is there a need for blood work? You may possibly need an EKG.

The point here is that the medical profession, over hundreds of years, has developed certain baseline measurements that reveal to the doctor where the body is out of alignment. The human body is an amazing organism with up to eleven different systems that work in harmony and cooperation to create health.[1] If one system or one part is not working, then you are going to negatively feel the results. In the same way, I believe we can measure the "vital signs" of a church and determine whether or not it is healthy.

Take Care of the Body and the Body Will Take Care of You

The illustration above is appropriate to consider because when Jesus describes the church, he says it is his body. Consider what the apostle Paul said to the church at Ephesus: "And he subjected everything under his feet and appointed him as head over everything for the church, which is his *body*, the fullness of the one who fills all things in every way" (Eph 1:22–23, emphasis added). Christ's church is not like a body; it is a body. It is his body.

In a similar passage, Paul says this: "Now you are the *body* of Christ, and individual members of it" (1 Cor 12:27, emphasis added). In Eph 3:6, Paul said that "The Gentiles are coheirs, members of the same *body*, and partners in the promise in Christ Jesus through the gospel."

The Body of Christ

This same thought is contained in 1 Cor 12:12–13 where Paul says, "For just as the *body* is one and has many parts, and all the parts of that *body*, though many, are one *body*—so also is Christ. For we were all baptized by one Spirit into one *body*—whether Jews or Greeks, whether slaves or free—and we were all given one Spirit to drink" (emphasis added). Again the apostle Paul says the church is Christ's body.

When we receive the gracious gift of salvation, we are baptized by the Spirit into the universal church, which is the body of Christ (1 Cor 12:13 and Eph 4:5). In Eph 4:11–12, 16, the apostle gives perhaps the clearest explanation of the inner workings of the church:

> And he himself gave some to be apostles, some prophets, some evangelists, some pastors and teachers, equipping the saints for the work of ministry, to build up the *body* of Christ. . . . From him the whole *body*, fitted and knit together by every supporting ligament, promotes the growth of the *body* for building up itself in love by the proper working of each individual part. (emphasis added)

Again this passage references the church as the "body of Christ." In addition, this passage notes that the body of Christ is to be built up and that it grows strong by "the proper working of each individual part." Stated negatively, if any parts in the body are not working "properly," the body will not be healthy.

How many parts of your body do you want working? We take great care to look after our bodies, and at the slightest indication something is not working properly, not only do we notice it, but we go to a doctor to find out exactly what is wrong. When we receive a diagnosis by the doctor, we are usually meticulous about following through and doing whatever is necessary to experience health once again—in my case, even to the point of major surgery. How far are you willing to go to help the body of Christ become healthy? Equipping and empowering members of the body to love Christ, love one another, and love their neighbors will enable a community of believers to become the visible body of Christ.

What Are Your Passions?

We are passionate about the health of our bodies. Shouldn't we be as passionate about the health of the body of Christ? Jesus wants all the parts of his body working. The apostle Paul devotes an entire chapter to this idea. See 1 Cor 12:4–20:

Now there are different gifts, but the same Spirit. There are different ministries, but the same Lord. And there are different activities, but the same God produces each gift in each person. A manifestation of the Spirit is given to each person for the common good: to one is given a message of wisdom through the Spirit, to another, a message of knowledge by the same Spirit, to another, faith by the same Spirit, to another, gifts of healing by the one Spirit, to another, the performing of miracles, to another, prophecy, to another, distinguishing between spirits, to another, different kinds of tongues, to another, interpretation of tongues. One and the same Spirit is active in all these, distributing to each person as he wills.

For just as the *body* is one and has many parts, and all the parts of that *body*, though many, are one *body*—so also is Christ. For we were all baptized by one Spirit into one *body*—whether Jews or Greeks, whether slaves or free—and we were all given one Spirit to drink. Indeed, the *body* is not one part but many. If the foot should say, "Because I'm not a hand, I don't belong to the *body*," it is not for that reason any less a part of the *body*. And if the ear should say, "Because I'm not an eye, I don't belong to the *body*," it is not for that reason any less a part of the *body*. If the whole *body* were an eye, where would the hearing be? If the whole body were an ear, where would the sense of smell be? But as it is, God has arranged each one of the parts in the *body* just as he wanted. And if they were all the same part, where would the *body* be? As it is, there are many parts, but one *body*. (emphasis added)

This passage teaches us several things about the health of the body.

1. Every Christian has at least one "manifestation of the Spirit" (spiritual gift).
2. There are many different types of spiritual gifts.
3. Even though the body of Christ has many parts, there is only one body.
4. All the parts of the body are important—not just the external (visible) but also the internal (invisible) parts.
5. Even if a part is not seen, it is still a part of the body.
6. God has placed the parts in the body "just as he wanted."
7. The body could not function if there were only one part.
8. All the parts working together form one body.

Putting It All Together

The apostle Paul is here explaining to us how the body of Christ functions. It is an organic system where all the parts work together. For a local church to be healthy, all the parts need to be working "by the proper working of each individual part." The most important vital sign in the body of Christ is to answer this question: Are all parts of the body working? Greg Ogden puts it this way:

> As we rediscover the church as a living organism, the body of Christ, church members have been called out of the audience to become players on the stage. Everyone has a part in this play. Every believer is a necessary part of the drama God is producing, the drama of salvation history. We are on stage together, pastors and people alike. There is no longer a select, professional union of actors. In the body of Christ, all the "actors" have a direct connection to the Producer, the Creator, and the Choreographer of History.[2]

Let me ask you an important question: Have all the believers in your church discovered their spiritual gift, and are they using it the way the Master intends?

It is not just the pastor's job to "feed the flock." Listen to Aubrey Malphurs: "Do you want to know if your church is effective? Look for disciples! While the Great Commission includes pastoral care, it's much broader than that."[3] The pastor's main job is to "equip" or "train" the members to grow spiritually *and* to use their gift in the proper way in the body. When all the parts are working "just as he wanted," then the body is healthy. Disciple making is about helping individuals develop to their full potential for Christ and his kingdom. This happens best in a healthy body where all the parts are functioning the way he intended.

To understand church health, we must understand that a body is the primary metaphor the New Testament employs to describe the church. The church of Jesus is his body. The human body is a wonderful and complex system of interrelated parts (1 Cor 12:1–31). Likewise, the church is an organic collection of systems that form a living organism. Unfortunately we have ignored the organic part and are more concerned with the health of the organization than the health of the individuals who comprise the organization.

The Wrong Starting Point

The starting point for most pastors is to measure the health of the organization, not the health of the individuals in it. Many churches measure the wrong things. Things—bodies, bucks, buildings, and perhaps even big shots—is the wrong emphasis. I believe the starting point in the New Testament (based on the passages above) is the health of the individual. Our focus as pastors is to get all the parts healthy (spiritual growth—"being") and to get all the parts working (spiritual activity—"doing"). When all the parts of the organism are healthy, then the organization (body) will be healthy. A healthy body of Christ is the perfect environment for disciple making. A body of believers that is spiritually formed—loving God, loving one another, and loving their neighbors—will be a healthy body of Christ.

There are many different perspectives about how to measure a church's health. Some people measure health by the attendance on Sunday morning. Some seek to find out how many buildings the church has. Some look at the church's bank account or balance sheet.

The world tries to measure health by the externals. Jesus is looking deeper. He is looking inward to see the condition of the body. In reality the body of Christ stays healthy exactly the same way the human body stays healthy. The human body is healthy and stays healthy as each part works the way it was designed to work. The body of Jesus is healthy and stays healthy as each disciple grows strong and fulfills his or her role in the body. Make no mistake, Jesus, like a wise and experienced physician, is analyzing and measuring the health of his body. We would be wise to follow his example.

In summary, spiritual formation within the body of Christ involves *all* the members becoming healthy. According to the letters written to the seven churches in Revelation, Jesus is evaluating his church. He has an intense desire for his church to be healthy. There are no perfect churches. They all have weaknesses because they are made up of imperfect people. However, equipping and developing every member to be healthy is job number one of church leaders.

⚊ Quote to Consider ⚊

*"From him the whole body, fitted and knit together
by every supporting ligament, promotes the growth
of the body for building up itself in love by the
proper working of each individual part."*

—EPH 4:16

⚊ Questions to Ponder ⚊

1. In your opinion, what percentage of your church is spiritually healthy?
2. How many members of the body of Christ are daily connecting to Christ in prayer and Bible reading?

3. What percentage of the members are connected to Christ, to one another, and to the mission of the church?

Notes

1. Amanda Robb, "What Are the Organ Systems of the Human Body?" Study.com, accessed April 27, 2018, https://study.com/academy/lesson/what-are-the-organ-systems-of-the-human-body.html.

2. Greg Ogden, *Unfinished Business: Returning the Ministry to the People of God* (Grand Rapids: Zondervan, 2010), 355–59. Kindle Edition.

3. Aubrey Malphurs, *Strategic Disciple Making: A Practical Tool for Successful Ministry* (Grand Rapids: Baker Books, 2009), 157. Kindle Edition.

Living Out Your Spiritual Identity in Christ

Dave Earley

I dentity theft: the fastest growing crime in America."[1] That was a headline recently. A few years ago, my niece had her identity stolen, and it was a nightmare. Without her permission, criminals were using her name, Social Security number, and credit card number to commit fraud and other crimes.

Identity theft is serious. While some identity theft victims can resolve their problems quickly, many spend thousands of dollars and months to years repairing damage to their good name and credit record. Some consumers victimized by identity theft may lose out on job opportunities or be denied loans for education, housing, or cars because of negative information on their credit reports.

Unfortunately, an even larger problem and greater crime is sweeping through Western Christianity at an alarming rate. I am talking about spiritual identity theft. A high percentage of the people who call themselves followers of Jesus suffer from spiritual identity theft.

In financial identity theft, thieves steal our financial identity for their gain. In spiritual identity theft, the devil steals our spiritual identity for our loss. While financial identity theft is serious, spiritual identity theft is exceedingly more serious. Loss of spiritual identity will keep you from experiencing victory over sin, fellowship with the Father, and power in the Spirit.

Your New Identity

As someone passionate about making disciples, I have entered discipleship relationships many times with many different types of people. When I first started trying to make disciples, I followed the prevailing philosophy of that time and piled spiritual discipline after spiritual discipline on the would-be disciple.

Some of them experienced amazing spiritual transformation. But others, well, not so much. Even though they were employing the disciplines, they kept struggling with the same old hurts, habits, and hang-ups. Discouraged, they often dropped out of the discipling relationship.

Then I did an in-depth study of Ephesians. One big truth that jumped out at me was that before Paul gave the Ephesians any spiritual practices to adopt, he reminded them of the spiritual position they had been given.

The letter to the Ephesians opens with these words, "Paul, an apostle of Christ Jesus by God's will: To the faithful saints *in Christ* Jesus at Ephesus" (Eph 1:1, emphasis added). The phrase *in Christ* or its equivalent occurs *165 times* in the letters of the apostle Paul to describe a believer's amazing spiritual identity!

At the moment of regeneration, the believer is placed into a blessed spiritual position that Paul refers to as being "in Christ." We are all baptized or placed into Christ's body (1 Cor 12:13; Rom 6:3–4). From this exalted position, the believer experiences every spiritual blessing in the heavenly places (Eph 1:3).

Here is a quick listing of some of the many spiritual blessings available to us "in Christ."

Identifying Marks of Being "in Christ"
"In Christ" I am:

1. Justified (Rom 3:24)
2. Alive to God (Rom 6:11)
3. The recipient of eternal life (Rom 6:23)
4. Void of all condemnation (Rom 8:1)
5. Loved (Rom 8:39)
6. Connected with others in the body of Christ (Rom 12:5)
7. Given a reason to boast (Rom 15:17)
8. Sanctified (1 Cor 1:2)
9. Established and sealed (2 Cor 1:21)
10. Victorious (2 Cor 2:14; Rom 8:37)
11. New (2 Cor 5:17)
12. Reconciled to God and given the ministry of reconciliation (2 Cor 5:18–19)

13. Liberated (Gal 2:4)
14. Blessed with the blessing of Abraham and the promise of the Holy Spirit (Gal 3:14)
15. Adopted (Gal 3:26; 4:4–7)
16. The owner of an identity more significant than social position, gender, or race (Gal 3:28; 5:6; 6:15)
17. Redeemed (Eph 1:7)
18. Made an heir (Eph 1:11; Gal 4:6–7)
19. Exalted to sit together in Christ in the heavenly places (Eph 2:6)
20. Graced (Eph 2:7)
21. A masterpiece created for good works (Eph 2:10)
22. Made a citizen of heaven (Eph 2:12–14, 19)
23. Given a promise (Eph 3:6)
24. Granted access to the throne of the Father (Eph 3:12; 2:18)
25. Forgiven (Eph 4:32)
26. Sainted (Phil 1:1; 4:21)
27. Given joy (Phil 3:3)
28. Called upward (Phil 3:14)
29. Promised life (2 Tim 1:1)
30. Strengthened in grace (2 Tim 2:1)
31. Saved (2 Tim 2:10; Eph 2:4–9)

As I study the New Testament, I continue to find new aspects of our identity in Christ. Beyond the thirty-one "in Christ" aspects mentioned above, at least another twenty aspects of our Christian identity are mentioned in Scripture that are not tied to the term *in Christ*. But the number of spiritual identifiers is not as significant as the need to grasp your identity in Christ.

Living out one's spiritual identity is essential for experiencing deep intimacy with God, walking in real integrity as a Christ follower, and fulfilling one's spiritual destiny. It is foundational for living in spiritual and emotional victory and liberty. It is vital for exercising authority in Christ.

Three Foundational Spiritual Identifiers

Saints

The word *saint* is used ninety-eight times in the Bible: thirty-three times in the Old Testament and sixty-five in the New. In fact, Paul's favorite term for a Christian was *saint*. He used it nine times in the book of Ephesians. Paul began most of his letters by addressing them to the "saints" (Rom 1:7; 1 Cor 1:2; 2 Cor 1:1; Eph 1:1; Phil 1:1; Col 1:1).

The Bible term for "saint" is the Greek word *hagios*. It means "holy, set apart, sacred, hallowed, worthy of reverence, awesome; set apart for God, exclusively his." Therefore, saints are awesome, holy people set apart exclusively for God!

Even after being saved, I still struggled with besetting sin in several areas. Before I was saved, the enemy lied to me and told me I *needed* to sin, I *wanted* to sin, and I *had* to sin. I was powerless against it. After salvation I tried to discipline myself not to sin, which made it harder to sin, but the lies would run through my head, and the sin would return. Then I got accountability partners, but when I got tired or discouraged, the lies would run through my head all over again, and the sin would come back.

One day I was studying this word *saint*, and the truth hit me: *As a saint, I am set apart from sin. I do not need to sin, want to sin, or have to sin.* As I renewed my mind with that truth, the power of sin was broken.

You don't become a saint *after* you die. If you have been saved, you are a saint right now. You became a saint the moment you are saved. You don't become holy after you get to heaven. You are right now. Believe it. Live like it. Enjoy it.

We do not have to wait until we get to heaven to have the power to say no to sin. We have the power "in Christ" as saints to say no to sin today. We do not have to wait until we get to heaven to have the desire for sin to be removed. It already has been removed "in Christ."

I don't know what your besetting sin is. It could be lust, greed, anger, anxiety, alcohol addiction, fear, envy, gluttony, or gossip. The truth is that if you are a saint, "in Christ" you do not *have to* commit that sin, you do not *need to* commit that sin, and you do not even *want to* commit that sin. You are no longer a victim of temptation and sin.

Saved

Prior to being "in Christ," we were in a spiritual sense the walking dead. In Ephesians 2, Paul describes what we were like *before* we were saved. He horrifyingly describes us as grotesque spiritual zombies, staggering around, following the commands of the devil, hungrily trying to satisfy our sinful natures.

> And *you were dead* in your trespasses and sins in which you previously lived according to the ways of this world, according to the ruler of the power of the air, the spirit now working in the disobedient. We too all previously lived among them in our fleshly desires, carrying out the inclinations of our flesh and thoughts, and we were by nature children under wrath as the others were also. (Eph 2:1–3, emphasis added)

But thankfully Paul did not end there. After painting the horrifying picture of us as the walking dead, Paul gives us the good news and tells us what it means for us to be the living saved.

> *But God*, who is rich in mercy, because of *his great love* that he had for us, *made us alive* with Christ even though we were dead in trespasses. You are *saved by grace*! He also *raised us* up with him and *seated us with him* in the heavens in Christ Jesus, so that in the coming ages *he might display the immeasurable riches of his grace through his kindness to us* in Christ Jesus. . . . For we are *his workmanship*, created in Christ Jesus for good works, which God prepared ahead of time for us to do. (Eph 2:4–7, 10, emphasis added)

As saved people, we go from being dead in our sins to being resurrected with Christ. No longer doomed, we are now loved. Instead of being dominated by the world and the flesh, we are seated with Christ in the heavens and stand throughout eternity as trophies of his grace!

But that is not all. In verse 10, the phrase *we are his workmanship* means we are his "special handiwork, craftsmanship, and masterpiece." The term is *poiema*, which sounds like our word *poem*, giving us the sense we are his poem, his song, his symphony, his magnum opus!

When God made us trophies of his grace, he did not make us stiff statues but living, breathing, walking, and talking masterpieces with the express purpose of doing good works. Of course, we do not perform good works in order to be saved (Eph 2:8–9). We do them because we have been saved.

Sons and Daughters

Too many of us believe God is our Father but inwardly feel like spiritual orphans. This is evidenced by the fact that we struggle with persistent feelings of loneliness, fear, unworthiness, rejection, distance from God our Father, and difficulties getting along with our spiritual brothers and sisters in Christ. Such struggles often are caused by unresolved hurts from our parents when we were at strategic points in our growing up. They are only resolved by experiencing the truth that God is our Father.

> When the time came to completion, God sent his Son, born of a woman, born under the law, to redeem those under the law, so that we might receive *adoption as sons*. And because you are sons, God sent the Spirit of his Son into our hearts, crying, *"Abba, Father!"* So *you are no longer a slave but a son*, and if a son, then God has made you an heir. (Gal 4:4–7, emphasis added)

Paul is reminding the Galatians that they have been redeemed. But he goes beyond that and tells them that in Christ they are now the legal sons and daughters of God.

God sent his own Son to buy us out of the slave market of sin. He not only set us free from slavery to sin, but he did it with the express purpose of adopting us as his own sons and daughters with full legal privileges of sonship.

> For he chose us in him, before the foundation of the world . . . *to be adopted* as sons through Jesus Christ for himself, according to the good pleasure of his will (Eph 1:4–5, emphasis added).

God's love for us and its expression in our adoption into his eternal family did not start in this world. It started back in eternity. Therefore, your adoption is not based on your talent, personality, or distinctiveness. It is rooted in God's eternal purpose and grace. Your adoption is not fragile or tenuous or uncertain. God will not adopt then find out you are unworthy and unadopt. He knows we are unworthy. Yet he chose us and predestined us for adoption anyway.

One awesome privilege of our adoption as God's sons and daughters is that we can "cry out *Abba*, Father." The term *cry* describes "a loud and earnest cry; a public announcement; a word of intensity." The term is used elsewhere for the croak of a baby bird for food. It is a heart cry, the expression of deep, desperate desire. This cry does not make us sons and daughters. It is the cry we make *because* we are sons and daughters.

The word *abba* is not a religious, business, political, or legal word. It is a family word. *Abba* originated as a babble term of affection and fondness used by small children for their fathers. It means "papa" or "daddy."

The privilege of being adopted into God's family and being able to "cry out Abba, Father" is overwhelming and multifaceted.

Crying Abba speaks of intimacy. God did not send his Son to make you a slave. He sent his Son to free you and to adopt you as his son or daughter.

Crying Abba speaks of identity. The people redeemed and adopted into God's family can know who they are, members of God's family.

Crying Abba speaks of dependency. Jesus cried Abba in the garden of Gethsemane the night he was betrayed (Mark 14:33–36).

Crying Abba speaks of security. When Paul speaks of the privilege of crying Abba in Romans 8, he stresses the fact that it assures our position in God's family and removes fear (Rom 8:14–16).

Crying Abba speaks of prosperity. In Galatians 4, Paul states, "So you are no longer a slave but a son, and if a son, then God has made you an heir"

(v. 7). An heir describes someone who receives an inheritance. We are our Father's heirs. He is rich. Therefore, we are rich!

Crying Abba speaks of our destiny. We are like the prodigal of Luke 15. When we return to our Father's house, we receive all the joys of finally being at home with our Father who loves us unconditionally, undeniably, unashamedly, unmistakably, and unrelentingly.

The Choice

The beauty of our new identity in Christ is that we now have a choice. We can face every situation either as a saint or as a sinner, as a son (or daughter) or as a spiritual orphan, as an heir or as a slave, as a victor or as a victim. Only as we live out our spiritual identity will we fully realize our spiritual possibilities.

— Quote to Consider —

"The story of your life is the story of a long and brutal assault on your heart by the one who knows what you could be and fears it."

—John Eldredge[2]

— Questions to Ponder —

1. Which of the thirty-one spiritual identifiers caught your attention? Why?
2. What did you learn about being a saint?
3. What aspect of being a son or daughter means the most to you?

Notes

1. Michelle Dargan, "Identity Theft: The Fastest Growing Crime in America," *Palm Beach Daily News*, March 24, 2013, accessed February 21, 2018, https://www.palmbeachdailynews.com/news/national/identity-theft-the-fastest-growing-crime-america/UOZ6sZ066zTE3k41vhZ43K.

2. John Eldredge, *Waking the Dead* (Nashville: Thomas Nelson, 2003), 149.

9 Walking in the Spirit

Dave Earley

One hundred and twenty-five years ago, Scottish author Robert Louis Stevenson wrote a novella titled *The Strange Case of Dr. Jekyll and Mr. Hyde*.[1] In Stevenson's story, mild-mannered Dr. Henry Jekyll has spent a great part of his life trying to repress the evil urges that spring up within him. So he creates a potion as an attempt both to express and hide the hidden evil within his personality. However, the potion transforms Henry Jekyll into the smaller, younger, self-indulgent, cruel, violent, lust-filled, evil Edward Hyde. The more Hyde is allowed to control Dr. Jekyll, the more evil he becomes. Mr. Hyde literally becomes the enemy within.

In the book, Dr. Jekyll tries to stop becoming Mr. Hyde by doing charity work. But when this fills him with pride, it only gets worse, and he turns into Hyde again. From that point, Hyde gets stronger and stronger, and Dr. Jekyll increasingly feels like a slave to Mr. Hyde. He finds himself feeling hopeless and helpless against his dark side. The only solution Jekyll can see is that he has to kill Mr. Hyde. But the only way to kill Hyde is to kill himself. So sadly the story ends in suicide.

Interestingly, the apostle Paul felt the same struggle Dr. Jekyll faced. What Paul wrote in Romans 7 could have been something Dr. Jekyll wrote.

A Christian's Journal

What I don't understand about myself is that I decide one way, but then I act another, doing things I absolutely despise. . . . I can't be trusted to figure out what is best for myself and then do it. . . .

For if I know the law but still can't keep it, and if the power of sin within me keeps sabotaging my best intentions, I obviously need help!

I realize that I don't have what it takes. I can will it, but I can't do it. I decide to do good, but I don't really do it; I decide not to do bad, but then I do it anyway. My decisions, such as they are, don't result in actions.

Something has gone wrong deep within me and gets the better of me every time. It happens so regularly that it's predictable.

The moment I decide to do good, sin is there to trip me up. I truly delight in God's commands, but it's pretty obvious that not all of me joins in that delight. Parts of me covertly rebel, and just when I least expect it, they take charge.

I've tried everything and nothing helps. I'm at the end of my rope. Is there no one who can do anything for me? (Rom 7:15–24 MSG)

Poor Dr. Jekyll should have read the next verse before he took his life.

What a wretched [pitiful, helpless, hopeless, miserable, defeated, discouraged] man I am! Who will rescue me from this body of death? *Thanks be to God through Jesus Christ our Lord!* (Rom 7:24–25, emphasis added)

Dr. Jekyll and Mr. Hyde is a disturbing story that ends in the suicide of Dr. Jekyll.

The gospel is a redemptive story, a good news story that gives us another option. We do not have to kill ourselves to be free of the evil inside. We can come to Jesus and let his death on the cross execute Mr. Hyde for us and breathe life into our lungs by his Spirit. He can free us from the power within and transform us into his image.

Let's be clear on this point. No one can realize their full spiritual transformation without learning to walk in freedom from the enemy within.

In Romans 8, Paul discusses the battle within and shows us how the gospel gives us freedom from the enemy within. First, he discusses the way we were *before* Christ (8:5–8). Then he reminds us who we *are now in* Christ (8:9–11). Then Paul shows us that through the power of the Holy Spirit we now have the power to make the right choice in Christ (8:12–17).

The Contrast
Romans 8:5–11

The Flesh. The flesh could be described as our Mr. Hyde. It is the sinful nature, the carnal nature, the nature set on fulfilling evil appetites, the do-it-yourself, self-adsorbed, self-focused enemy within. It is the part of us that is fully alive to selfish, sinful temptations. It is the magnet that pulls us away from good, away from God, and away from the people of God.

The Spirit. The Spirit is the Holy Spirit of Jesus. In this passage, living "according to the Spirit" refers to our new nature in Christ. It is the God-focused nature, the part of us set on fulfilling the desires of God. It is characterized by God-reliant, God-absorbed, God-focused living. It is that part of us that is keenly alive to good. Think of the Spirit in us as the magnet that pulls us to good, God, and to the people of God. The Spirit gives us life, real life in Christ.

Prior to Christ We Were "in the Flesh"
Romans 8:5–8

> For those who live according to *the flesh* have their minds set on the things *of the flesh*, but those who live according to the Spirit have their minds set on the things of the Spirit. Now the mind-set of *the flesh* is death, but the mind-set of the Spirit is life and peace. The mind-set of *the flesh* is hostile to God because it does not submit to God's law. Indeed, it is unable to do so. Those who are in *the flesh* cannot please God. (Rom 8:5–8, emphasis added)

In Rom 8:5–8, with just a few words, Paul provided a rather extensive description of the life in the flesh. He painted an ugly picture of living as enslaved victims of sin and self. He noted several grisly characteristics of a person who is given over to the flesh.

Controlled by the Sinful Nature

Prior to being born again, we "lived according to the flesh." We were dominated by it. Mr. Hyde had the upper hand and called the shots in our lives. King Self sat on the throne of our hearts.

Desirous of the Things That Gratify the Sinful Nature

A "mind-set" (v. 6) is "a basic orientation, a bent." It includes our affections, will, and thought patterns. Prior to Christ, our basic orientation was toward the flesh, and our thoughts revolved around pleasing the flesh.

Dead to the Things of God

When Paul uses the word *death*, he is referencing "being unresponsive." To be spiritually "dead" is to be unresponsive to the things of the Spirit. Paul also used "death" to reference being "separated from, distanced from." To be spiritually "dead" is to be distanced from God by the sin in our lives (Isa 59:2). Living in the flesh is a spiritual killer.

Defiant toward God

The flesh cannot coexist with God. It refuses to bow the knee to the King of kings. It will not submit to the will, way, and words of the Lord of lords. Because its entire orientation is away from God, the flesh is inherently incapable of carrying out God's will. The flesh not only does not want to submit to God and his Word; it could not even if it wanted to.

Displeasing to God

Paul is clear: "Those who are in the flesh cannot please God" (Rom 8:8).

Displaying Distorted, Wicked Behaviors

In another passage, Paul describes the panoply of perverted, sinful expressions that are produced when the flesh is left unchecked.

> Now the *works of the flesh* are obvious: sexual immorality, moral impurity, promiscuity, idolatry, sorcery, hatreds, strife, jealousy, outbursts of anger, selfish ambitions, dissensions, factions, envy, drunkenness, carousing, and anything similar. I am warning you about these things—as I warned you before—that those who practice such things will not inherit the kingdom of God. (Gal 5:19–21, emphasis added)

Summary

Prior to receiving Christ, a person is the enslaved victim of the flesh, with desires that pull defiantly away from God and stubbornly toward self and sin. Lost people are unresponsive to the things of God. They view God as their enemy and rebel against him and his law. Left to itself, the flesh-dominated life produces all sorts of ugly behaviors and attitudes. The flesh on its own will produce perverted, sinful expressions. No wonder Paul said living dominated by the flesh makes it impossible to please God.

Therefore, the notion of experiencing spiritual transformation while living in the flesh is ridiculous. The two are mutually exclusive. It is impossible to experience spiritual transformation in the flesh.

That is all bad news.

But the good news is that in Christ there is an alternative to life in the flesh. We can experience life in the Spirit.

In Christ, We Are Now "in the Spirit"
Romans 8:9–11

> *You, however, are not in the flesh, but in the Spirit*, if indeed the Spirit of God lives in you. If anyone does not have the Spirit of Christ, he does not belong to him. Now if Christ is in you, the body is dead because of sin, but the Spirit gives life because of righteousness. And if the Spirit of him who raised Jesus from the dead lives in you, then he who raised Christ from the dead will also bring your mortal bodies to life through his Spirit who lives in you. (Rom 8:9–11, emphasis added)

The Holy Spirit is mentioned only one time in the first seven chapters of Romans. But in the beginning part of chapter 8, Paul discusses the Spirit twenty times! He describes life in the Spirit in sharp contrast to life in the flesh.

Hosts of More Than "Phenomenal Cosmic Power"

Several years ago, when my boys were young, we allowed them to watch the animated movie *Aladdin*. In the movie, the young man Aladdin finds a lamp in the magical Cave of Wonders. Residing inside the lamp is a genie, an all-powerful spirit full of life and bursting with positive energy.

In perhaps the most memorable scene in the movie, the genie, played by the late Robin Williams, is trying to explain to Aladdin all of the amazing power and potential the genie makes available to him. At the high point, the genie shouts:

> "PHENOMENAL COSMIC POWER
> . . . Itty, bitty living space."

Isn't that similar to what we have as the hosts of the Spirit? He is God. He has infinite, immense, unlimited, supernatural power. Yet he resides in us (Rom 8:9). With so much energy, strength, and authority available for good, we have all we need to live lives pleasing to God.

Alive Because of Christ's Righteousness

We *were* spiritually dead, separated from God because of our sin. But in Christ we *are* made alive because of his righteousness. The righteousness of Jesus has been applied to our account (2 Cor 5:21). As ones in the righteousness column, we are not separated from God but are united with him and his life. This not only means we have a new life in Christ and an eternal home in heaven; it also means we have the possibility of a full, free, fulfilling life in the Spirit.

Guaranteed a Resurrection

The Spirit of the living God is alive in us. Therefore, we cannot stay dead. We have a guarantee that our existence will not end as a corpse in a grave. We will experience the resurrection of our bodies.

Producers of Beautiful Spiritual Fruit

Just as life given over to the flesh produces perverted sinful practices, life given over to the Spirit exudes amazingly attractive character qualities. In the parallel passage to Romans 8, Paul also reveals the glories of life in the Spirit.

> But the fruit of the Spirit is love, joy, peace, patience, kindness, goodness, faithfulness, gentleness, and self-control. The law is not against such things. (Gal 5:22–23)

In Christ, We Can Choose to Live in the Spirit
Romans 8:12–17

> So then, brothers and sisters, we are not obligated to the flesh to live according to the flesh, because if you live according to the flesh, you are going to die. But if *by the Spirit you put to death the deeds of the body,* you will live. For all those led by God's Spirit are God's sons. You did not receive a spirit of slavery to fall back into fear. Instead, you received *the Spirit of adoption,* by whom we cry out, "*Abba,* Father!" The Spirit himself testifies together with our spirit that we are God's children, and if children, also heirs—heirs of God and coheirs with Christ—if indeed we suffer with him so that we may also be glorified with him. (Rom 8:12–17, emphasis added)

We do not have to live under the domination of the flesh a moment longer. "In Christ" any obligation to the flesh was broken. "In Christ" we can choose how we will live and what will be our dominating factor, the flesh or the Spirit.

The Spirit-dominated life is available "in Christ." But it must be chosen. We can choose to face each circumstance out of who we used to be (a person controlled by the flesh) or who we now are "in Christ" (a person controlled by the Spirit).

How to Live in the Spirit

Say No to the Flesh

Because our obligation to the flesh is broken, we no longer have to listen to it. We have the power to say *no* to the flesh. We are obligated to *be who we are*, not who we *used to be*. As we saw in the previous chapter, we are saved, saints, and spiritual sons and daughters of the Most High God.

Bury the Flesh and Live in the Spirit

In the power of the Spirit, we can habitually choose to declare the power of the flesh to be dead. It is gone. "In Christ" Mr. Hyde has no authority to tell us what to do. He has no strength to make us obey him. Beyond that, he has been put to death. So we need to point at his tombstone and go on living under the influence of the Spirit.

Follow the Leadership of the Spirit

The phrase *led by God's Spirit* (Rom 8:14) speaks of continual submission to the Holy Spirit. We submit to him and allow him, not the flesh, to call the shots.

Live Like a Child of God Instead of a Slave to Sin

The Lord God has not only pardoned our crimes and let us out of prison, but he has also made us his own children. We are no longer slaves to sin. We are the children of God.

We *were* controlled by the sinful nature as slaves to sin. We could not keep from sinning.

But in Christ we *are* children of God, under no obligation to sin. The Holy Spirit is present, willing, and able to empower our lives. He gives us both the desire and the ability to say *no* to the flesh and sin and to say *yes* to God.

Replace the Old Lifestyle with the New

> To take off your former way of life, the old self that is corrupted by deceitful desires, to be renewed in the spirit of your minds, and to put on the

new self, the one created according to God's likeness in righteousness and purity of the truth. (Eph 4:22–24)

The tangible display of being free of the enemy within is replacing the attitudes, habits, actions, and words of the old lifestyle (dominated by the flesh) with new ones.

Live under the Influence of the Holy Spirit

And don't get drunk with wine, which leads to reckless living, but *be filled by the Spirit*: speaking to one another in psalms, hymns, and spiritual songs, singing and making music with your heart to the Lord, giving thanks always for everything to God the Father in the name of our Lord Jesus Christ, submitting to one another in the fear of Christ. (Eph 5:18–21, emphasis added)

When people are drunk with alcohol, they are saturated to the point of control. The alcohol controls their thoughts, words, and actions. In like manner, Paul encourages the Ephesians to be so permeated with the Holy Spirit that he controls their lives. The means, as well as the results, of being Spirit filled are making music in their hearts, living grateful lives, and choosing a place of submission with others. In a similar passage, Paul states that the same activities are means and results of being filled with God's Word (Col 3:15–21).

— Quote to Consider —

*"Being a Christian and living the Christian life
are supernatural. God's Spirit, the Spirit of Christ,
lives in us and brings about changes that could
never and would never be made without him so
that Jesus Christ is glorified in what we do."*

—JOHN PIPER[2]

— Questions to Ponder —

1. What surprised you about life in the flesh?
2. Which better describes your life: living in the flesh or living in the Spirit?
3. What aspect of walking in the Spirit do you need to apply?

Notes

1. Robert Louis Stevenson, *The Strange Case of Dr. Jekyll and Mr. Hyde* (London: Longman's, Green, and Co., 1886).

2. John Piper, "Why and How We Walk According to the Spirit," sermon given December 2, 2001, at Bethlehem Baptist Church, Minneapolis, accessed February 12, 2017, http://www.desiringgod.org/messages/why-and-how-we-walk-according -to-the-spirit.

10

Sweating in God's Gym

Dave Earley

In January the gyms are full. People have made New Year's resolutions to get fit, lose weight, get buff, and become stronger. You can join a gym for as little as $10 a month or as much as $20,000 a year.

When it comes to spiritual formation, God has a gym where you can get truly fit—with the type of fitness that won't last a few weeks or even a few years but the type that lasts forever. God has a gym where you can go deeper in your relationship with him and be transformed into being more like Jesus.

Run Hard, Train Hard

In the first century, the Olympian Games were not the biggest sporting event in Greece. The most important was the Isthmian Games in Corinth. Paul spent several years in Corinth making tents. Many of those tents likely were used by those who came from around the empire to enjoy the Isthmian Games.

Paul no doubt watched the athletes training for the races and wrestling matches that dominated the games. He used the graphic image of an athlete in training to exhort the Corinthian church to go all out in their spiritual growth.

> Don't you know that the runners in a stadium all race, but only one receives the prize? Run in such a way to win the prize. Now everyone who competes exercises self-control in everything. They do it to receive a perishable crown, but we an imperishable crown. So I do not run like one who runs aimlessly or box like one beating the air. Instead, I discipline my

body and bring it under strict control, so that after preaching to others, I myself will not be disqualified. (1 Cor 9:24–27)

A closer look at this paragraph reveals the intensity with which Paul regarded spiritual discipline. When Paul told the Corinthians to "run to win," he used a word (*trecho*) that described "giving everything you had, spending all your strength, exerting total effort." When he spoke of athletes "exercising self-control" he used a word (*agonezomi*) from which we get our word *agony*. When he spoke of "disciplining" his body (*hupopeazo*), he used the image of a boxer "beating himself black and blue." The phrase "bring it under strict control" is from a word (*doulagogeo*) that was used of "making someone your slave" or "being a slave driver."

His point was that as athletes intensely train for physical progress, the Corinthians needed to put just as much effort into their spiritual growth. So do we.

Sweat in God's Gym

Train yourself in godliness. For the training of the body has limited benefit, but godliness is beneficial in every way, since it holds promise for the present life and also for the life to come. (1 Tim 4:7–8)

Sounding like a spiritual fitness coach, Paul told Timothy, you must "*train yourself in godliness.*" "Train yourself" (*gymnazo*) is the word from which we get our word *gymnasium*. As we noted previously, it means "to go into the gym, strip down, and sweat."

This training has three aspects.

First, it includes adding spiritual exercises to our lives. Time-tested disciplines such as Bible reading, prayer, and keeping a journal, among others, are ways we can spiritually go into God's gym and sweat each day. The second half of this book is a detailed discussion of the primary spiritual disciplines of the Christian life.

Second, spiritual training involves wise abstinence. Athletes not only need to add certain exercises to their lives, but they also need to cut out certain activities and attitudes that limit their growth. As the author of Hebrews encourages us, "Let us lay aside every hindrance and the sin that so easily ensnares us. Let us run with endurance the race that lies before us, keeping our eyes on Jesus" (Heb 12:1–2). If we want to become more like Jesus, we must cut out attitudes and activities that pull us in the opposite direction.

Third, spiritual training involves consistency. The word *discipline* or *train* in the original is a present tense verb. It implies consistent, ongoing, daily practice. Godliness does not happen overnight. It is a transformation from glory to glory, little by little, day by day (2 Cor 3:18). Every day we need to position ourselves to be transformed by the Spirit of the Lord into the image of Jesus. In this text, when Paul implored Timothy to "train yourself in godliness," he was telling him to practice those disciplines that will make you more like God. Spiritual formation is the result of vigorously practicing spiritual discipline.

Spiritual Discipline Is . . .

As we have seen, spiritual formation is the process of being changed to be more like Jesus. As we discussed in chapter 3, spiritual formation is a partnership where God does his part and we do ours (Phil 2:13). Spiritual discipline is our part in the spiritual transformation process. It is the human effort we make to press into God's presence so his life can transform our lives. It is our strategy for spiritual progress. Spiritual disciplines are specific spiritual exercises we do to position ourselves to be transformed by the Holy Spirit into the image of Jesus.

Spiritual Disciplines Are . . .

What are the spiritual practices that transform us into the image of Jesus? I remember an old preacher referring to them as "the things I do to get myself under the spout where the glory pours out."

Since the spiritual disciplines are many and varied, perhaps it is most helpful to give both general descriptions of them and specific examples. In general, spiritual disciplines are:

- Holy habits that propel our pursuit of God and the character of Christ.
- Spiritual exercises the Holy Spirit uses to train and transform us into the image of Jesus.
- Divine disciplines that maintain and deepen our relationship with God.
- Concrete actions that connect us to Jesus and allow us to more deeply abide in him.
- The means by which we lay the pipe to access the sanctifying grace of the living water.
- Aids to living under the influence of the Spirit.
- Spiritual practices that position us for and open us to more of God's work in our lives.
- Means of accessing the power of the Holy Spirit.
- Eternal exercises that keep us on the path toward God, with God, and for God.
- Means of transforming grace.

- Activities we can do so God can do in us what we can't do.
- Acts of obedience done because we love God and others.

Examples of Spiritual Disciplines

There are many spiritual disciplines. In the third section of this book, we discuss fifteen holy habits and primary practices of spiritual growth. We organize them under the three primary commands of Jesus: love God, love one another, and love your neighbor.

Love God: The Upward Disciplines

- Taking in the Word of Christ
- Prayer
- Journaling
- Fasting
- Stillness, Silence, and Solitude

Love One Another: The Inward Disciplines

- Doing Life Together
- Participating in a Healthy Small Group
- How to Love One Another
- Accountability
- Practiced at Home

Love Your Neighbor: The Outward Disciplines

- Praying for Your Neighbors
- Being Light to Your Neighbors
- Sharing the Good News with Your Neighbors
- Loving the Least of These
- Loving Your Enemies

Necessary Attitudes for Maximum Benefit from Spiritual Disciplines

Intentionality

Remember, the goal of spiritual formation is transformation into the image of Jesus. The point of practicing a spiritual discipline is to position yourself so the Holy Spirit can transform you. Practicing the disciplines is not an end it itself. The goal is Christlikeness. The disciplines are merely a means to the end.

My oldest sons were on their middle school's wrestling team. Part of the training involved push-ups and weight lifting. The goal was to strengthen the team to be better able to perform the skills needed to win wrestling matches.

On my sons' team were twin brothers. They paid little attention to technique and strategy. Instead they focused their attention almost exclusively on the push-ups and weight lifting (especially on doing biceps curls) in order to get bigger arms. As a result, they indeed had big arms. But they were unable to win matches against opponents' better wrestlers who had focused more on technique.

In a similar manner, it is pointless to read the Bible for hours if you do not allow the Holy Spirit to apply the truth of Scripture to change your life.

Frequency

In order to get in good physical condition, you need to exercise more than once. Physical fitness is the result of frequent and consistent exercise. A physical body is transformed little by little from weak and flabby to strong and lean after months of ongoing exercise.

In the same way, you cannot get in good spiritual condition by practicing a spiritual discipline once. Spiritual fitness is the result of frequent and consistent spiritual exercise. A person's beliefs, attitudes, behaviors, and personality are transformed little by little, day after day by the Spirit of the Lord as the individual draws closer to him through the regular practice of spiritual disciplines.

Humility

A chief character trait of Jesus that we are to grow in is humility. Paul said, "Adopt the same attitude as that of Christ Jesus . . . he humbled himself by becoming obedient to the point of death—even to death on a cross" (Phil 2:5, 8). We don't practice spiritual disciplines to prove we are better than someone else. We practice them to draw closer to Jesus and become more like him. We practice spiritual disciplines because we cannot become more like Jesus without them.

Dependency

We don't practice spiritual disciplines to reach a place of independence from God. We practice them because we are dependent on God. As we discussed in chapter 2, the branch is utterly dependent on the vine for life and must be connected to it to produce fruit. Jesus is the vine. Without him, we "can do nothing" (John 15:4).

Expectancy

When Moses practiced the spiritual discipline of meeting with the Lord, it was done in an attitude of expectancy (Exod 33:7–10). The people stood as he walked past them to enter the tent of meeting. The pillar of cloud signifying the manifest presence of the Lord hovered at the doorway. Inside, the Lord spoke with him face to face. Moses left with his countenance transformed.

We should not practice the disciplines merely to relieve guilt or to feel good about checking off a box on a spiritual growth plan. We need to practice our disciplines with the same attitude of expectancy that Moses had entering the tent of meeting. We are coming to connect with God, and as a result we will be transformed by his presence.

Variety

In physical fitness there is value to changing our routines. Otherwise our minds become bored, our energy lags, and our muscles stop progressing.

Most of us get in a rut with our spiritual disciplines. Doing only the same spiritual disciplines over and over can cause us to plateau spiritually. We find ourselves just going through the motions. Occasionally we need to change our disciplines to challenge and stretch our spiritual muscles.

Difficulty and Intensity

Oliver Wendell Holmes Jr. stated, "Man's mind, once stretched by a new idea, never regains its original dimensions."[1] Occasionally we need to be stretched to be changed. For years I have practiced the discipline of fasting one day a week. A few years ago, it had become such a routine that it lost its spiritual impact. So I decided to fast for several days. The greater degree of difficulty caused me to rely on the Lord more intensely.

The Tool That Makes It Easier

After I got saved, I tried to be consistent in having what my friends called "quiet time," which was simply reading the Bible and praying every day. But after the initial thrill wore off, I became more sporadic in maintaining my quiet time.

Frequently I would get excited and start a new discipline like keeping a journal, memorizing Scripture, or fasting, only to quit after a short time. I just couldn't stay consistent, let alone make progress.

Finally I decided I was going to give myself the best shot at success. So I bought a new journal. Then I created a spiritual growth plan.

Spiritual Growth Plan

Benjamin Franklin, a founding father of the United States, was also a leading printer, satirist, political theorist, politician, scientist, inventor, civic activist, statesman, and diplomat. He also published the popular *Poor Richard's Almanack*. In it he noted, "By failing to prepare, you are preparing to fail."[2]

Without a plan, we typically have great intentions for spiritual growth but little progress. Planning creates a map to get from here to there.

Business experts claim that "every minute you spend in planning saves 10 minutes in execution; this gives you a 1,000 percent Return on Energy!"[3] Read that again. One minute of planning saves ten minutes of doing. Wow!

That means careful planning yields a return of ten times, or 1,000 percent, on your investment of mental, emotional, and physical energy. Therefore, spending a meaningful period of time reflecting on strategy and goals *before* taking action is almost always a wise course of action for any individual or institution.

We are all busy. None of us has time to waste. Life is not a dress rehearsal. We get one shot at life. It is up to us to make the most of it. If we don't, we won't get to try it again. Planning helps us best use the time we have been given.

How to Develop Your Spiritual Growth Plan

Select areas for growth. Earlier in this chapter, we listed fifteen spiritual disciplines. Select five or six in which you need to grow. For instance, you might include: reading the Word, prayer, journaling, self-discipline, exercise, loving the least, and using my spiritual gifts.

Set SMART goals. The letters SMART make a mnemonic acronym providing criteria that guide us in setting effective goals. The letters stand for **S**pecific, **M**easurable, **A**ttainable, **R**elevant, and **T**ime related. A noneffective goal for Bible reading would be something like, "Read my Bible." A SMART goal for Bible reading may state, "Read three chapters every day for the next thirty days." Other examples of SMART goals:

- Private prayer—fifteen minutes every morning.
- Journaling—make an entry daily for a month.
- Exercise—go to the gym for an hour three days a week.
- Loving the least—serve the homeless men in the outreach center every Tuesday night for a month.
- Use my spiritual gifts in a weekly place of service every Sunday night.

- Corporate worship—participate every Sunday morning.
- Tithing—give first 10 percent of all to God through my local church.
- Fellowship—participate in small group every week.

Make a chart for your spiritual growth plan. On the top row, list the date in columns 2–8. In the second row, place the days of the week. Then in the first column starting with row 3, put the disciplines you will work on. Each day you fulfill your goal for a specific discipline, place a check in the corresponding box.

— Quote to Consider —

"Each of us can grow and improve. If you choose to grow, and commit to taking steps of growth daily, you will be on your way to reaching your potential. If you keep learning and growing every day over the course of many years, you will be astounded by how far it will take you."

—JOHN MAXWELL[4]

— Questions to Ponder —

1. What spiritual disciplines are you currently practicing?
2. Which ones do you need to add? Why?
3. Do you use a form of a spiritual growth plan?
4. Will you start using a spiritual growth plan?

Notes

1. Oliver Wendell Holmes, *The Collected Works of Justice Holmes: Complete Public Writings and Selected Judicial Opinions of Oliver Wendell Holmes,* 1st ed., ed. Sheldon Novick (Chicago: University of Chicago Press, 1994), 148.

2. Ben Franklin and Bob Blaisdell, *Poor Richard's Almanack and Other Writings* (Mineola, NY: Dover Publications, 2013), 25.

3. Brian Tracy, "Plan Ahead and Increase Productivity," Brian Tracy International, accessed May 23, 2016, https://www.briantracy.com/blog/time-management/plan-ahead-and-increase-productivity.

4. John Maxwell, "Are You Ready to Reach Your Potential?" The John Maxwell Co., accessed February 1, 2012, http://www.maxwellplan.com.

Date	Monday	Tuesday	Wednesday	Thursday	Friday	Saturday	Sunday
Bible Reading							
Prayer							
Journaling							
Exercise							
Loving the Least							
Use of Spiritual Gifts							

11

Putting to Death the Deeds of the Flesh

Rod Dempsey

One aspect of spiritual formation is battling the many and varied temptations we face on a daily basis. Spiritual formation is not only "putting on." There is also a commitment to eliminate the harmful residual effects of the fall. It is a daily battle to discourage, prevent, and eliminate anything and everything that exalts itself against the goal of becoming more and more like Jesus.

I live in the state of Virginia. A few years ago, our state was invaded by a terrible enemy. The enemy's name? "Stink bug." Now for those of you who may be unfamiliar with stink bugs, they are insects that stink. The Environmental Protection Agency gives the official description: "The brown marmorated stink bug, *Halyomorpha halys*, is an invasive pest that is present throughout much of the United States. The species is native to Asia and was introduced into the United States in the mid-1990s, possibly stowing away in a shipping container."[1] The website goes on to say that stink bugs reproduce quickly, are damaging to crops, and currently pesticides are not effective in controlling them. The website outlines eight suggestions to prevent stink bugs from entering your home because they can cause quite a fright if they happen to fly in your home and land on a person. Sometimes in the excitement, the stink bugs may get squashed. When they do, they certainly, as the name implies, stink. To prevent stink bugs from entering your home, a person must be vigilant and take precautions.

Now you may ask what stink bugs have to do with spiritual formation. Spiritually speaking, we have enemies that want to invade our lives. When they do penetrate our spiritual lives, they can cause quite a disruption. These enemies—the world, the flesh, and the devil—must not be allowed entrance into our homes/lives. If we are not vigilant or if we leave doors open (mind, body, spirit), they will be glad to come in and cause a stink. In our area, the stink bugs congregate outside our home in our screened porch. They wait until the door opens, and then they try to come inside. The only way I have found to prevent that from happening is to exterminate the "stinkers" before they enter the home. So usually two or three times a day, I go on "stink bug patrol." Using a mixture of soap and water, I spray the creatures, and within a few seconds they die.

Killing Sin

This earthy illustration has at least two spiritual parallels. In our spiritual formation, we have many enemies (e.g., lust of the flesh, lust of the eyes, and the pride of life), and they are trying to come into our lives (mind, body, spirit). These enemies will cause terrible disruption, and they will cause our lives to stink if left unchecked. They remain a threat day after day, week after week, and year after year. In our lifetimes, the threat never ceases. The second point of this illustration is that we must daily go on "stink bug patrol" and mortify, or put to death, the enemies of our spiritual growth. This patrol is about eliminating the enemies of our soul before they enter our lives and cause problems not only for us but for everyone around us as well. The Scriptures are clear that our sinful flesh is constantly trying to gain entrance and influence in our lives:

1. "For the flesh desires what is against the Spirit, and the Spirit desires what is against the flesh; these are opposed to each other, so that you don't do what you want" (Gal 5:17).
2. "Now the works of the flesh are obvious: sexual immorality, moral impurity, promiscuity, idolatry, sorcery, hatreds, strife, jealousy, outbursts of anger, selfish ambitions, dissensions, factions, envy, drunkenness, carousing, and anything similar" (Gal 5:19–21).
3. "So then, brothers and sisters, we are not obligated to the flesh to live according to the flesh, because if you live according to the flesh, you are going to die. But if by the Spirit you put to death the deeds of the body, you will live" (Rom 8:12–13).

We see from these passages that we have a natural enemy, and that enemy is our own fleshly appetites that wage war on our souls. Paul describes this battle in several places but perhaps most succinctly in Romans 7:

> For I know that nothing good lives in me, that is, in my flesh. For the desire to do what is good is with me, but there is no ability to do it. For I do not do the good that I want to do, but I practice the evil that I do not want to do. Now if I do what I do not want, I am no longer the one that does it, but it is the sin that lives in me. So, I discover this law: When I want to do what is good, evil is present with me. For in my inner self I delight in God's law, but I see a different law in the parts of my body, waging war against the law of my mind and taking me prisoner to the law of sin in the parts of my body. What a wretched man I am! Who will rescue me from this dying body? Thanks be to God through Jesus Christ our Lord! So then, with my mind I myself am serving the law of God, but with my flesh, the law of sin. (Rom 7:18–25)

Paul is describing the struggle the believer faces daily with the resident desire to go our own way, do our own thing, and rebel against God's ways. James describes the process this way: "But each person is tempted when he is drawn away and enticed by his own evil desire. Then after desire has conceived, it gives birth to sin, and when sin is fully grown, it gives birth to death" (Jas 1:14–15). We must both develop habits that promote godly living and disengage from habits that grieve and quench the Holy Spirit, who enables us and empowers us to follow Christ. Paul details some helpful steps for us in Colossians 3, which is a summary of Romans 6–8:

> So if you have been raised with Christ, seek the things above, where Christ is, seated at the right hand of God. Set your minds on things above, not on earthly things. For you died, and your life is hidden with Christ in God. When Christ, who is your life, appears, then you also will appear with him in glory. Therefore, put to death what belongs to your earthly nature: sexual immorality, impurity, lust, evil desire, and greed, which is idolatry. Because of these, God's wrath is coming upon the disobedient, and you once walked in these things when you were living in them. But now, put away all the following: anger, wrath, malice, slander, and filthy language from your mouth. Do not lie to one another, since you have put off the old self with its practices and have put on the new self. You are being renewed in knowledge according to the image of your Creator. (Col 3:1–10)

The focus for us in this chapter is verse 5, which states in effect, "Therefore, since we have died (Romans 6), we must now be in the business (present tense) of putting to death what belongs to our worldly nature." This sounds similar to what Paul says in Gal 5:24: "Now those who belong to Christ Jesus have crucified the flesh with its passions and desires." Paul continues in Colossians 3 to give us a list of some fleshly desires to be putting to death: "sexual immorality, impurity, lust, evil desire, and greed." Another passage that details some works of the flesh that we should not be allowing to guide our thoughts and actions is Gal 5:19–21:

> Now the works of the flesh are obvious: sexual immorality, moral impurity, promiscuity, idolatry, sorcery, hatreds, strife, jealousy, outbursts of anger, selfish ambitions, dissensions, factions, envy, drunkenness, carousing, and anything similar.

John gives us further instruction concerning the avenues of temptation and how the things of this world draw our singleness of devotion and love away from Christ.

> Do not love the world or the things in the world. If anyone loves the world, the love of the Father is not in him. For everything in the world—the lust of the flesh, the lust of the eyes, and the pride in one's possessions—is not from the Father, but is from the world. And the world with its lust is passing away, but the one who does the will of God remains forever. (1 John 2:15–17)

The broad categories of sinful desire the enemy uses to entrap and ensnare us, and to shift our affections from Christ to things in the world, are the lust of the flesh, the lust of the eyes, and pride in one's lifestyle.

So, how do we put these fleshly desires "to death"? How do we kill these "stink bugs" in our lives? The process can be summarized in this little poem:

> Two natures beat within my breast.
> The one is foul, the one is blessed.
> The one I love, the one I hate.
> The one I feed will dominate.
> —Anonymous

Puritan pastor John Owen put it this way, "Do you mortify; do you make it your daily work; be always at it while you live; cease not a day from this

Put Off: Starve the Flesh → Put On: Feed the Spirit → Walk in the Power of the Spirit work; be killing sin or it will be killing you."[2] "Be killing sin, or it will be killing you." That pretty well sums up this chapter. At this point, let me ask, Do you have a plan, a strategy to be killing sin in your life?

Replace the Old Habits

You may be practicing disciplines of engagement, but are you equally practicing disciplines of disengagement? Yes, we may be "putting on," but are we paying equal attention to "putting off"? The Scriptures place an equal emphasis on both disciplines. There are good habits that aid and assist the Holy Spirit to have greater influence in our lives, but there are also bad habits that feed the flesh, grieve the Spirit, and possibly quench the work of the Spirit. Consider the following suggestions for crucifying or killing the flesh:

- Kill the sin of greed by being generous.
- Kill the sin of fear by stepping out in faith/obedience.
- Kill the sin of lust by finding your source of love in Christ.
- Kill the sin of gossip by speaking well of others.
- Kill the sin of pride by practicing humility.
- Kill the sin of overeating by fasting.
- Kill the sin of overspending by sacrificial giving.
- Kill the sin of anger by speaking words of kindness.
- Kill the sin of harsh/filthy language by speaking uplifting words.
- Kill the sin of selfish ambition by promoting others.
- Kill the sin of drunkenness or losing control by being filled with the Spirit.

Are you killing sin? Are you crucifying the flesh? The enemy has been at this for a long time and has many tricks, snares, and temptations. We must be vigilant in not only starving the flesh but also resisting the temptation, going the extra mile, and turning the temptation into an opportunity for "letting our light shine before men." As Jesus said in the Sermon on the Mount:

> You have heard that it was said, An eye for an eye and a tooth for a tooth. But I tell you, don't resist an evildoer. On the contrary, if anyone slaps you on your right cheek, turn the other to him also. As for the one who wants to sue you and take away your shirt, let him have your coat as well. And if anyone forces you to go one mile, go with him two. Give to the one who asks you, and don't turn away from the one who wants to borrow from

you. You have heard that it was said, Love your neighbor and hate your enemy. But I tell you, love your enemies and pray for those who persecute you, so that you may be children of your Father in heaven. (Matt 5:38–45)

This of course sounds similar to Paul's instructions to the church at Rome in Rom 12:14–21:

- Bless those who persecute you; bless and do not curse.
- If your enemy is hungry, feed him.
- If someone wrongs us, we should not take our own revenge, but we should leave room for God's wrath.
- If an enemy is thirsty, give him something to drink.

And to the church of Ephesus in Eph 4:25–32:

- Since you put away lying, speak the truth to one another.
- No longer should a person steal, but rather should work and give to those in need.
- We should not engage in foul language, but we should speak only what is good to build up those around us.
- We should be kind and compassionate and forgive others because God has forgiven us.

It is not enough to put to death the deeds of the flesh. We must break the old habits (dehabituation) and replace them with new habits and disciplines (rehabituation). What are you wrestling with? What is your plan to overcome the "stink bugs" that seek to gain entrance into your soul? Follow the advice of Jesus and Paul and replace the old with the new way in Christ. Here are some principles to consider in this fight:

1. Spiritual formation involves consistently putting to death the desires and deeds of the flesh by walking in the power of God's Spirit.
2. Putting to death the deeds of the flesh requires that we starve the flesh and simultaneously strengthen the Spirit.
3. Starving the flesh means we intentionally limit negative input from the flesh, the world, and the devil.
4. Walking in the Spirit means the believer will experience victory over the flesh.
5. When we do not feed the Spirit, or worse, if we are feeding the flesh (leaving doors open), we are too weak to withstand the attacks of the world, the flesh, and the devil.

6. Be serious in the pursuit of killing sin (stink bugs) in your life. To paraphrase what Jesus said, "If your hand offends you, cut it off. If your eye offends you, pluck it out" (Matt 18:8–9). Now we know this is not to be taken literally, but it does mean that we are to be serious in dealing with the "sin that so entangles us" (Heb 12:1).

7. The goal of the Christian life is not external conformity or mindless action but a passionate love for God that causes us to act.

8. Continually ask friends to help you adopt good habits (habituation) and get rid of bad habits (dehabituation).

9. Make a plan to put on good habits and make a plan to put off bad habits. Work out your salvation with fear and trembling.

— Quote to Consider —

"Discipleship to Jesus ideally means, in Evangelical piety, living interactively with his resurrected presence (through his word and people) as we progressively learn to lead our lives as he would lead our lives if he were we."

—DALLAS WILLARD[3]

— Questions to Ponder —

1. From the categories "lust of the flesh," "lust of the eyes," and "love of the world," which category gives you the most challenge?

2. What is one bad habit that you need to "put to death" in your life right now?

3. What is a good habit that could replace your bad habit?

Notes

1. "Brown Marmorated Stink Bug," EPA, accessed February 22, 2018, https://www.epa.gov/safepestcontrol/brown-marmorated-stink-bug.

2. John Owen, *Overcoming Sin and Temptation*, eds. Kelly M. Kapic and Justin Taylor (Wheaton: Crossway, 2006), 50.

3. Dallas Willard, "Christ-Centered Piety," accessed March 16, 2018, http://www.dwillard.org/articles/individual/christ-centered-piety.

12

Three-Directional Love

Rod Dempsey

Spiritual formation is primarily about becoming more and more like God. The apostle John tells us succinctly that "God is love" (1 John 4:8). Believing in and receiving the good news of the gospel is our introduction to this God of love. As we are introduced to him and as we spend time with him, we should become more like him and become more loving. In fact, the first fruit of walking in and being controlled by the Spirit of God is love. As we become more loving, our influence and impact on the world around us become tangible.

I met my wife in the winter of 1980. We met in college. A mutual friend introduced us while I was doing laundry. The smell of the detergent, the banging of the dryers, the hot stifling air in the room. It was so romantic. In spite of the surroundings, we had a great conversation, and she made an immediate impression on me. After I finished folding my clothes and as I was walking back to my dorm, I said to myself, *She could be the person I marry.* The following year, on top of the World Trade Center in New York City, I asked her to be my wife. The next year, we were married, and for more than thirty-five years now, I have had the privilege of knowing her as my wife. She is godly. She is beautiful. She is kind. She is strong. She is smart. She is determined. She is a wonderful representation of the continuing work of God's grace in a human being. To say I love her would be too simplistic because human love is a difficult thing to quantify and describe. It has many facets. Is it an emotion? Yes. Is it an action? Yes. Is it difficult? Yes. Is it easy? Yes. Does it require commitment? Yes. Can it be lost? Yes. Is it conditional? Seemingly. Is it a choice? Yes. This concept called love has many characteristics.

God's love, though, is different from human love. It is similar in some ways, but it is pure. When God loves a person—and God loves every person—he loves them individually and unconditionally. God's love never ends. We see God's love most clearly in the gospel. "For God loved the world in this way: He gave his one and only Son, so that everyone who believes in him will not perish but have eternal life" (John 3:16). This is the crux of the gospel. The good news is that God's love prompted him to save us. The Creator God comes to the rebellious creation and lays down his life so that the creation can be reconciled to the Creator. When we come to know Christ, we begin to experience God's love, and he wants us to emulate his love. God's love is humble and self-sacrificing. The apostle Paul explains this type of love to the Philippian church:

> Everyone should look out not only for his own interests, but also for the interests of others. Adopt the same attitude as that of Christ Jesus, who, existing in the form of God, did not consider equality with God as something to be exploited. Instead he emptied himself by assuming the form of a servant, taking on the likeness of humanity. And when he had come as a man, he humbled himself by becoming obedient to the point of death—even to death on a cross. (Phil 2:4–8)

God's love as seen in Jesus is an others-oriented, need-meeting type of love. God wants this type of love to characterize his followers. It is a love that sacrifices for others. It is a humble love that does not feel the need to exalt but to serve. It is a love whose highest ambition is obeying the Father. It is a love that causes people to "empty" themselves in service of others. This is how Henry Drummond explains the process, "God is love. Therefore love. Without distinction, without calculation, without procrastination, love."[1] Consider what the apostle John says, "Dear friends, let us love one another, because love is from God, and everyone who loves has been born of God and knows God. The one who does not love does not know God, because God is love" (1 John 4:7–8). God's Word gives us some parameters regarding how we are to love and, as a result, become more like Christ. Neil Cole more recently describes the three aspects a little differently,

> In our movement the DNA is the key component of organic church. Our life giving code is within each disciple (a result of internalizing and activating/obeying the gospel) and is the most important part of being organic. The DNA is Divine Truth (relating to God—the great commandment), Nurturing Relationships (relating to one another—the second greatest command) and Apostolic Mission (relating to the world—the great commission).[2]

Loving God (relating to God), loving one another (nurturing relationships), and loving our neighbors (apostolic mission) is the DNA of a follower of Jesus.

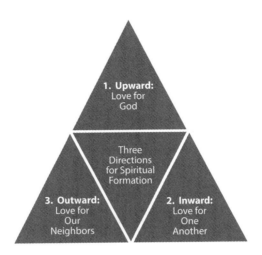

Upward

Throughout the Bible we are commanded to love God, love one another (fellow believers), and love everyone, everywhere, all the time. Jesus explains to the Pharisees what God expects concerning love:

> When the Pharisees heard that he had silenced the Sadducees, they came together. And one of them, an expert in the law, asked a question to test him: "Teacher, which command in the law is the greatest?" He said to him, "Love the Lord your God with all your heart, with all your soul, and with all your mind. This is the greatest and most important command. The second is like it: Love your neighbor as yourself. All the Law and the Prophets depend on these two commands." (Matt 22:34–40)

We are to love God with all our heart, soul, and mind. Our love for God is to be all encompassing and all consuming. Heart, soul, and mind. To make this practical, this is where the disciplines come into focus. We can sharpen our love for God, love for one another, and love for our neighbors by responding to his love and developing habits and disciplines that deepen our love. For instance, when my wife and I were first dating, we were away from each other for one summer while in school. As a result, we wrote each other love letters every day.

Now I am not saying that the prose contained in these letters rose to a Shakespearean level, but they were heartfelt expressions of love. I remember going to the mailbox each day with excitement and anticipation. I could not wait to read the words my beloved had taken the time and effort to write down on paper. Her words gave me encouragement. Her words gave me confidence. Her words gave me joy. Her words gave me hope for the future. As I read her letters, I got to know her better. I was beginning to learn what was important to her. I began to learn what she liked and what she didn't like. As I read her letters, I made mental notes to remember and put into practice things I knew would please her. I also made mental notes to avoid things that she didn't like. Getting to know her through her letters gave me meaningful things to talk about when we spent time together. In like manner, we can deepen our love for God by getting to know him through reading his letters and talking with him through prayer.

You can probably tell from this human illustration what it can and should be like as we read God's love letter to us (the Bible). We know that God loves us. He sent his Son to die in our place. We know that "His divine power has given us everything required for life and godliness through the knowledge of him" (2 Pet 1:3). Our source of power and strength is accessed "through the knowledge of him." Our knowledge of his teachings through his Word is our access to life and godliness, and we need to take this seriously. Reading God's words empowers our communication with him. We each have 168 hours in a week, and I believe we should allocate at least one hour a day to hearing, reading, studying, memorizing, and meditating on God's Word and spending time in his presence in prayer. This is how we get to know who God is and how he wants us to live. Simply put, what if every believer consistently invested one hour a day reading God's Word and getting to know him in a personal way through prayer? What would happen to a church if every believer were reading God's Word like a love letter? I believe if every believer in a church read God's Word like a precious love letter and looked forward to spending time with him, that church would experience an immediate revival. Consider what Jesus, through the apostle John, says to the church of Ephesus:

> But I have this against you: You have abandoned the love you had at first. Remember then how far you have fallen; repent, and do the works you did at first. Otherwise, I will come to you and remove your lampstand from its place, unless you repent. (Rev 2:4–5)

The church at Ephesus had abandoned their first love, and they were in danger of having God's presence and blessing removed from their midst. Now keep in mind that this is the same church to which Paul gave this instruction,

"Husbands, love your wives, just as Christ loved the church and gave himself for her to make her holy, cleansing her with the washing of water by the word" (Eph 5:25–26). Christ loves the church, gives himself up for the church, and cleanses the church through the washing of the Word. His Word is what cleanses us and makes us spotless and blameless. He does this to present the church to himself in splendor. Years after the Ephesians received that teaching, the Spirit of God instructed John to tell them that something was wrong—and this is a terrible indictment—they had "abandoned their first love."

Any and every church can experience revival if they will daily hear, read, study, memorize, and meditate on God's words. The author of the book of Hebrews describes God's Word this way, "For the word of God is living and effective and sharper than any double-edged sword, penetrating as far as the separation of soul and spirit, joints and marrow. It is able to judge the thoughts and intentions of the heart" (Heb 4:12). The first direction we must direct our love is upward. We are to respond to God's love by intentionally spending time hearing, reading, studying, memorizing, and meditating on his Word, so we can actively love him back.

Inward

The next direction we must direct our love is inward. Jesus tells his disciples in the upper room that he has a "new" commandment for them. This new commandment is in addition to loving God with all of our heart, soul, and mind. This new commandment pertains to loving our brothers and sisters in the family of God. Consider Jesus's teaching, "I give you a new command: Love one another. Just as I have loved you, you are also to love one another. By this everyone will know that you are my disciples, if you love one another" (John 13:34–35). Jesus reiterates this command in John 15:12, "This is my command: Love one another as I have loved you." The way we love our brothers and sisters is to follow all of the "one anothers" in the New Testament and use our spiritual gifts to build one another up in the Lord's service. The phrase *one another* occurs more than fifty times in the New Testament, and the phrase is always connected to points of action. Here is a partial list (more on this in chapter 20) of how we can practice our love for one another (emphasis added):

- *"Love one another"* (John 13:34).
- *"Love one another deeply. . . . Outdo one another* in showing honor" (Rom 12:10).
- *"Live in harmony with one another"* (Rom 12:16).

- *"Accept one another"* (Rom 15:7).
- *"Instruct one another"* (Rom 15:14).
- *"Greet one another"* (Rom 16:16).
- *"Agree with one another"* (1 Cor 1:10 NIV).
- *"Serve one another through love"* (Gal 5:13).
- "With patience, *bearing with one another in love"* (Eph 4:2).
- *"Be kind and compassionate to one another, forgiving one another"* (Eph 4:32).
- *"Speaking to one another* in psalms, hymns, and spiritual songs" (Eph 5:19).
- *"Submitting to one another* in the fear of Christ" (Eph 5:21).
- "In all wisdom *teaching and admonishing one another"* (Col 3:16).
- *"Encourage one another daily"* (Heb 3:13 NIV).
- *"Watch out for one another* to provoke love and good works" (Heb 10:24).
- *"Don't criticize one another, brothers and sisters"* (Jas 4:11).
- *"Confess your sins to one another and pray for one another"* (Jas 5:16).
- *"Be hospitable to one another* without complaining" (1 Pet 4:9).
- "All of you *clothe yourselves with humility toward one another"* (1 Pet 5:5).
- *"Have fellowship with one another"* (1 John 1:7).

Jesus commanded us to love one another. Fortunately for us, the authors of the New Testament explained and illustrated for us how to obey this command: by practicing the "one anothers"! This new command of loving one another is in addition to the two great commandments to love God and to love our neighbor. When taken together, obedience and adherence to these three commands is the complete picture of what a spiritually formed follower of Jesus looks like. The others-oriented service and ministry to members in the body of Christ is different from the world's self-interest and self-absorption. Imagine what would happen if every member in your church had a daily, disciplined practice of using their gifts, talents, and abilities and followed all of the "one anothers" in the New Testament (more on this in chapter 20).

Outward

To complete the circle, we are commanded not only to love God and love one another. We are also commanded to "love our neighbor as ourselves." As we love God and as we love one another, we begin to show that God is living among us, and the visible presence of Christ begins to be seen and felt in our community. Our love for God and for one another should be a major apologetic to the unbelieving world. The message of Christ, who loved so much that he died in our place, should not only be heard; it should also be seen, felt, and experienced. Methodism founder John Wesley was among the numerous figures in church history who believed personal piety and love of neighbors worked hand in hand in the Christian life. Wesley stated in a sermon:

> But what good works are those, the practice of which you affirm to be necessary to sanctification? First, all works of piety; such as public prayer, family prayer, and praying in our closet; receiving the supper of the Lord; searching the Scriptures, by hearing, reading, meditating; and using such a measure of fasting or abstinence as our bodily health allows. Secondly, all works of mercy; whether they relate to the bodies or souls of men; such as feeding the hungry, clothing the naked, entertaining the stranger, visiting those that are in prison, or sick, or variously afflicted; such as the endeavouring to instruct the ignorant, to awaken the stupid sinner, to quicken the lukewarm, to confirm the wavering, to comfort the feebleminded, to succour the tempted, or contribute in any manner to the saving of souls from death. This is the repentance, and these the "fruits meet for repentance," which are necessary to full sanctification.[3]

Wesley believed followers of Jesus should be involved in loving their neighbors by practicing "acts of mercy" (more on this in chapter 26). We can intentionally develop daily habits and disciplines that will help us love our neighbors, but it requires effort and focus. Dave Ferguson, with Verge Network and Exponential, has come up with an acrostic explaining how to BLESS our neighbors:

- B—Begin with prayer. We want you to ask, "God how do you want me to bless the people in the places you've sent me?"
- L—Listen. Don't talk, but listen to people, their struggles, and their pains in the places God has sent you.
- E—Eat. You can't just check this off. It's not quick. You have to have a meal or cup of coffee with people. It builds relationships.
- S—Serve. If you listen to people and you eat with people, they will tell you how to love them, and you'll know how to serve them.
- S—Story. When the time is right, we share the story of how Jesus changed our life.[4]

Imagine if every member of your church intentionally blessed their neighbors. What would your church look like? What would your community look like? The church of Jesus Christ shows itself to be the body of Christ as its members love God with their whole heart (upward), love one another (inward), and love their neighbors (outward).

— Quote to Consider —

"Now is our time. By far the most powerful 'church-growth
plan' ever implemented is that of the Great Commission.
Its incredible effect on the world in the times immediately
following its impartation was due to the whole life
transformation it brought to millions of ordinary people
who, as disciples, were taught to do and lead others to
do 'all things, whatsoever I have commanded you.'"

—DALLAS WILLARD[5]

— Questions to Ponder —

1. Which type of love do you need to work on most: upward (love for God), inward (love for one another), or outward (love for your neighbors)?
2. What is your plan to develop some new habits in that area?
3. Who can hold you accountable to develop some new habits to love God, love one another, and love your neighbors?

Notes

1. Henry Drummond, *The Greatest Thing in the World* (London: Hodder and Stoughton, 1880), 6; accessed December 29, 2017, https://www.jesus.org.uk/sites/default/files/media/documents/books/others/drummond_greatest_thing.pdf.

2. Neil Cole, *Church 3.0: Upgrades for the Future of the Church* (New York: Jossey-Bass Leadership Network Series, 2010), 7. Kindle Edition.

3. John Wesley, "The Scripture Way of Salvation," Wesley Center Online, accessed December 29, 2017, http://wesley.nnu.edu/john-wesley/the-sermons-of-john-wesley-1872-edition/sermon-43-the-scripture-way-of-salvation/.

4. Davd Ferguson, "Five Ways to Bless Your Neighbors," Verge, accessed February 23, 2018, https://www.vergenetwork.org/2012/12/27/five-ways-to-bless-your-neighbors-dave-ferguson.

5. Dallas Willard, "Whole Life Transformation," accessed March 16, 2018, http://www.dwillard.org/articles/individual/foreword-whole-life-transformation.

Part 3

The Practices and Disciplines of Spiritual Formation

The Upward Disciplines—
Loving God

13 Taking in the Word of Christ

Rod Dempsey

I transferred to a Christian college when I was nineteen years old. I had spent years trying to live for Christ and failed many times. There were times when I genuinely wanted to follow Christ, but I seemed to have no power to resist the urges and temptations I was facing. I wanted to follow Christ. The desire was there, but the ability was not. The first or second night I was in my dorm room, a resident assistant walked into my room and, after exchanging pleasantries, asked, "What did you get out of God's Word today?" I was taken aback. I mumbled something about the fact that it had been a busy day and I was just getting settled. But I remember thinking I had never been asked that question before and I did not like it. The next night, the RA came into my room again, and we discussed the day's events. Then much to my chagrin, he asked the same question again: "What did you get out of God's Word today?" BOOM. Yikes! I was caught flat-footed again. Once more I explained I was getting things sorted out in a new environment and so forth and so on. This time my thinking changed from, *Who does this person think he is?* to *Hmmm, maybe I need to make some changes to my schedule and make room for reading God's Word.* I also figured he probably was going to keep on asking the same question.

The next morning I picked up the Bible, and for the first time I started reading God's Word for myself. I started reading Genesis 1 and then chapter 2 and 3 and 4. The more I read, the more I wanted to read. This was something new and powerful in my life. I could not wait until the RA came into my room and asked the question again. Sure enough he did, and this time I was able to say I had read God's Word and it was wonderful.

Over the next few months, I continued to read God's Word every day, and the RA and I struck up a close spiritual friendship that extends to this day. That RA's name was Dave Earley, the coauthor of this book. God used that simple question—What did you get out of God's Word today?—to change my habits and cause me to adjust my schedule to allow time for reading God's Word. God's Word was flowing into my mind, my heart, and my soul, and it was beginning to change me from the inside out. Let me ask the same question: What did you get out of God's Word today? The answer to that question has the power to change your life, because the Word of God is "living and active" (Heb 4:12). In my case, I had committed my life to Christ, but the Spirit of God through the Word of God was not transforming me. This process reminds me of what Paul wrote in Rom 12:1–2:

> Therefore, brothers and sisters, in view of the mercies of God, I urge you to present your bodies as a living sacrifice, holy and pleasing to God; this is your true worship. Do not be conformed to this age, *but be transformed by the renewing of your mind,* so that you may discern what is the good, pleasing, and perfect will of God. (emphasis added)

Even though I had presented my body to Christ many times, I was not experiencing the good, pleasing, and perfect will of God, because my mind was not being renewed by the Word of God. I was seemingly powerless to resist the temptations and urges I faced. Jesus addresses this in John 8:30–32:

> As he was saying these things, many believed in him. Then Jesus said to the Jews who had believed him, "If you continue in my word, you really are my disciples. You will know the truth, and the truth will set you free."

Jesus is our final authority, and he is the one who instructs us to "continue in [his] word." What does this mean? This means we are to listen to and obey his words. From Genesis to Revelation, the Bible is the Word of God, and as such it is the Word of Christ. Therefore, we should be hearing, reading, studying, memorizing, and meditating on the Word of Christ consistently—so much so that the "living and active" Word of God is bending our hearts, our minds, and our wills to align with the good, pleasing, and perfect will of God. These disciplines will lead us to better understand and obey Christ, who is himself the Word of God (cf. John 1:1–4). He is the object of our study, and he is the pattern for our lives. Donald Whitney says, "No Spiritual Discipline is more important than the intake of God's Word. Nothing can substitute for it. There simply is no healthy Christian life apart from a diet of the milk and meat of Scripture."[1]

Sometimes, however, we may get the incorrect impression that mere knowledge of God is the supreme goal of spiritual formation. While cognitive knowledge is crucial, sometimes bare knowledge without warmhearted personal devotion to Christ can lead to a modern-day form of Gnosticism. Now do not misinterpret what I am saying. I am not saying knowledge is unimportant. Knowledge of God's Word is important as it leads our hearts, minds, and wills to bend our path toward following Christ. Knowledge without accompanying personal application is what I'm warning against.

Martin Luther, the great reformer of the church, referred to Scripture as "the swaddling-clothes and the mangers in which Christ lies."[2] As a mother goes to a cradle to find her baby, we go to the Bible to find Jesus. We must never focus only on the cradle without paying attention to the baby. George Mueller wrote, "I saw that the most important thing I had to do was to give myself to the reading of the Word of God, and to meditation on it. . . . What is the food of the inner man? Not prayer, but the Word of God; and . . . not the simple reading of the Word of God, so that it only passes through our minds, just as water runs through a pipe, but considering what we read, pondering over it, and applying it to our hearts."[3] We read God's Word, and we ponder over it, applying it to our hearts and lives. We do not read God's Word just for information but for obedience. Consider the warning James gives:

> But be doers of the word and not hearers only, deceiving yourselves. Because if anyone is a hearer of the word and not a doer, he is like someone looking at his own face in a mirror. For he looks at himself, goes away, and immediately forgets what kind of person he was. But the one who looks intently into the perfect law of freedom and perseveres in it, and is not a forgetful hearer but a doer who works—this person will be blessed in what he does. (Jas 1:22–25)

We are to be doers of the Word, not hearers only. We must not preach and teach the Scriptures without a systematic plan to help train listeners to become doers of the Word of Christ. We worship Jesus by obeying Jesus. We obey Jesus as we hear, read, study, memorize, and meditate on the words of Christ. Now I would like to turn our attention to some of my favorite ways of taking in the Word of God.

Hearing

This one is easy. Go to church every week and take notes on what you hear. On your way home, discuss one or two things you learned from the sermon. Later, share that information with someone. At first glance, this might sound simplistic. However, consider an analysis that concluded that "less than 20 percent of Americans regularly attend church—half of what the pollsters report."[4] For the longest time many pollsters believed 40 percent of Americans were attending church. However, it may be that while 40 percent say they attend church weekly, only about 20 percent actually attend. In contrast to the contemporary dearth of church attendance, the author of Hebrews emphasizes coming together regularly with other believers:

> And let us watch out for one another to provoke love and good works, not neglecting to gather together, as some are in the habit of doing, but encouraging each other, and all the more as you see the day approaching. (Heb 10:24–25)

Make sure you are attending church every week. Make sure you are taking notes. Make sure you are discussing what you are learning. Moreover, make sure you are sharing what you are learning with others. Give serious attention to hearing the Word of Christ, and let it lead you to Christ.

Reading

Again, there are many ways to take in the Word of God, but my favorite way to daily immerse myself in God's Word is a simple plan called the *One Year Bible*. It is a daily reading system where you read a little from the Old Testament, a little from the New Testament, a little from Psalms, and a couple of verses from Proverbs. I like to call it a balanced diet from the Word of God. You can either purchase a hard copy of the *One Year Bible* or you can read the online version.[5] Before I start reading, I pray a simple prayer along the lines of "Lord, speak to me today through your Word." It only takes about fifteen minutes to read the collected passages. Then I write down one or two verses I feel I need for that day or I feel the Holy Spirit prompting me to consider. I have used this method for more than thirty years, and it works for me. Now, I realize that there are many different ways to read God's Word. You can check out a variety of Bible reading plans at Bible Gateway.[6] I am sure you can find at least one plan of Bible reading that will work for you.

Studying

To study the Word of God, you need three essential commodities. First, you need time. Second, you need a place. Third, you need a plan. Let us look at these one at a time:

Time

Let us state the obvious: everyone is busy—or at least we all think we are busy. You truly may be busy. However, the real question is not about how busy you are. The real question is, What are your priorities in life? According to one estimate, the average person makes about 35,000 decisions each day![7] Just think about the numerous decisions we face:

- What to eat
- What to wear
- What to purchase
- What we believe
- What jobs and career choices we will pursue
- How to vote
- Who to spend our time with
- Who we will date and marry

- What we say and how we say it
- Whether or not we would like to have children
- What we will name our children
- Who our children spend their time with
- What they will eat[8]

Remember the conversation Jesus had with Mary and Martha concerning priorities. The story reveals that if we choose the one necessary thing, the Lord may say to us, "You have made the right choice."

> While they were traveling, he entered a village, and a woman named Martha welcomed him into her home. She had a sister named Mary, who also sat at the Lord's feet and was listening to what he said. But Martha was distracted by her many tasks, and she came up and asked, "Lord, don't you care that my sister has left me to serve alone? So tell her to give me a hand."
>
> The Lord answered her, "Martha, Martha, you are worried and upset about many things, but one thing is necessary. Mary has made the right choice, and it will not be taken away from her." (Luke 10:38–42)

The right choice in our daily onslaught of choices is to spend time hearing, reading, and studying God's Word. That is the "one thing that is necessary."

Place

Now this sounds easy, but it may require more effort than you think. You need a place of quietness free of distractions. When I was in college, I had three roommates, and there was rarely a time during the day that I was alone. It is hard to study anything, much less God's Word, with noise and distraction all around. So I decided to find a place where I could get alone with God and his Word. After looking around, I found a room where I could go early in the morning and be alone. I remember well that as I closed the door behind me, it seemed as if the Spirit of the Lord came in right behind me, and we sat down together to discover Jesus revealed in his Word. You need a quiet place. Discipline yourself to find a quiet place free of distractions.

Plan

As has already been mentioned, a lot of plans are available to the person who is serious about studying God's Word.[9] However, let me share a simple plan that is easy to remember. It is called the STUDY method. I do not remember where I picked it up, but I have used it for many years, and it is the method I share with my students every semester as I teach spiritual formation. It is a simple acrostic that goes like this:

S—Summarize the passage:

- What does it say?
- What does it mean?
- *Put into your own words the main idea in a few sentences.*

T—Title. Give the passage a title that summarizes the main idea.

U—Uplifts. Write down one to two encouraging ideas or thoughts from the passage.

D—Difficulties. Write down anything that is unclear from the passage for future study or further clarification.

Y—Your verse. Write out word for word the verse you believe God is leading you to meditate on.

Memorizing

One of the first books I read after I surrendered my life to Christ was a biography of Dawson Trotman. The title of the book is *Daws: The Story of Dawson Trotman, Founder of the Navigators.* I discovered that Dawson started memorizing Scripture as a child in order to win a contest in a church. Reading this book and the powerful testimony of how God used the Navigators and the power of Scripture memory caused me to develop the same discipline.

The plan I followed is one I recommend to you, and it is so simple. It starts with purchasing three-by-five index cards and simply writing out the verse or passage you want to memorize on one or more cards. Say the verse aloud fifteen to twenty times. Then close your eyes and try to remember the verse. If you have trouble, read the verse or passage again fifteen to twenty times and again close your eyes and repeat the verse or passage. Continue until you have the verse memorized word for word. You may object and say, "I can't memorize." But you can. You do all the time. It is a matter of priorities. Spiritual formation is a matter of engaging in the habits and disciplines that feed the Spirit and starve the flesh. Scripture memory is a discipline just like any other discipline. It requires attention and effort. Today I have hundreds of verses memorized, and my life and ministry are much richer for committing to memory the "living and active" Word of God. Yours will be too.[10]

Meditating

Meditating is perhaps the easiest discipline because it is a natural result of continually hearing, reading, studying, and memorizing God's Word. When I say it is the easiest, I do not mean to imply it does not require effort. It does. Yet there is a simplicity to meditating, because it is merely the discipline of getting the most out of your hearing, reading, studying, memorizing, and meditating. Here are a few suggestions from Donald Whitney for meditating on Scripture:

- Memorize the text.
- Emphasize different words in the text.
- Rewrite the text in your own words.
- Formulate a principle from the text. What does it teach?
- Think of an illustration of the text. What picture explains it?
- Look for applications of the text.
- Ask how the text points to the law or the gospel.
- Ask how the text points to something about Jesus.
- Ask what question is answered or what problem is solved by the text.
- Pray through the text.
- Create an artistic expression of the text.[11]

Conclusion

The purpose of hearing, reading, studying, memorizing, and meditating on God's Word is not just for head knowledge, but it is instead to encourage us to obey the Word of God. Obedience to Jesus Christ in our thoughts, attitudes, words, and actions is our highest goal. It is about spiritual transformation. The transformation begins when we believe the gospel: the good news of how Jesus came to this earth to be the sacrificial Lamb of God and to take our sin penalty and satisfy the holy wrath of God against our rebellion. The transformation continues as we daily make choices to align our words, thoughts, attitudes, and actions with God's will. As we daily choose to follow the promptings of God's Spirit and to "train ourselves in godliness" (1 Tim 4:7), the Spirit of God assumes greater control over our "old man," and we begin to experience the fruit of the Spirit. As our words, thoughts, attitudes, and actions are transformed into the image of Christ by the Spirit of God, the image of God is revealed in our daily interaction with the world he has created. We become more loving people. Our love for God, one another, and our neighbors becomes the visible apologia for the verbal proclamation of the gospel. Being leads to doing.

∼ Quote to Consider ∼

"For the word of God is living and effective and sharper than any double-edged sword, penetrating as far as the separation of soul and spirit, joints and marrow. It is able to judge the thoughts and intentions of the heart."

—Heb 4:12

∼ Questions to Ponder ∼

1. Of the five ways to take in the Word of Christ (hearing, reading, studying, memorizing, and meditating), which do you need to work on most?
2. What is your plan to develop this area?
3. Who can you ask to hold you accountable for the development of this area?

Notes

1. Donald S. Whitney, *Spiritual Disciplines for the Christian Life* (Carol Stream, IL: NavPress, 2014), 22. Kindle Edition.

2. Martin Luther, "Introduction to the Old Testament," 1523, accessed December 29, 2017, http://www.godrules.net/library/luther/NEW1luther_f8.htm.

3. George Mueller, *A Narrative of Some of the Lord's Dealings with George Muller, Written by Himself, Jehovah Magnified. Addresses by George Muller Complete and Unabridged,* 2 vols. (Muskegon, MI: Dust and Ashes, 2003), 1:272–73.

4. Kelly Shattuck, "7 Startling Facts: An Up Close Look at Church Attendance in America," ChurchLeaders.com, December 14, 2017, accessed December 29, 2017, https://www.churchleaders.com/pastors/pastor-articles/139575-7-startling-facts-an-up-close-look-at-church-attendance-in-america.html.

5. "One Year Bible Reading Plan Download," One Year Bible Online, accessed February 23, 2018, http://www.oneyearbibleonline.com/reading-plan-downloads.

6. "Welcome to Scripture Engagement," Bible Gateway, accessed February 23, 2018, https://www.biblegateway.com/resources/scripture-engagement.

7. Dr. Joel Hoomans, "35,000 Decisions: The Great Choices of Strategic Leaders," *Leading Edge Journal,* accessed February 23, 2018, https://go.roberts.edu/leadingedge/the-great-choices-of-strategic-leaders.

8. Hoomans.

9. "How to Study the Bible," accessed February 23, 2018, https://www.navigators.org/resource/how-to-study-the-bible/.

10. Dawson Trotman, "Converted through Scripture Memorization," Sermon Index, accessed April 27, 2018, http://img.sermonindex.net/modules/newbb/viewtopic_pdf.php?topic_id=48530&forum=34.

11. Justin Taylor, "17 Ways to Meditate on Scripture," The Gospel Coalition, accessed February 23, 2018, https://www.thegospelcoalition.org/blogs/justin-taylor/17-ways-to-meditate-on-scripture.

14 Prayer

Dave Earley

King David was an astounding man. He was an incredible leader, an invincible warrior, a top-flight musician, a cunning general, a popular songwriter, and a beloved monarch. On top of that and foundational to it, David was a man whose heart beat in rhythm with God's (Acts 13:22).

The secret of his greatness can be found in a simple statement David made describing how he handled fierce opposition: "But I am a man of prayer" (Ps 109:4 NIV).

In the Hebrew, this multiword phrase is only two words, which can be translated literally: "But I prayer." The Hebrew word for prayer (*tĕphillah*) could describe an intercession, a supplication, or a song. Some translate this word in the context of Psalm 109 as "I give myself to prayer" (NKJV and ESV), or "But I resort to prayer" (AMPC), or "But I am in prayer" (NASB). I especially like the way Adolph Saphir renders the phrase as "I prayer" or "I am prayer."[1] Prayer was such a part of David's life that it defined his life. His life was prayer.

The Foundation of Spiritual Formation

Prayer is the foundational spiritual discipline. In a sense nearly all other spiritual disciplines incorporate prayer. It is a primary means for spiritual transformation. Since God is the agent of spiritual formation and prayer is communicating with and connecting to God, prayer is a primary tool by which God transforms us into his image. It is essential in maintaining our relationship with him.

Prayer Is . . .

Prayer is the one discipline we can and should practice as we practice the other disciplines. Prayer makes all the others better.

In a simple sense, prayer is communicating with God. Spiritual growth can be hindered when we get stuck in a rut of only communing with God a few ways. Effective prayer has a variety of expressions.

The following descriptions of prayer help give an understanding of how simple yet varied prayer is.

1. Talking directly with God
2. Listening to God's voice
3. Practicing the presence of God
4. Opening yourself for spiritual heart surgery
5. Telling God everything going on in your life
6. Begging God to intervene and effect change in circumstances
7. Praising God for who he is
8. Thanking God for what he has done
9. Asking God for help
10. Standing in the gap before God on behalf of others
11. Counseling with the most trustworthy adviser in the universe
12. Declaring the worthiness of Jesus
13. Petitioning God to supply needs
14. Crying "Abba" to your heavenly Father
15. Asking forgiveness
16. Bowing before the supreme majesty
17. Sharing with a trusted friend
18. Silently enjoying a lover's companionship
19. Asking for mercy
20. Taking authority over the enemy
21. Releasing your spiritual debtors

Read back through the list slowly. Note the images that leap out at you. Why do those particular images get your attention?

Prayer Because . . .

Christian prayer is a stunning and staggering privilege. To us prayer is free and easily available. But even though it is free, it is not cheap or unimportant.

Jesus paid a bloody, exorbitant, overwhelming price. Prayer is an overwhelming privilege. Remember, Jesus died to make it possible for us to pray. Christ went to the cross, offering his life and shedding his blood to make it possible for the veil of the temple to be torn (Matt 27:50–51; Heb 6:19–20; 10:19–22) and for us to have direct access to the Father (Eph 2:18; Heb 4:14–16; 10:12–14).

Prayer is not only an amazing privilege; it also provides powerful possibilities and real answers. It can influence the affairs of our lives and the lives of those for whom we pray. Below is a partial list of the blessings and benefits of prayer.

1. Prayer puts us in the place to be transformed into the image of Jesus (2 Cor 3:18; Exod 33:7–11).
2. Prayer yields provision for daily needs (Matt 6:11).
3. Prayer is a means to obtain healing mercy for ourselves and others (Matt 9:27; 20:30–31; 15:22; 17:15).
4. Prayer raises up laborers for the harvest (Matt 9:36–38).
5. Prayer yields justice for God's elect (Luke 18:1–8).
6. Prayer is the place we surrender our wills to God's (Luke 22:42).
7. Prayer is how we abide in Christ (John 15:4–5; Eph 3:16–19; Col 1:9–10).
8. Prayer relieves worry and replaces it with peace (Phil 4:6–7; Ps 29:11; Isa 26:3).
9. Prayer is how our sins are forgiven and cleansed (1 John 1:9; Matt 6:12).
10. Prayer gives protection and security when we are afraid (Ps 34:4; 56:3; 2 Cor 1:8–11).
11. Prayer is one means to obtain the grace we desperately need (Heb 4:16).
12. Prayer is how we cast our burdens upon the Lord (1 Pet 5:6–10; Ps 55:22).
13. Prayer gives us wisdom for challenges we face (2 Chr 1:10; Prov 2:3–6; Jas 1:5).
14. Prayer provides power and perseverance to defeat Satan and overcome his schemes (Luke 22:32; Eph 6:18; Jas 4:7).
15. Prayer takes us deeper into intimacy with the Lord (Ps 27:4–8; 73:25–26).

Read back through the list slowly. Note the benefits that leap out at you. Why do those particular benefits get your attention?

Prayer Forms

Because prayer is communication with an infinite God, there are many ways to pray. The majority of the prayers offered in the Bible fit into seven categories.

1. Thanksgiving

David not only practiced the discipline of thanksgiving, but he also prescribed it for all Israel, assigning Levites to make a permanent practice of giving thanks to the Lord. He even wrote a prayer of thanks for them to sing.

> Give thanks to the LORD; call on his name; proclaim his deeds among the peoples. . . . Give thanks to the LORD, for he is good; his faithful love endures forever. (1 Chr 16:8, 34; see also Ps 106:1; 107:1; 136:1)

When Solomon finished the temple and was bringing the ark to reside there, he instructed all the Levites, the musicians, and the singers to give thanks to the Lord (2 Chr 5:12–13). Judah's king Jehoshaphat faced a fearsome threat from three armies. When God promised to fight for them, Jehoshaphat came up with one of the most bizarre battle plans in history. It was based entirely on thanksgiving and resulted in an amazing victory (2 Chr 20:21).

A great way to apply the discipline of thanksgiving prayer is to make your own thanksgiving list. The list could include these areas:

- *Spiritual* blessings like the Bible, answered prayer, heaven, forgiveness, the Holy Spirit, and the church. Try to list at least ten.
- *Physical* blessings like sight, the ability to walk, taste, and smell.
- *Material* blessings like clothes, food, a car, furniture, books, and so forth.
- *Financial* provisions.
- *Lessons* God has been teaching you lately.
- *Trials* he has seen you through and how they have benefited your life.
- Key *people* in your life: family members, friends, spiritual mentors, pastors, teachers, and missionaries.

2. Adoration or Praise

Praise is essentially a positive response to the person of God. Jesus taught us to begin our prayers with praise when he said, "This, then, is how you should pray: 'Our Father in heaven, *hallowed be your name*'" (Matt 6:9 ESV, emphasis added). Nehemiah opened his prayer with praise, referring to the Lord as *"the great and awe-inspiring God who keeps his gracious covenant with those who love him and keep his commands"* (Neh 1:5, emphasis added). More than a hundred times David uses the word *praise* in his prayers recorded in Psalms.

Praise and thanksgiving are always good places to begin when we pray (Ps 100:4). By beginning with God, we are stating our priorities and putting our needs into perspective.

We can apply this form of prayer by praising God for his unique attributes. He alone is infinite, eternal, omnipotent, omniscient, omnipresent, and perfect. We can also praise him for his titles and roles: Creator, King of kings and Lord of lords, Savior, Counselor, Shepherd, Physician, Deliverer, and only true God. We can praise him for his love, compassion, mercy, kindness, grace, generosity, truth, justice, righteousness, and holiness. We can worship him for his unsurpassed excellences such as glory, majesty, and beauty.

3. Simple Prayer

Simple prayer is carrying on a consistent conversation with God about the daily stuff of life. It is conversing with the Father about all of our thoughts, events, hurts, sorrows, joys, and questions freely and openly because he listens. It is sanctifying the ordinary by turning all the typical events and experiences of daily life into prayer.

In college I came across a little book called *The Practice of the Presence of God.* It was written by a monk named Nicholas (later known as Brother Lawrence).[2] He was a large and awkward man who was always breaking things. His job was washing pots and pans and cleaning a large kitchen. Yet he loved God with all his heart. He set a goal for himself to practice the presence of God all day long. This continual practice of the presence of God is the essence of simple prayer.

Nicholas discovered that the way to sense God's presence all day was to have lots of conversations with him throughout the day. In fact, he thought it was shameful to cut off a conversation with God. His goal was to form the habit of talking to God all the time. The key was continually loving God and recognizing him as intimately present and, therefore, addressing him with every thought.

4. Surrender

In order to expand our hearts and grow our faith, the Lord calls us to surrender every aspect of our lives to him. Such surrender is worship.

> Therefore, brothers and sisters, in view of the mercies of God, I urge you to present your bodies as a living sacrifice, holy and pleasing to God; this is your true worship. (Rom 12:1)

Abraham modeled surrender when he offered the Lord his most prized possession: his son Isaac. After an excruciating wait of more than twenty years, Abraham received Isaac supernaturally, yet God called him to sacrifice Isaac as an ultimate act of worship (Gen 22:1–5).

Jesus demonstrated surrender when he prayed in the garden of Gethsemane. As he looked into the wrenching agony he was about to face in serving as the sacrifice for humankind's sins, he was brought to the point of ultimate surrender: "Father, if you are willing, take this cup away from me—nevertheless, not my will, but yours, be done" (Luke 22:42).

One way to practice surrender in prayer is to list the things you hold most dear. Then give each one to the Lord, asking that only his will be done.

5. Supplication

Jesus taught us the daily discipline of supplication prayer when he commanded, "Therefore, you should pray like this. . . . Give us today our daily bread" (Matt 6:9–11). Most of the prayers recorded in Scripture are prayers of supplication. Asa received a great victory for Israel when he cried out to the Lord for help (1 Chr 14:11). Daniel was delivered from the lions after praying for help (Dan 6:11). Nehemiah received the king's blessing, protection, and provision to return to Jerusalem and rebuild the walls as a result of supplication (Nehemiah 1). The Psalms are filled with petitions for help (Ps 38:22; 40:13; 46:1–2; 56:9; 70:1, 5; 79:9; 121:1–2; 124:8).

The Bible is filled with prayers people effectively prayed for themselves. They include:

- Wash away my guilt (Ps 51:2).
- Enlarge my territory (1 Chr 4:10 NIV).
- Grant me wisdom (2 Chr 1:10).
- Grant me success (Neh 1:11 NLT).
- Strengthen my hands (Neh 6:9).
- Send me (Isa 6:8).
- Lord, help me (Matt 15:25).

6. Intercession

Intercessory prayer is standing in the gap on behalf of others. It is our way of loving others by asking God to meet *their* needs. It is asking God to bless others in the same ways we desire him to bless us.

Jesus lived intercession. His entire ministry is identifying with us, standing in our stead, and going to God the Father on our behalf. As a leader, he prayed for his followers. In speaking of his Twelve, he said, "I pray for them" (John 17:9). In speaking of his then-future followers like us, he said, "I pray . . . also for those who believe in me through their word" (John 17:20). Now in his exalted home in heaven, Jesus is the One "who is even at the right hand of God, who also makes intercession for us" (Rom 8:34 NKJV) who "always lives to make intercession" for us (Heb 7:25 NKJV).

Bible Prayers for Others

- Good health; spiritual progress and prosperity; walk in the truth (3 John 1:2–4).
- Increasing, overflowing love; strengthened hearts; blameless holiness (1 Thess 3:11–13).
- Abounding, accurate, and appropriate love; discern the best over the good; blameless purity; bear righteous fruit (Phil 1:9–11).
- Know and experience God deeply and progressively; know and experience all God has for them in terms of hope, calling, and lifestyle (Eph 1:17–19).
- Know God's will; live worthy of and pleasing to God; bear spiritual fruit; grow in their knowledge of God; grow in spiritual strength and endurance; live a life of gratitude (Col 1:9–12).
- Be made fit for what God has called them to be; that God would energize and fulfill their spiritual ideas and efforts; that Jesus would be glorified in them (2 Thess 1:11–12).
- Unfailing faith; use all their mistakes to ultimately help others (Luke 22:31–32).

7. Confession

The discipline of confessing sin in prayer involves letting the sin in our hearts break our hearts. It is seeing sin as God sees it. It is letting the pain that our sin caused the Father and Jesus on the cross fill our thoughts, stir our emotions, and change our wills. It is saying the same thing about our sins that God says.

> If we confess our sins, he is faithful and righteous to forgive us our sins and to cleanse us from all unrighteousness. (1 John 1:9)

The word *confess* means "to say the same thing," which basically means we say the same thing about our sin that God says. Sin is not a mistake, a mess-up, an error, or a misbehavior. It is sin. It is wrong. It must be forgiven. It needs to be washed off our record and purified from our hearts. We must accept responsibility for our sin and confess it—not excuse it, rationalize it, or blame it on someone else.

Prayer Suggestions

When it comes to developing the discipline of prayer, we often have good intentions but poor follow-through. Here are four practical aids in developing your prayer life.

Time. Have a set time or times when you pray each day.

Amount of time. Have an amount of time blocked out for daily prayer.

Place. Have a place or places where you pray each day.

Record. Have a place where you record prayer requests and answers.

— Quote to Consider —

*"Sometimes we think we are too busy to pray. That also
is a great mistake, for praying is a saving of time. . . .
God can multiply our ability to make use of time. If
we give the Lord his due, we shall have enough for all
necessary purposes. In this matter seek first the kingdom
of God and his righteousness, and all these things shall be
added to you. Your other engagements will run smoothly
if you do not forget your engagement with God."*

—CHARLES SPURGEON[3]

— Questions to Ponder —

1. On a scale of 1 to 3, with 1 being low and 3 being high, how would you rate your prayer life?
2. Do you have a time or times set aside for daily prayer?
3. Do you have a place or places for daily prayer?

Notes

1. Adolph Saphir, *Lectures on the Lord's Prayer*, as quoted in C. H. Spurgeon, *The Treasury of David*, vol. 5, *Psalms 104–118* (1869; reprt., Grand Rapids: Baker Book House, 1981), 173.

2. Brother Lawrence, *The Practice of the Presence of God* (Grand Rapids: Revell, 1967).

3. Charles Spurgeon, "Pray without Ceasing," Metropolitan Tabernacle Pulpit, A Sermon Delivered on Lord's Day Morning, March 10, 1872, accessed February 24, 2018, https://www.spurgeon.org/resource-library/sermons/pray-without -ceasing#flipbook/.

15 Journaling

Dave Earley

In my early thirties, I was blindsided by what became a long nightmare season of severe illness, adversity, and burnout. I had been raised to keep my emotions bottled up and to keep my questions to myself. That approach was not working. I got depressed.

In my season of suffering, I read and reread the book of Job. As I read the ancient account of a man in a similar situation, I was astounded by the frank and honest manner in which he addressed and questioned God. I envied his raw directness.

I was stirred by a deep longing for a safe place to air my confusing, conflicting emotions and admit my selfish, sinful attitudes. I wanted to vent and question without repercussion. I wanted to muse over the Scriptures in a personal fashion. Longing for a fresh way to dialogue, deal, discuss, and dream with God, I began to journal. Thus began my daily counseling sessions with the master Counselor.

I had heard about the benefits of journaling in the past and had tried to practice the discipline a few times. But it never stuck. This time it was different. I poured out what I was feeling in hope the act of putting pen to paper would clarify and cleanse the ugly emotions stirring in my heart.

It worked.

Oh, my first efforts were not polished or pretty. But that really isn't the point of journaling. You do not have to sanitize or spruce up your words. Sometimes you just vomit out what you have and feel better as a result.

Since then journaling has been a constant spiritual discipline in my life. I write in my journal almost every day. In it I keep up-to-date on my spiritual/ personal growth plan. It contains the various intercessory prayer, thanksgiving, surrender, and Bible promise lists I am using. I record meaningful quotes from my reading. In my journal, I keep a calendar with significant events and opportunities. I record things I don't want to forget. I write out prayers, list fears, and ask God tough questions. I am a big fan of the spiritual discipline of journaling. It keeps me sane and centered.

Journaling Is . . .

A journal is a safe and sacred place to record your deepest or most mundane thoughts, feelings, fears, dreams, ideas, questions, and emotions. A journal is a record of the works and ways of God in your life. It can include daily events and your reflections about them, insights into Scripture, prayer requests, meaningful quotes, and your personal growth plan.

Keeping a journal is a way to practice meditation, contemplation, and meaningful reflection. It is a means of organizing and understanding your spiritual journey.

Why Journal?

I have personally experienced many overlapping benefits by practicing reflection through journaling:

Legacy

Many Bible characters and noted saints of the past practiced journaling. When I journal, I am doing something that has been done for thousands of years by the people of God. For example, the book of Job is his account of a struggle with suffering and the sovereignty of God. Lamentations describes Jeremiah's feelings about the fall of Jerusalem.

Many of the psalms contain the spiritual journal of David. He tells us what he was thinking and how he was feeling at the best and worst times of his life. As such, the psalms are not always pretty or nice. Some of the psalms are raw and real, painful and poignant. As we read them, we discover that developing stark honesty and painful thoroughness in the presence of God helps us become whole.

Meditation

Journaling is an aid in meditating on the Lord and his Word. For example, when the Israelites were transitioning from forty years of wandering in the desert to settling in the Promised Land, God gave Joshua clear instructions regarding meditation on the law. He promised prosperity and success as a result.

> This Book of the Law shall not depart from your mouth, but you shall meditate on it day and night, so that you may be careful to do according to all that is written in it. For then you will make your way prosperous, and then you will have good success. (Josh 1:8 ESV)

The book of Psalms opens with similar instruction and promise.

> How happy is the one who does not walk in the advice of the wicked or stand in the pathway with sinners or sit in the company of mockers! Instead, his delight is in the LORD's instruction, and he meditates on it day and night. He is like a tree planted beside flowing streams that bears its fruit in its season and whose leaf does not wither. Whatever he does prospers. (Ps 1:1–3)

Notice the rewards of meditating on God's law:

- *Stability*—a tree planted
- *Productivity*—yields its fruit
- *Durability*—leaf does not wither
- *Prosperity*—he prospers

My initial attempts at journaling involved writing down a verse of Scripture and then writing out my thoughts about the meaning and application of that Scripture. I found life and joy in personalizing Scripture and turning the words of the Bible into the words of my prayers.

Pep Talk

We all need spiritual pep talks on occasion. At one point in his spiritual journey, David felt the need to give himself a pep talk. In his pep talk, he spoke of the need for all of us to pour out our hearts before God. Journaling is a safe place to do that.

> Rest in God alone, my soul, for my hope comes from him. . . . Trust in him at all times, you people; pour out your hearts before him. God is our refuge. (Ps 62:5–8)

Remembrance

Journaling creates a place to remember the works of the Lord. For example, Psalm 77 is a record of Asaph's struggle through a season of trouble (vv. 1–3). He felt far from God, abandoned, and alone (vv. 7–9). His solution? Recall the power of God in the past.

> I will remember the Lord's works; yes, I will remember your ancient wonders. I will reflect on all you have done and meditate on your actions. (Ps 77:11–12)

In times when I have been discouraged, I have gone back to an old journal. There I have read how, when I was at a similar place in the past, God came through on my behalf.

Discernment and Direction

Reflection helps discern meaning in what is going on around you. It helps reveal the Holy Spirit's pattern of guiding you in the past and, thereby, helps you determine God's direction for your future.

Gratitude

Keeping a journal helps you record and cultivate gratitude for the way the Lord has been and is currently at work in your life.

Awareness

Honest contemplation through journaling yields a deepening awareness of the Lord's active presence with and in you.

Reflection

Using a journal provides a place to ponder the picture the Lord is painting with our lives. Our shallow culture has become one of reacting instead of reflecting. Staring at a blank page forces you to think through what happened and how you feel about it. As you put words down, ideas, principles, and lessons untangle and gain clarity.

Organization

A journal can bring order to your interior world. In my journal, I maintain my spiritual growth plan and keep a record of my prayer requests and answers. I record places I hope to visit in the future, people who have blessed me, favorite quotes from my current reading, and many other things that would probably be lost or otherwise forgotten.

Developing Transparency

Journaling provides a safe place for me to vent frustration, put words to thoughts, and confess sin.

Listening

Keeping a journal has greatly helped me learn to hear God's still small voice.

Trust

Journaling is a record that God indeed answers prayer. That record increases our trust in him. In my journal, I maintain a section of prayer lists. On a daily basis, I pray for my family, myself, my ministry, my friends, and so on. If I ever wonder whether God is real and answers prayer, I can pull out an old journal and see how God answered.

Enhancement of the Other Disciplines

My journal is my best tool to help me use various disciplines in my spiritual development. The back few pages of my journal contain my spiritual growth plan.[1] I divide a single page into twenty-one columns and ten rows. Along the top are the days of the week and the dates. Down the left column is a listing of the ten to twelve disciplines I am pursuing during that three-week period. These may include Bible reading, prayer, physical exercise, serving my wife, journaling, communicating with my grown children, fasting, reading, and writing.

The columns and rows create boxes I check off at the end of the day if I did the discipline. After a few days, I can tell easily how I am doing in my various disciplines.

How to Journal

The key to effective journaling is remembering *why* you are doing it. The purpose is to look honestly into the face of Jesus and be changed to be more like him. Keeping a journal is simply a tool to help you get there.

Therefore, there is no right way to keep a journal. Your way is the right way *if* you use it to help you grow into the image of Christ. Just as everyone is a little different, the way people keep journals is also different. Try various methods until you find what works for you.

An Example

If you are new to this, it may help you to have an example. So I will tell you what I do. But as you read what I do to journal, realize that I know of no one else who does it exactly like I do.

I use my journal from front to back *and* from back to front. As I said previously, my back pages contain my spiritual growth plan, followed by my prayer lists. This is followed by written-out Scripture verses I want to pray through and quotes I want to remember. Then come ideas I have about various things and lists of things I want to remember.

The front of my journal reads chronologically. At the top of the page is the date. Then I usually write "Yesterday . . ." and discuss some of the things that happened.

Then I write "Today . . ." and describe some of what I have on the calendar for that day or need to add. Then I turn that to-do list into a prayer list.

That is often followed by a four-paragraph prayer.

Paragraph 1. *Thanks*—"God, I thank you for . . ."

Paragraph 2. *Praise*—"God, I praise you because you are . . ."

Paragraph 3. *Confession*—"God, I acknowledge . . ."

Paragraph 4. *Supplication*—"The three big things I ask for today are . . ."

When the front half of the journal runs into the back half, I start another journal. I usually go through a journal in three months. I use simple spiral notebooks that are six inches wide and eight inches long. I get them at an office supply store.

Suggestions for Getting Started

Maybe you want to get started but are stumped. You have the notebook, but a white page is staring at you. Or you have the file created, but a blank computer screen mocks you. So let me give you a few prompts that you may find helpful to break into the discipline of journaling.

1. Write the word *Yesterday* . . . and go from there. Record both the event and how you feel about it.
2. As a starting entry for each day, try listing the one verse or idea from your Bible reading that impressed you most. Meditate on that for a few minutes. Then record your insights and impressions. Write down

questions—things about the passage you do not understand. But don't turn this into a mere exegesis exercise. Make it personal.

3. Picture Jesus sitting across from you. What would you say to him? Write this down. Write out one thing you are afraid to tell Jesus. Then tell him why you have been afraid.

4. Write the words *I think God is trying to teach me* . . . and go from there.

5. Write down prayers and requests. Review these often and see how God has responded to your prayers.

6. Write down a list of your "impossible prayers."

7. Each page of your journal could include responses to self-examination questions, such as *In the last twenty-four hours, have I* . . .

   - Served and shown love to my spouse? My kids?
   - Spent some quality time with God?
   - Relied on the Lord in every area of my life?
   - Confessed my sins?
   - Thanked the Lord for his blessings?
   - Used the time wisely that God has given me?
   - Read through my journal?
   - Served someone who could not pay me back?
   - Maintained a pure mind and heart?
   - Thought or spoken kindly to family and friends?
   - Meditated on God's Word?

More Advice

These three simple reminders apply to other spiritual disciplines as well.

Any Journaling Is Better Than None

Every day's journal entry will not be a work of art or a literary masterpiece. Maybe you did not say it poetically or spell it correctly. That's not the point. The point is to get honest before God and look into the face of Jesus. The point is to connect with God more deeply than you would otherwise.

Therefore, there are days I don't make any entries. I may simply check off the appropriate spiritual growth plan boxes and pray through a few of my lists and call it good. Other days I write page after page of what is happening, or what I am thinking, or what God is doing. Journaling can be fruitful at any level of involvement.

Persist through the Dry Times

There are days when I am basically going through the motions. I am doing it by discipline and faith, not feeling and delight. Some days I break through dryness into meaningful moments with God. Sometimes not. The dry season may last one day, or several days, or even weeks.

But journaling is a holy habit in my life that has proven over the years to pay rich rewards. Eventually the breakthrough comes, and I feel God's presence in a tangible way. Or I see clearly what had previously been foggy.

Get Started

Like all spiritual disciplines, journaling does you no good until you start doing it.

⚊ Quotes to Consider ⚊

"Used appropriately, a journal can be a mirror in the hands of the Holy Spirit in which He reveals His perspective on our attitudes, thoughts, words, and actions."

—DONALD WHITNEY[2]

"This is what you do when you journal. You are recording God's grand, epoch-spanning redemptive story as it unfolds in your limited, temporal sphere of existence here on earth. Your journal has the potential to record the continuation of the Holy Spirit's work in our world!"

—ADAM FELDMAN[3]

⚊ Questions to Ponder ⚊

1. What was the most compelling thing you read in this chapter?
2. What would be a few good reasons for you to keep a journal?
3. Will you try to journal several times a week for the next month?

Notes

1. See chapter 10 for information on setting up your own spiritual growth plan.

2. Donald Whitney, *Spiritual Disciplines for the Christian Life* (Colorado Springs: NavPress, 1997), 254.

3. Adam L. Feldman, *Journaling: Catalyzing Spiritual Growth through Reflection* (Ellicott City, MD: Milltown Publishing, 2013), 10.

16 Fasting

Dave Earley

If you were a Christ follower in the first few centuries of church history, one of the spiritual disciplines you likely practiced was the discipline of fasting. Epiphanus, who authored what could be considered the first Christian encyclopedia, asked rhetorically, "Who does not know that the fast of the fourth and sixth days of the week (Wednesday and Friday) are observed by Christians throughout the world?"[1]

Church historian Justo Gonzalez offers further insight into the early Christian weekly fasts.

> There were indeed times set aside for sorrow for one's sins, in particular during the two weekly days of fasting, which the church adopted from Jewish practice. At an early date, however, at least some Christians began fasting, not on Tuesdays and Thursdays, like the Jews, but rather on Wednesdays and Fridays. It may be that this shift took place in commemoration of the betrayal and the crucifixion.[2]

The early church also fasted for several days prior to Easter. Later this fast became a series of one-day fasts each week for the six weeks leading up to Easter. It was also customary for Christians to fast in preparation for their baptism.[3]

The Discipline of Fasting Is . . .[4]

Fasting has long been an ally in spiritual formation. Fasting, as practiced in the Bible, means "not to eat" or "self-denial." In the Old Testament, the word *fast* is derived from the Hebrew term *tsom*, which refers to the practice of self-denial. In the New Testament, the Greek word is *nestia*, which also refers to self-denial.

A normal fast involves fasting from all food but not from water (Matt 4:2). A partial fast is the restriction of one's diet as opposed to complete abstention (Dan 10:3). Fasting may also include skipping a meal consistently or abstaining from certain foods or other activities. Many of us have enjoyed the benefit of a media fast from television, movies, and the internet.

Typically fasts in the Bible went for one complete twenty-four-hour period, usually from sundown to sundown. As we previously mentioned, the early church fasted two days every week, Wednesday and Friday. Pharisees fasted Tuesday and Thursday. Other biblical fasts went from three to forty days.

The Bible includes both individual and corporate fasts. Corporate fasts could involve the whole church (Acts 13:1–4) or even the entire nation (Jonah 3; Esther 4; 2 Chronicles 20).

Fasting Because . . .

When I started college, I was challenged to adopt the spiritual discipline of fasting. So I read every passage in the Bible regarding fasting. I started out asking, "Why should I fast?" I was looking for benefits of fasting. But soon the question in my mind changed from "Why fast?" to "Why don't I fast more often?" Here are some biblical teachings related to fasting.

1. Jesus fasted prior to launching his ministry in power (Luke 4:1–14).
2. Fasting obeys the implied command of Jesus, "When you fast . . ." (Matt 6:16–18).
3. Fasting is a secret service to God. We can express the deepest desires of our hearts. God, who sees in secret, promises to reward it openly (Matt 6:4, 6, 18).
4. Fasting was/is to be practiced to prepare for the return of Jesus, the Bridegroom (Joel 2:15–18; Luke 2:57; 5:33–35).
5. Fasting with desperate prayer gave Hannah a stunning answer to prayer (1 Sam 1:7ff). Even though she had long been barren, she conceived a special son, Samuel, who would shake a nation with his prayers.
6. David practiced the discipline of fasting. He advocated fasting as a means to empathize with a sufferer and develop humility (Ps 35:13; 69:10).

7. Fasting yielded a plan and provision for Nehemiah to return to Jerusalem and rebuild the walls (Neh 1:4).
8. Fasting pleases God by undoing the chains of injustice, setting the oppressed free, and providing for the hungry, the homeless, and the naked; it causes righteousness to shine, healing to come, and God's glory to surround you. It leads to answered prayer (Isa 58:6–14).
9. Daniel practiced fasting to purify his soul and body and was rewarded with better health and increased favor in Babylon (Daniel 1).
10. Fasting made it possible for Daniel to receive revelation from the Lord (Dan 10:2–3).
11. Fasting opened the door of the gospel to the Gentiles (Acts 10:30–31).
12. Fasting aided decision making and launched the missions movement (Acts 13:1–4).
13. Fasting aided the selection of the first Gentile church leaders (Acts 14:23).
14. Fasting is a spiritual service. Anna, a widow in her eighties, served the Lord with fasting day and night (Luke 2:37).

My Big Requests

During my first few years of college, I fasted one day a week. But as a junior in college, I launched a three-day fast with lots of intense prayer. I had four major requests that I needed/wanted to see happen in the next thirty days:

1. That God would miraculously provide me with enough money to help my friend cover a bill so he could stay in school.
2. That I would lead fifty souls to Christ.
3. That God would give me a mentor.
4. That God would spare the lives of and heal three students who were severely injured in an automobile accident.

Within thirty days, the answers were coming in: All three of the students in the accident turned the corner, and we knew they would all live. One of my professors agreed to mentor me. Unexpectedly I received a check in the mail for enough money to help a friend pay his bill and remain in school. While the fifty souls request seemed too aggressive, God was gracious. On the last day of the fast, I spoke at a youth event, and nearly thirty young people gave their lives to Christ. That brought my number for the month to fifty.

A Major Monetary Miracle

In 1971 Jerry Falwell started Liberty University. During its first twenty-five years, Liberty grew rapidly from a handful of students to more than ten thousand in its various programs. Classroom buildings and dorms were built on a cash-only basis, with most of the cash coming from supporters of Falwell's television program.

When scandals rocked the religious broadcasting world, contributions to every ministry decreased dramatically. The university continued to grow and build. Soon the university was staring at more than $100 million in debt. Liberty risked losing its accreditation because of its excessive debt. The loss of accreditation would spell the end of the school. Falwell said, "With this crisis, I had to fast, and fast seriously."[5]

Falwell felt impressed by the Lord to go on a forty-day fast to pray for miraculous financial provision. He began July 20, 1996, and abstained from all food until September 1. He drank water, took a vitamin daily, and drank some vegetable juice every few days. The fast, however, did not go as he had planned.

> I kept asking God for money, but He impressed upon my heart that I needed to get close to Him, to listen to Him, and trust Him. When I asked for money, God told me not to ask for money, but to learn to know Him better. I had several lessons to learn before I could ask for money. As I ended that first forty-day fast, I felt I had learned what God wanted to teach me. But I did not have an answer about money.[6]

Falwell needed to learn how to deal with God on a deeper level. Then he was ready to proceed. He said, "After resuming my normal diet for twenty-five days, God told me I could ask Him for money. So I went back on another forty-day fast that began September 25, 1996, ending on November 4."[7]

God responded.

First the university received a huge cash gift that erased long-term mortgage debt. Second, they got more money that put the university into a place of financial health. Third, all accreditation sanctions were removed, and accreditation was affirmed for the next decade.

Over the past several years, the answers to prayer from Falwell's fasts have continued to roll in. By 2016, Liberty's enrollment included 15,000 residential students and more than 100,000 online students. It became the largest evangelical Christian university in the world. The campus has recently experienced a $1 billion transformation. And the school has an endowment of more than $1 billion.

Fasting and Revival

The revival movement born in New England in the early eighteenth century has been called the Great Awakening. In many ways, it began with a pastor named Jonathan Edwards and fasting. Burdened about the unconverted members of his church, Edwards fasted for twenty-two hours before giving his famous sermon "Sinners in the Hands of an Angry God."[8]

Several years later in England, George Whitefield and the Wesley brothers, John and Charles, were influenced by a praying group of Christians known as the Moravians. Soon they experienced what Whitefield later called "a Pentecostal season." Days and nights were spent praying and fasting. When these young men began to preach, they had such power that crowds swelled to hear their words. They soon took to preaching outside where the crowds numbered into the thousands.[9]

Charles Finney saw entire towns shaken with revival during the early 1800s. He and his co-laborers were intense prayer warriors who spent days fasting and praying. As a result, as many as a million people or more were swept into the kingdom of God. An estimated 85 percent of professed converts in the Finney revival remained true to the Lord.[10]

In 1857 in New York City, during what is now called "the Laymen's Prayer Revival," Christians fasted and prayed during their lunch hours as they attended noon interdenominational prayer meetings in churches near their places of employment. Soon these lunchtime prayer meetings spread to other major cities of the eastern seaboard. By May 1859, 50,000 people had been converted to Christ through fasting and prayer.

Fasting Advice

Before You Begin

1. Determine how long you plan to fast and what type of fasting you will practice. Will you be fasting for one meal, or one full day, or three days, or a week? Will you be abstaining from just solid food, or food *and* juice, or TV, or the internet, or social media, or sweets?
2. Review some of the reasons for fasting mentioned in this chapter and set some objectives for your fast.
3. Prepare yourself spiritually by repenting of sin. Fasting cleanses your body while confession cleanses your heart.
4. Prepare yourself physically by cutting down to smaller meals a few days prior, especially prior to taking on a long fast of a week or more.

5. Plan to be less busy during the period you will be fasting. One of the goals is to be able to concentrate on God as much as possible.

6. Set aside ample time to spend with God.

7. Consider the effect fasting may have on prescription medications. Some medications have to be taken with food. Can you skip a day or two? Can you take your medication with juice?

Other Practical Advice and Observations

1. Try to limit physical activities during your fast.

2. Drink a lot of liquid.

3. Be prepared for some headaches or joint pain as your body detoxes. The headaches may be worse if you fast from nicotine and/or caffeine.

4. Build up gradually. Start with one meal. The next time go for a whole day. Then fast for three days. Then a week.

5. Most people can fast one to three days regardless of the busyness of their schedule.

6. You may tell others about your fast but do not boast. Since my wife plans and prepares the meals, I let her know ahead of time when I will not be eating.

7. The longer the fast, the more gradually it needs to be broken. Do not break a longer fast with a heavy meal.

Still More Advice and Encouragement

1. If you have never fasted before, try it. You really have nothing to lose and much to gain.

2. You don't have to be a spiritual giant in order to fast.

3. Your fast does not have to be a forty-day fast to be effective.

4. If you fast regularly, realize that most of the time there is no great accompanying spiritual experience. Fasting is a spiritual discipline that allows God to transform you little by little, step-by-step, as you humble yourself and seek his face.

5. Fasting is good for your body. You may feel lousy the first day or two you fast, because fasting causes your body to detox. However, after fasting you feel better than before.

6. Consider fasting one day a week for twenty-four hours, from sundown the first day to sundown the next day. That is the model practiced by the disciples.

7. Remember, the God who sees in secret will reward openly. Fasting is a secret service that can aid in bringing open answers to prayer.

⤙ Quote to Consider ⤚

"Fasting is the most powerful spiritual discipline of all the Christian disciplines. Through fasting and prayer, the Holy Spirit can transform your life."

—BILL BRIGHT[11]

⤙ Questions to Ponder ⤚

1. Have you ever practiced fasting as a spiritual discipline?
2. Do you regularly practice fasting as a spiritual discipline?
3. How do you plan to apply this discipline in your life this month?

Notes

1. Epiphanus, as quoted in Wesley Duewel, *Mighty Prevailing Prayer* (Grand Rapids: Zondervan, 1990), 180.

2. Justo Gonzalez, *The Story of Christianity: The Early Church to the Dawn of the Reformation* (San Francisco: HarperOne, 2010), 27.

3. Elmer Towns, *Fasting for Spiritual Breakthrough* (Ventura, CA: Regal, 1996), 26.

4. Some of this material appears in Dave Earley, *Prayer: The Timeless Secret of High-Impact Leaders* (Chattanooga: AMG, 2008), chapter 6. Used by Permission.

5. Jerry Falwell, quoted in Elmer Towns, *Fasting Can Change Your Life* (Ventura, CA: Regal, 1998), 19.

6. Towns, 19–20.

7. Towns, 20.

8. Elmer Towns and Douglas Porter, *The Ten Greatest Revivals Ever* (Ann Arbor: Servant Publications, 2000), 63.

9. Wesley Duewel, *Revival Fire* (Grand Rapids: Zondervan, 1995), 49–80.

10. Duewel, 92–93.

11. Bill Bright, "Your Personal Guide to Fasting and Prayer," Bill Bright, accessed February 24, 2018, https://www.cru.org/us/en/train-and-grow/spiritual-growth/fasting/personal-guide-to-fasting.html.

17 Stillness, Silence, and Solitude

Dave Earley

I was always an active kid. I spent much of my early elementary years in the corner or visiting with the principal simply because I could not keep still. I remember once when my mom came home from an open house at my school. The first thing she said was, "Dave, why didn't you tell me where your desk was?"

I said, "I did. I said that it was next to the teacher's."

She shook her head and sighed, "Yes, but when you said 'next to the teacher's,' I thought you meant the front row. I did not think you meant right up *next to* the teacher's."

In first grade, the girl who sat in front of me was extremely tall. Her name was Patricia. She was one of those always perfect, always clean, always quiet, straight-A, teacher's pet types. You know the type. Maybe some of you were that type. I wasn't. I got bored too easily. I was always saying, "Hey Patricia, look at that. Hey Patricia, watch this." And probably a dozen times every day she would turn around and say, "Keep still, Dave Earley. You won't learn anything. Keep still." I can still hear her voice telling me, "Keep still."

The best day of first grade was the only time Patricia ever got in trouble. She got in trouble because, of all things, she was turned around talking.

She was telling *someone* to keep still.

Do you know what? There are times I hear God say, "Dave, keep still. You won't learn anything. Quiet your soul, son. Slow down. Get off the fast lane. Jump off the treadmill. Stop doing. Start being. Be still."

I wonder, does God ever say to you, "Be still. I can't do anything with you because your world is too busy, too cluttered, too crowded, and too loud. You are busy about many things, and you are neglecting the one thing that is most needed. Your world is too loud to hear my voice. It is too cluttered to see my hand. It is too crowded to feel my touch"?

At these times we need to practice the disciplines of stillness, silence, and solitude.

One of the more challenging truths I have read in the last few years comes from the pen of John Ortberg on a subject he calls "slowing." He writes, "Jesus urged his disciples to take time out. Following Jesus cannot be done at a sprint. If we want to follow someone, we can't go faster than the one who is leading."[1]

The Spiritual Discipline of Stillness and Silence

The discipline of stillness and silence is ceasing physical activity so we may experience spiritual growth. Stillness is not so much the absence of noise as it is the presence of the divine whisper. It is being silent before God so we might listen to God. Silence is creating space in our crowded souls so that God may fill them with himself.

"Know That I Am God"

A few years ago, as I was preparing to teach on Psalm 46, one phrase jumped off the page and grabbed my heart: "Be still, and know that I am God" (v. 10 NIV).

The word translated "know" can be understood as "intimately experience." In other words, this verse says, "Be still and intimately experience God." As I read this verse, I realized that when my heart is not still, I am not experiencing God.

God speaks through a still small voice. When I am not still, I am unable to see God or feel God. Without the discipline of stillness and silence, I would not experience God, or as much of God, as much as I desire.

"Hear My Voice"

My sheep hear my voice, I know them, and they follow me. (John 10:27)

The context of this verse is Jesus claiming his ability to give his disciples eternal life. The verb tense indicates his sheep hear his voice *more than once.* They *continue* to hear his voice that they may *continue* to follow him. The word *know* speaks of intimate, personal experience.

Put this all together, and you'll see that Jesus told his disciples they were to develop a lifestyle of hearing his voice in order to live in relational obedience to him. Obviously we can't hear his voice if we are doing all the talking. There-fore, listening in stillness and expectant silence is an essential discipline for us to develop.

There are times when the Lord says, "Be quiet. Stop talking. Stop analyz-ing. Just listen. You are not ready to *follow* my voice until you are quiet enough to *hear* my voice."

"Taste and See That the LORD Is Good"

I love all of David's psalms, but possibly my favorites are those he wrote while running from Saul in the wilderness. I call them the Fugitive Psalms. One of the Fugitive Psalms I especially like is Psalm 34. He wrote it after having to pretend to be crazy to escape the Philistines. I'd expect him to whine about his misfortune, but he did not. Instead he determined to praise the Lord. As he did, he mused on the blessings he had received from the Lord and then made an amazing observation.

> Taste and see that the LORD is good. How happy is the person who takes refuge in him! (Ps 34:8)

The question that arises is how and where David learned to taste the good-ness of the Lord. The answer is in seasons of silence and solitude. As a shep-herd, he had spent long periods alone with the sheep. But he was not alone. The Lord was with him, and David learned to cultivate that relationship.

Create Space

Stillness prayer is creating space in our crowded souls so God may fill them with himself. Our hearts get so crowded—crowded with worries, fears, frustra-tions; crowded with wants and desires and wishes; crowded with good things, crowded with bad things. But whatever it is, it can easily crowd out God and drown out his voice.

A few years ago, I spent forty-eight hours in the disciplines of silence, still-ness, solitude, journaling, and prayer. I was alone with God. I was in a hotel room in a distant city. At first it was uncomfortable. It was hard for me to get truly still. It was hard for me just to be quiet before God.

Writing in my journal, I slowly and silently worked through several types of prayer: adoration, confession, thanksgiving, and surrender. As I reached a certain level of stillness, the Holy Spirit began to unload my crowded heart. It felt awkward, yet good, to sense him carrying burdens out of my soul and off of my shoulders. I struggled with a sense of uneasiness, because I was making nothing happen, yet something was definitely happening.

As my heart became less crowded, God became more real. His presence tenderly, quietly, peacefully began to flow into the newly vacated areas of my soul. I began to discern God's heartbeat slowly, deeply, firmly, pounding out love and hope with each beat. His still small voice gave me an encouragement and a plan for the next chapter in my life. As I experienced a great calming in my soul, I realized just how tense, stressed, anxious, busy, cluttered, and empty I had let myself become in the previous months.

The best part of my forty-eight hours of silence and stillness was not the forty-eight hours themselves, although they were wonderful. The best part was the space created during those forty-eight hours. I now had more room for God. For months afterward, I felt, heard, and tasted God more often, more deeply, and more clearly than before.

The Discipline of Solitude

The discipline of solitude is the close cousin of silence and stillness. Generally they are practiced together. Solitude as a discipline involves shutting ourselves away *from* people so we can shut ourselves away *with* God. It is escaping the sound of human voices so we can hear the voice of God. It is the voluntary abstinence from our normal patterns of activity and interaction with people for a time in order to rediscover that our strength and well-being come from God alone.

Henri Nouwen has noted, "Without solitude it is virtually impossible to lead a spiritual life."[2] Why is this so? Because in solitude we are freed from our bondage to clatter, clutter, and crowds, so we can hear, feel, touch, taste, and know God. In solitude we learn to let go of all else so that we might grab hold of God. We find a healthy detachment from the world and a special attachment to God.

Jesus's Long Day

What a busy, draining day! Jesus got up that morning and went to the synagogue and taught the people. As Jesus taught with authority, a demon-possessed man cried out, "What do you have to do with us, Jesus of Nazareth? Have you come to destroy us? I know who you are—the Holy One of God!" (Mark 1:24).

Jesus cast out the demon and freed the man from his agony. Then Jesus and some of his disciples went to Simon Peter's house, where his mother-in-law was sick in bed with a fever. Jesus healed her, and she got up and fixed them a meal.

News of the freeing of the demon-possessed man and the healing of Peter's mother-in-law spread all afternoon. By evening sick and demon-possessed people began to line up. According to Mark 1:33, the crowd was so large that "the whole town was assembled at the door." Jesus was busy late into the night healing the sick and freeing the demonized.

Now that's a draining day of teaching, healing, and casting out demons! Yet, as I read this passage in Mark's Gospel, what is amazing to me is not Jesus's long day but what he did the next morning.

> Now in the morning, having risen a long while before daylight, He went out and departed to a solitary place; and there He prayed. (Mark 1:35 NKJV)

How did Jesus combat the fatigue of a draining day of ministry? He practiced solitude prayer. Notice carefully what he did:

"In the morning . . . a long while before daylight." Jesus chose a solitary time.

"He went out and departed." Jesus chose a solitary act to distance himself from people for a time.

"To a solitary place." Jesus chose a solitary place.

"He prayed." Jesus used solitude from people as a sanctuary to be with the Father, and he prayed.

Jesus got away from others so he could get away with the Father. He sought physical solitude in order to address his spiritual needs. He not only got still before God, but he also got alone with God. He practiced the discipline of solitude.

This was his secret for staying fresh, sharp, full, centered, and on track. During his three and a half years of intense ministry, he used solitude to keep his spiritual tank full and his emotional batteries charged.

Don't we need to learn to do the same?

You may be thinking, *Yeah, but he was the Son of God.*

And I say, "Yes, and if the Son of God needed to practice solitude prayer, *how much more* do you and I? If the Son of God needed to get up early and go to a solitary place and pray, *how much more* do you and I?"

The sad reality is that most of us are too busy, too crowded, and too cluttered to stay spiritually sharp, full, charged, and optimally useful to God, others, and even ourselves. Most of us have lives filled with too much activity, too much noise, and too much time with people for us to have much left for God. Our lives are so full of stuff—good stuff, perhaps, but still stuff—that there is little room for God. All of us must learn the art of solitude in prayer.

Spiritual Strength and Renewal

Solitude is an essential secret of spiritual freshness, fullness, centeredness, and strength. I know I desperately need those graces, especially spiritual strength. Isaiah gives us insight about how to derive strength from God.

> Even the youths shall faint and be weary, and the young men shall utterly fall, but those who wait on the LORD shall renew their strength; they shall mount up with wings like eagles, they shall run and not be weary, they shall walk and not faint. (Isa 40:30–31 NKJV)

Notice that great mental, emotional, spiritual fortitude is with those who "wait on the LORD." This waiting involves time and speaks of place. The spiritually strong are those who have a time and place for seeking the Lord in solitude.

Spiritual Reward

Jesus not only practiced solitude in prayer, but he also encourages us to practice it. He spoke of going into our "closet" so that the God who sees in secret may reward openly:

> But when you pray, go into your private room, shut your door and pray to your Father who is in secret. And your Father who sees in secret will reward you. (Matt 6:6)

Stillness, Silence, and Solitude Advice

Practice These Disciplines out of an Attitude of Seeking God

Another of David's Fugitive Psalms from the wilderness is Psalm 63. In it he compares his thirst for water with his thirst for God. As is true with all the disciplines, but especially these, they are to be practiced as part of your passionate pursuit of God. Remember, you are doing the disciplines in order to deepen the relationship.

> God, you are my God; I eagerly seek you. I thirst for you; my body faints for you in a land that is dry, desolate, and without water. (Ps 63:1)

Determine to Practice Stillness, Silence, and Solitude Regularly

Have you formed the holy habit of meeting with God daily in quiet time and in the secret place? Those people who could be called spiritual successes, those who have developed spiritual depth, those who have tasted and seen that God is good, those who have run and not grown weary and walked and not fainted—those are people who have established the habit and discipline of a daily time alone with God in his Word and in prayer.

In addition to the daily time alone with God, let me encourage you to carve out a special time of secret and solitude with God on a consistent basis. Maybe it will be first thing in the morning. Possibly it will be late at night. Maybe it will be at midday. Maybe it will be an afternoon each week. Or overnight once a month.

Plan a Spiritual Retreat

After Jesus launched his itinerant ministry, his fame grew. The crowds multiplied, the pace increased, the stakes amplified, and the energy expended increased. So how did Jesus deal with the pressures of high-impact ministry? He often went on spiritual retreats.

Yet he often withdrew to deserted places and prayed. (Luke 5:16)

Spiritual retreats have been a great joy and aid to my interior life. They have helped ease my distress from the pressures of family or ministry and untangled gnarled ministry issues.

Get started today.

— Quote to Consider —

"The person who wants to arrive at interiority
and spirituality has to leave the crowd behind
and spend some time with Jesus."

—THOMAS À KEMPIS[3]

— Questions to Ponder —

1. Have you ever practiced stillness, silence, and solitude as a spiritual discipline?
2. Do you regularly practice stillness, silence, and solitude as a spiritual discipline?
3. How do you plan to apply this discipline in your life this month?

Notes

1. John Ortberg, *The Life You've Always Wanted* (Grand Rapids: Zondervan, 1997), 84.

2. Henri Nouwen, as quoted in Richard J. Foster and James Bryan Smith, *Devotional Classics* (San Francisco: HarperCollins, 1990), 95.

3. Thomas à Kempis, as quoted in Richard J. Foster and Emilie Griffin, *Spiritual Classics* (San Francisco: HarperCollins, 2000), 149.

The Inward Disciplines—
Love One Another

18

Doing Life Together

Dave Earley

In 1700, Count Nikolaus Ludwig von Zinzendorf was born into wealth and nobility. In his early twenties, Nikolaus was approached by a persecuted Christian group of Moravians requesting refuge on his estate. Zinzendorf granted their request and, seeing their authentic and deep devotion, joined them in what became an amazing Christian community. A few years later, he left public life to help lead them full time.

Under his leadership the large group of several hundred was divided into smaller groups for fellowship and held to a tight code of Christian behavior. Soon the remarkable religious refugee community experienced a powerful outpouring of the Holy Spirit. The result was a continuous prayer meeting covering every hour of every day for a hundred years.

The emphasis on prayer launched a radical commitment to costly missions. Upon arriving at the shores of their destinations, the Moravian missionaries would unload their few belongings and then burn the ships. They planned to die on the field sharing the gospel. What they started has been called the birth of the modern missionary movement.

For Zinzendorf everything flowed out of the unity of the community. The people he pastored forged a powerful structure of intentional relationships, doing life together, corporate prayer, and global evangelism that still impacts us today. He saw the heart of pure Christianity when he said, "There can be no Christianity without community."[1]

The Discipline of Doing Life Together

Zinzendorf was right. There is no Christianity without community. Therefore, any efforts at spiritual formation are remiss unless they include the discipline of doing life together.

The Western practices of individualism and isolation are foreign to New Testament Christianity. The New Testament is a corporate book. First-century churches shared life *together*, gathered *together*, read the Scriptures *together*, and applied the Scriptures *together*. The blessings and challenges of knowing, loving, serving, listening to, eating with, worshipping with, and simply being with others is a primary tool the Holy Spirit uses to shape us into the image of Jesus.

Jesus Valued and Practiced Gathering Together in Community

Those who would be the disciples of Jesus must practice the disciplines of Jesus. If we want to live as Jesus lived, we must do as Jesus did. One of the main things Jesus did was invite a handful of men to gather together with him in an intense, ministry-focused, close-knit community (Mark 3:13–14).

Involvement in community with others was a primary spiritual discipline in the life of Jesus Christ. Just as it was then, following Jesus today means following him into relationships with other Christ followers. The question we must ask is, "If Jesus, the Son of God, felt the need to be involved in community, *how much more* should you and I be involved in community?"

Jesus Prayed for His Followers to Live in Unity and Community

> I pray not only for these, but also for those who believe in me through their word. May they all be one, as you, Father, are in me and I am in you. May they also be in us, so that the world may believe you sent me. (John 17:20–21)

The cry of Jesus's heart for his church was that we "may be one." Unity is best facilitated in community. Theologian J. I. Packer believes as much, writing, "How can God's one family, locally and denominationally separated, be enabled to look like one family? . . . By wisdom in structuring and small groups within congregations."[2]

The First Christians Gathered Together in Community

The first Christians made several serious commitments. One primary focus of their devotion was to "the fellowship." The sacred record describes the DNA of the first church by stating, "They devoted themselves to the apostles' teaching, to the fellowship, to the breaking of bread, and to prayer" (Acts 2:42).

If you were a first-century Christian in Jerusalem, you experienced Christianity in two locales, the temple courts and the homes of the members. "Every day in the temple, and in various homes, they continued teaching and proclaiming the good news that Jesus is the Messiah" (Acts 5:42; see also Acts 2:46).

First- and second-century churches in other cities met primarily in homes. This makes sense as the first church building was not constructed until the second or third century AD. As the early church spread through the world, its primary meeting place was in the homes of the people. There they experienced fellowship.

The Greek term for *fellowship* is *koinonia*, meaning "sharing life together." Asbury Seminary professor Howard Snyder observed, "It is my conviction that the koinonia of the Holy Spirit is most likely to be experienced when Christians meet together informally in small group fellowships."[3]

Gathered Together, the Church Functions as the Body of Christ

The apostle Paul's favorite term for the church was "the body of Christ." He taught that the physical body was in many ways similar to the church. Just as separate body parts combine to form one physical body, in like manner separate individuals become inseparable parts of Christ's body, the church.

Paul emphasized that no single part could survive on its own. Every part relied on the others. The body functions best as a symphony of dependency. He stated plainly, "The eye cannot say to the hand, 'I don't need you!' Or again, the head can't say to the feet, 'I don't need you!'" (1 Cor 12:21).

John Ortberg notes, "We are created to draw life and nourishment from one another the way the roots of an oak tree draw life from the soil."[4]

The Author of Hebrews Strongly Advocated Gathering Together

We don't know what human penned the book of Hebrews. We do know that under the leadership of the Holy Spirit, the people valued the importance of the spiritual discipline of consistently gathering together.

> And let us consider [thoughtfully] how we may encourage one another to love and to do good deeds, not forsaking our meeting together [as believers for worship and instruction], as is the habit of some, but encouraging one another; and all the more [faithfully] as you see the day [of Christ's return] approaching. (Heb 10:24–25 AMP)

Gathering Together in Community Reflects the Image of God

Let us make man in our image. (Gen 1:26)

Note the use of the words *us* and *our* in Gen 1:26. They remind us that God has always existed as an eternal community of tri-unity. God is Father, Son, and Holy Spirit. All are distinct persons, yet all are vitally linked as one God.

From this text and others, Garth Icenogle draws a powerful conclusion, "God as Being exists in community. The natural and simple demonstration of God's communal image for humanity is the gathering of small groups."[5]

Doing Life Together in Community Expresses Our DNA

As God was creating the world, he made an interesting observation about humanity's need for community: "It is not good for the man to be alone" (Gen 2:18). From this text we clearly see that even before the fall, God said isolation was not the ideal state. Humans needed to be in community with other humans. It is part of the human DNA.

So God created man in his own image. (Gen 1:27)

Man's being made in the image of God includes the existence of embedded relational identity. It is impossible to find the fulfillment of our communal craving in ourselves, as God does. We must find it in one another. In other words, we not only have a God-shaped void; we also have an *others-shaped void* etched into our hearts. We cannot be healthy or fully human without others. We will not be fulfilled until our relational void is filled. This relational hunger is an identifying mark of our humanity.

Bill Donahue and Russ Robinson write, "God chose to embed in us a distinct kind of relational DNA. God created us all with a 'community gene,' an inborn, intentional, inescapable part of what it means to be human." They continue: "This 'relational DNA' or 'community gene' helps explain why churches need small groups. People don't come to church simply to satisfy spiritual needs. They come to us internally wired with a desire for connection. . . . Their hunger for togetherness is an inescapable mark of humanity."[6]

Community Life Is Beneficial

Solomon, the world's wisest man, observed the benefits of interdependence to be numerous. Accomplishment, help, warmth, and support are more accessible to those in community than those outside of it.

It's better to have a partner than go it alone. Share the work, share the wealth. And if one falls down, the other helps, But if there's no one to help, tough! . . . By yourself you're unprotected. With a friend you can face the worst. Can you round up a third? A three-stranded rope isn't easily snapped. (Eccl 4:9–12 MSG)

Consistently gathering in a healthy small group within your local church has the power to create community and connectedness. It can foster real fellowship. Biblical fellowship involves participating in life with others to the point of knowing them, feeling their hurts, sharing their joys, and encouraging their hearts. Chuck Swindoll describes what happens when real fellowship occurs: "Fences come down. Masks come off. Welcome signs are hung outside the door. Keys to the doors of our lives are duplicated and distributed. Joys and sorrows are shared."[7]

Suggestions for Gathering Together

Community is a living reality as the life of Jesus flows through his people. When we gather in his name, he is there meeting with us (Matt 18:20).

Some atmospheres kill community and others grow it. The epistles are full of injunctions that promote the growth and health of vibrant Christian community.

Affection

Love one another deeply as brothers and sisters. (Rom 12:10)

Greet one another with a holy kiss. (Rom 16:16; see also 1 Cor 16:20; 2 Cor 13:12)

Greet one another with a kiss of love. (1 Pet 5:14)

New Testament Christianity put a premium on affection and giving one another a hearty greeting. Greeting breaks the ice and lowers defenses. We live in a high-tech, low-touch world. One major reason people get involved in a group is they want a safe, high-touch environment. Learn to greet one another with an appropriate touch. In some cultures this would be shaking hands. In others it's a hug. In others it's a kiss. Remember: as touch goes up, defenses come down; as touch increases, receptivity increases.

Acceptance

> Therefore accept one another, just as Christ also accepted you, to the glory of God. (Rom 15:7)

> Therefore let us not pass judgment on one another any longer, but rather decide never to put a stumbling block or hindrance in the way of a brother. (Rom 14:13 ESV)

When people sense a spirit of criticism or self-righteousness, they either close down or begin to find fault. A spirit of criticism will suck the life out of a community. On the other hand, acceptance becomes fertile soil for fostering relationships. We must give others the freedom to be themselves. We also must not look at one another through the lens of criticism or self-righteousness.

Active Sharing

> Carry one another's burdens; in this way you will fulfill the law of Christ. (Gal 6:2)

> Rejoice with those who rejoice; weep with those who weep. (Rom 12:15)

Neal McBride wisely notes an obvious yet often overlooked reality when he writes, "Not all groups are really groups. Some are merely a collection of individuals with the appearance of a group. . . . The members assume that by calling themselves a group, they become one."[8]

Real community requires two parties. First, one person must open up and authentically share the hard, painful, challenging, frustrating aspects of his or her life. Second, the others must step into the person's pain and help that person walk through it. When this happens, something else happens: people enter into true community, the healing grace of God is poured out, and broken places are made healthy and whole.

Authenticity and Acknowledgment

A Christian gathering should be a safe place. People should be able to express their greatest struggles in an atmosphere of authenticity and acknowledgment.

Christian community is to be lived in the light. Sin dulls light and destroys fellowship. Christians must deal with their sin. Nothing builds community like honest confession to one another and prayer for one another.

> If we walk in the light as he himself is in the light, we have fellowship with one another, and the blood of Jesus his Son cleanses us from all sin. If we

say, "We have no sin," we are deceiving ourselves, and the truth is not in us. If we confess our sins, he is faithful and righteous to forgive us our sins and to cleanse us from all unrighteousness. (1 John 1:7–9)

Therefore, confess your sins to one another and pray for one another, so that you may be healed. (Jas 5:16)

Forgiveness

Let all bitterness, anger and wrath, shouting and slander be removed from you, along with all malice. And be kind and compassionate to one another, forgiving one another, just as God also forgave you in Christ. (Eph 4:31–32)

Grudges and resentment create walls and kill community. We must refuse to allow bitterness to grow by choosing to forgive one another.

Encouragement

Therefore encourage one another and build each other up as you are already doing. (1 Thess 5:11)

And let us watch out for one another to provoke love and good works, not neglecting to gather together, as some are in the habit of doing, but encouraging each other, and all the more as you see the day approaching. (Heb 10:24–25)

The word *encouragement* speaks of coming alongside another to provide courage. Living for God in a godless world can be a fearful challenge. Everyone needs a team behind them saying, "You can do it. Don't quit."

Resolve Conflict

Live in harmony with one another. Do not be proud; instead, associate with the humble. Do not be wise in your own estimation. (Rom 12:16)

Often, during the first few months of getting to know one another in a small group, conflicts arise. Yet the potential for conflict is always present. No two people are alike. Therefore, it is just a matter of time until conflict results. To try to deny or avoid disagreement is to kill true community. To resolve it builds community.

— Quote to Consider —

"We have made a terrible mistake! For most of this century we have wrongly defined soul wounds as psychological disorders and delegated their treatment to trained specialists. Damaged psyches aren't the problem. The problem is disconnected souls. What we need is connection! What we need is a healing community!"

—Larry Crabb[9]

— Questions to Ponder —

1. Are you in some sort of small, face to face weekly Christian gathering?
2. Which of the reasons to participate in community caught your attention and why?
3. Which of the ingredients for better Christian community would enhance your group's level of fellowship?

Notes

1. Nikolaus Ludwig von Zinzendorf, quoted in "Nikolaus von Zinzendorf: Christ-Centered Moravian 'brother,'" in *131 Christians Everyone Should Know*, ed. Mark Galli (Nashville: Holman Reference, 2000), 311.

2. J. I. Packer, "The Church in Christian Thought," Department of Theology, Regent College, Vancouver, BC, Canada, 1996.

3. Howard Snyder, *The Problem of Wineskins Revisited* (Houston: TOUCH Publications, 1996), 91.

4. John Ortberg, *Everybody's Normal Till You Get to Know Them* (Grand Rapids: Zondervan, 2002), 21.

5. Garth Icenogle, *Biblical Foundations of Small Group Ministry* (Downers Grove: InterVarsity, 1994), 13.

6. Bill Donahue and Russ Robinson, *Building a Church of Small Groups* (Grand Rapids: Zondervan, 2001), 24.

7. Charles Swindoll, *Dropping Your Guard* (Waco, TX: Word, 1983), 22.

8. Neal McBride, *Real Small Groups Don't Just Happen* (Colorado Springs: NavPress, 1998), 11.

9. Larry Crabb, *Connecting* (Nashville: Word, 1997), 6.

19 Participating in a Healthy Small Group

Rod Dempsey

Spiritual formation has many elements and three main directions, but it happens in one primary location. It happens best in a small group of Christ followers who love God, love one another, and are actively loving their neighbors. Its three main directions are: (1) Upward. We are to love God with our entire being. (2) Inward. On two separate occasions, Jesus commanded his disciples to "love another," and throughout the New Testament we are exhorted to live out the "one anothers" by showing love for our brothers and sisters in the body of Christ. Our love for one another is so powerful it can be a witness to the world of the fact that Christ lives in our hearts. (3) Outward. In the great commandments Jesus instructs his followers to love our neighbors as much as we love ourselves! Now that is a deep and impactful love. The three directions and the disciplines associated with each of them help us show that God—who is love—is present among his people and that the love of God is what the world needs now.

This three-directional love (love for God, love for one another, and love for our neighbor) is to be lived out in a community of believers. This community of believers comes together and determines to live differently and to be the visible body of Christ to the world. This community is called a church, and inside this church are smaller groups that take the commands of Christ and apply them to their own lives. The context for living out the commands of Jesus is a healthy small group. In this chapter, we will explore elements and components of healthy, growing, and multiplying groups.

Got GROUP?

Do you remember the ad campaign entitled, "Got Milk?" The ad would appear with a well-known star sporting a milk moustache. The star, looking debonair, would talk about the benefits of drinking milk and would always end the advertisement with the question, "Got milk?" Let me ask you a question: "Got GROUP?" This is a simple acrostic whose letters represent some of the most important elements in developing healthy small groups.

Guided by a Leader

John Maxwell said, "Everything rises and falls on leadership."[1] In a small-group context where people are seriously looking to live out the commands of Jesus, some sort of spiritual leader or coordinator is essential. Simply put, if you don't have a leader, it won't happen. Encouraging, equipping, and empowering people to grow in their love for God, love for one another, and love for neighbor are some of the most challenging aspects of ministry. Group leadership is an intentional pursuit and it is personal. Leadership is not about, "What can you do for me?" but rather, "What can I do for you?" It begins with a heart that asks the question, "How can I help you grow and become more like Christ?"

When a small-group leader understands this process, then he or she is in the business of true spiritual leadership. In order for a group to succeed, group leaders need to view their role as drawing out the new creation God has in mind for every individual in the group. When you do this, then you are a true leader.

Regular Meeting Times

I prefer weekly, but every other week will work if you have a good way to connect with people in the off weeks. Meeting monthly will not work if you are serious about helping the people in your group grow *and* develop. If you are meeting monthly, a person can miss one meeting, and it may be two full months before you see that person again. If you are trying to shepherd the flock of God with integrity, this is not acceptable. In two months' time, the enemy, who prowls about like a roaring lion, may easily use his tricks of deception, discouragement, and disillusionment to defeat one of your group members. Meeting weekly is best because people need to gather to share God's love and gifts with one another and with the world.

Open God's Word and Discuss

The Bible tells us in Heb 4:12, "For the word of God is living and effective and sharper than any double-edged sword, penetrating as far as the separation of soul and spirit, joints and marrow. It is able to judge the thoughts and intentions of the heart." Among the many things we do when we meet together as a small group, we must take responsibility to open the Word of life. The Bible has the power to change people's lives from the inside out. Consider Rom 12:2: "Do not be conformed to this age, but be transformed by the renewing of your mind, so that you may discern what is the good, pleasing, and perfect will of God." Studying and applying the Word of God can change us from what we are to what God has in mind for us.

United in Service

In the new commandment (John 13:34–35), Jesus exhorts us to "Love one another. Just as I have loved you, you are also to love one another." The second chapter of Acts describes the love the early church had for one another in this way, "They sold their possessions and property and distributed the proceeds to all, as any had need" (v. 45). They did this to meet needs that were coming to the forefront in that early gathering of believers. Additionally, Paul reminds the church at Ephesus that Christ's victory means supernatural abilities have been given to his people: "Now grace was given to each one of us according to the measure of Christ's gift. For it says: 'When he ascended on high, he took the captives captive; he gave gifts to people'" (Eph 4:7–8).

Every believer has at least one spiritual gift, and that spiritual gift should be used to build up the body of Christ—to minister to and serve others inside their group and out in the community.

Here is a list of ways people in your group can discover and use their spiritual gifts:

1. Lead the icebreaker portion of the group.
2. Lead the group's prayer time.
3. Plan the worship segment of group life.
4. Record and keep track of the group's prayer requests, and communicate those requests to all group members.
5. Send cards and letters to absentees.
6. Plan the group's refreshment schedule.
7. Plan the group's fun activities.
8. Plan the group's outreach efforts and activities.
9. Host the group.
10. Become an apprentice with an eye to starting a new group.
11. Lead the group discussion.
12. Start a new group to reach a new neighborhood or network.

Spiritual gifts are designed to strengthen the body and to serve the world. When we are using his gifts in our small groups or in our community, it is as if Christ were still present in the world today. Spiritual gifts are the visible extension of the hands and feet of Jesus to the world. When we use his gifts to serve and minister to people, they will sense his presence. Remember this truism: "People don't care how much you know until they know how much you care."[2]

Pray for One Another

In addition to studying and applying the Word, praying for and *with* one another is what separates a Christ-centered small group from a civic club. Prayer changes things. Hudson Taylor wrote of his desire "to move men, through God, by prayer alone."[3] Jesus put it this way: "Again, truly I tell you, if two of you on earth agree about any matter that you pray for, it will be done for you by my Father in heaven" (Matt 18:19).

What separates the church from secular groups is the spiritual content (Word of God) and spiritual encouragement (prayer). People get together in civic settings all across the country every day. The church must be different! Something amazing happens every time you ask someone the question, "How can I pray for you?" It is equally amazing what happens when two or three people begin to agree on something and petition our heavenly Father. Don't underestimate the power of small-group prayer when you meet together. I have heard Jerry Falwell say many times, "Nothing of eternal significance ever happens apart from prayer."[4]

This simple acrostic can help you determine whether those you lead each week are one of God's small groups or just another civic club. So I ask you again, "Got GROUP?"

GROUP Dynamics

As we continue to examine what a healthy group looks like, we must consider the internal dynamics of mobilizing the membership toward ministry and mission. Hebrews 4:12 says, "For the word of God is living and effective and sharper than any double-edged sword, penetrating as far as the separation of soul and spirit, joints and marrow. It is able to judge the thoughts and intentions of the heart." One of the primary reasons a person comes to a small group is to study and apply the life-changing Word of God. Fellowship is fun. Serving people is great. Praying for others and being prayed for is awesome. However, real life change takes place as we come in contact with the living and active Scriptures.

To ensure you are accurately sharing and applying truths from the Word, you should have some good curriculum (or a good set of questions) and learn how to study your Bible.

You want your group to grow not only in quantity but also in *quality*. If you focus on quality, you will gain quantity as a by-product. It is important that you are serious about breaking open the living and active Word of God.

This chapter provides several suggestions regarding the preparation of a good small-group discussion. These suggestions will be especially helpful if your church does not provide you with a weekly agenda to follow based on your pastor's sermon (which is a great way to reinforce what's being taught and tie your group to the larger church body). You could develop your own outline of the Sunday morning service if your church does not provide one.

Curriculum

A number of theologically sound publishing ministries have small-group curricula covering hundreds of Bible passages and topics. Make sure you choose discussion guides that will move your group past simple or complex Bible study and into life application and ministry to one another (more on this below).

Preparing Your Own Discussion Guide

If you are preparing your own outline from Scripture without using a curriculum, get approval from your pastor or small-group coach. They can help you shape and improve your outline or pass it along to other leaders who aren't as skilled as you in designing a discussion guide.

As you prepare, use these pointers to develop lesson objectives that foster a transformational gathering:

- Determine what you want the group to *learn* or gain through the discussion.
- Determine what or how you want them to *feel* after the meeting.
- Determine what you want to *do differently*, *more deeply*, or *start doing* as a group and as individuals through what you've learned and experienced in the meeting.
- Allow time for gender-specific accountability and interaction with questions related to loving God, loving one another, and loving our neighbors.

Once these objectives have been made clear, you'll do a far better job of creating the right questions based on any Scripture you choose.

Icebreakers

Make sure you have some good icebreaker questions at the beginning of your discussion. This is most important when you have first-time visitors or when your members are mentally preoccupied with other things (a deadline at the office or an argument with a family member at dinner before the meeting, just to name a few).

Reading the Bible Passage

Always read the passage or verse from the Bible. Invite other members to follow along or read a verse or two per person when the passage is long. This will encourage your members to bring their Bibles to your small group and personally read and dig for new truths. It also grounds your discussion.

Observation Questions

Questions that are specific to the passage or outline you are covering will start to get people thinking and talking. So ask one or two observation questions about the passage. For example: Who is speaking in this passage? Who was being spoken to? Where did the event described take place?

Discussion Questions

When discussing a passage, ask questions such as:

- What does it say?
- What does it mean?
- How can you apply this to your life?
- Is anything standing in the way of applying it immediately?

Try to have at least one question in the middle of your outline that you can use to go around the room and involve everyone.

Application Questions

Create a good set of application questions at the end of the lesson. Make sure you answer the question "So what?" for the entire lesson. By the time people leave the group meeting, they should be challenged to put something specific into practice. In the application section make sure you guide the group toward personal interaction with unbelievers and you plan group action for reaching out to friends, relatives, associates, neighbors, and classmates.

General Guidelines

- Avoid lecturing (or doing all the talking), even if you have to bite your tongue to keep quiet and just ask the questions. The Word of God is powerful. If you read it as a group, ask open-ended questions, and then make personal application, your members will find opportunities to confess sin, share deeply, and apply what is being discussed.
- Determine what you are hoping to accomplish with the discussion. Some leaders find it helpful to keep a journal of what they were hoping to accomplish in meetings and whether or not it happened. A simple journal is a great way to keep track of your expectations and gives you solid information to discuss with your coach or pastor when asked how your meetings are going.
- Don't let the discussion get off track. Keeping your goals in mind will help you remember this.

If you keep these basics in mind, then God's Word—the "two-edged sword"—will have a powerful effect on the members of your group. Remember, quality will always produce quantity. Spiritual formation in a healthy community of believers is a discipline that can have tremendous impact on an individual, a group, a church, and an entire community.

— Quotes to Consider —

"[John] Wesley wasn't persuaded that someone
had made a decision for Christ until that person
became involved in a small group."

—JOEL COMISKEY[5]

"When the New Testament was written, the typical church
was so small that it was, in essence, a small group."

—LARRY OSBORNE[6]

— Questions to Ponder —

1. Are you meeting regularly with your group to pray, to study the Word, and to apply what you are learning?
2. Does your group have GROUP?
3. How is your group engaging in Christ's mission?

Notes

1. John Maxwell, *The 21 Indispensable Qualities of a Leader: Becoming the Person Others Will Want to Follow* (Nashville: Thomas Nelson, 2007).

2. Theodore Roosevelt, Good Reads, accessed February 24, 2018, https://www.goodreads.com/quotes/34690-people-don-t-care-how-much-you-know-until-they-know.

3. Hudson Taylor, *A Retrospect* (1894; reprt., Sun City Center, FL: Revival Press, 2015), 18.

4. Jerry Falwell, in "All Night of Prayer Gives Students Sense of Unity," *Liberty Champion*, September 6, 2011, accessed February 24, 2018, https://www.liberty.edu/champion/2011/09/shifting-focus-to-prayer.

5. Joel Comiskey, *Home Cell Group Explosion: How Your Small Group Can Grow and Multiply* (Houston: TOUCH® Publications, Inc., 2002), 23.

6. Larry Osborne, *Sticky Church* (Grand Rapids: Zondervan, 2008), 45.

20 How to Love One Another

Dave Earley

Christians in the first century did more than follow a religion, ritual, creed, or doctrinal statement. They had a vibrant relationship with God *and* with the other Christ followers. For them spiritual formation was not a program; it was a communal relationship.

A New Commandment

Along with the two great commands of loving God and loving our neighbors, Jesus gave a third command, the new commandment.

> I give you a new command: *Love one another*. Just as I have loved you, you are also to *love one another*. By this everyone will know that you are my disciples, if you *love one another*. (John 13:34–35, emphasis added)

To Jesus, living in loving community with others was a distinguishing mark of discipleship. This high-level commitment to loving one another was important as these first Christians faced the challenge of persecution from both the Romans and the Jews. They not only wanted to be together; they *needed* to be together. By being together, they received the encouragement, prayer, esteem, support, provision, and care not available anywhere else.

Through the centuries it has been verified that effective spiritual formation happens in the context of relationships. People are diverse in personality, intelligence, interests, talents, and social status. Because of these differences, people can rub each other the wrong way. Also, people, even redeemed people, are flawed and frustrating, broken and bothersome. Trying to get along and live in community with imperfect people is challenging. Therefore, living in community is an ideal environment for spiritual formation.

As we discussed earlier, effective, biblical, spiritual formation stretches us in three directions: upward, as we love God; outward, as love our neighbors; and inward, as we love one another. Loving one another describes the aspects of spiritual formation that revolve around our relationships in the body of Christ.

Fortunately, the writers of the New Testament gave some helpful guidance in *how to* love one another—*how to* get along and thrive in Christian community. Their guidance is largely found in the "one another" commands of the New Testament.

The "One Another" Commands

Based on the overriding command to "love one another" (John 13:34–35), Jesus, Paul, James, Peter, and John give several specific relational imperatives. The New Testament records more than thirty of these clarifying relational imperatives.

The Thirty-Two "One Another" Commands of the New Testament

1. "Love one another" (John 13:34–35; 15:12, 17; 1 John 3:11; 3:23; 4:7, 11, 12; 2 John 1:5; Rom 13:8; 1 Pet 1:22; 4:8).
2. "Be at peace with each other" (Mark 9:50).
3. "Wash one another's feet" (John 13:14).
4. "Love one another deeply as brothers and sisters" (Rom 12:10).
5. "Outdo one another in showing honor" (Rom 12:10).
6. "Live in harmony with one another" (Rom 12:16).
7. "Let us no longer judge one another" (Rom 14:13).
8. "Accept one another, just as Christ also accepted you" (Rom 15:7).
9. "Instruct one another" (Rom 15:14; Col 3:16).
10. "Greet one another with a holy kiss" (Rom 16:16; 1 Cor 16:20; 2 Cor 13:12; 1 Thess 5:26; 1 Pet 5:14).
11. "When you come together to eat, welcome one another" (1 Cor 11:33).
12. "Have the same concern for each other" (1 Cor 12:25).
13. "Carry one another's burdens" (Gal 6:2).
14. "With patience, bearing with one another in love" (Eph 4:2; Col 3:13).
15. "Be kind and compassionate to one another" (Eph 4:32).
16. "Forgiving one another" (Eph 4:32; Col 3:13).
17. "Submitting to one another in the fear of Christ" (Eph 5:21).

18. "In humility consider others as more important than yourselves" (Phil 2:3).

19. "Do not lie to one another" (Col 3:9).

20. "Admonishing one another" (Col 3:16).

21. "Increase and overflow with love for one another" (1 Thess 3:12).

22. "Encourage one another" (1 Thess 4:18; 5:11; Heb 3:13; 10:25).

23. "Build each other up" (1 Thess 5:11).

24. "Watch out for one another to provoke love and good works" (Heb 10:24).

25. "Do not criticize one another" (Jas 4:11).

26. "Do not complain about one another" (Jas 5:9).

27. "Confess your sins to one another" (Jas 5:16).

28. "Pray for one another" (Jas 5:16).

29. "Love one another" (1 Pet 3:8).

30. "Be hospitable to one another without complaining" (1 Pet 4:9).

31. "Just as each one has received a gift, use it to serve others" (1 Pet 4:10).

32. "Clothe yourselves with humility toward one another" (1 Pet 5:5).

Primary "One Another" Commands of the New Testament

It is difficult to remember all thirty-two "one another" commands (admittedly, all translations of Scripture don't use the phrase *one another* in all the passages above). But three create the foundation for practicing the others.

1. Honor One Another

> Love one another with brotherly affection. Outdo one another in showing honor. (Rom 12:10 ESV)

Although he has been theological in the first eleven chapters, by the twelfth chapter of Paul's letter to the Romans, he gets practical. When he gives relational advice, loving one another by honoring one another is central. The word Paul chose for "honor" in the original language speaks of "placing high value on" others. It means "prefer," "give precedence to," "defer to," and "revere" them.

Paul adds that we are to "honor one another *above* ourselves." We are to put others above ourselves. Let others have the credit. Turn the focus on them, not us.

The grammar carries the idea that when we compete with others, it is not to make ourselves look good. But instead we are to compete to see who can honor others the most.

Below is a chart that shows the difference between actions that honor others and actions that take advantage of them. See which ones you are already good at and which ones you need to work on.

Actions That Honor Others	Actions That Dishonor Others
Actively trying to help them look good even at your own expense	Trying to make yourself look good at someone else's expense
Words of appreciation and affirmation	Disapproval, criticism, cut-downs
Give credit	Take credit
Take the initiative to clear up misunderstandings	Refuse to resolve misunderstandings
Only criticizing in private	Criticizing in front of others
Asking others for their opinions	Failing to seek the opinions of others
Updating people on their status, progress, or anything else that may affect them	Keeping people in the dark and purposely withholding information
Impartiality	Favoritism
Giving your full attention, active listening	Disinterest
Noticing when others need encouragement and giving it	Being insensitive, failing to notice the feelings of others

Honoring others creates the climate in which Christian community can flourish. It is a spiritual discipline that helps us and others become more like Jesus.

2. Serve One Another

Wash one another's feet. (John 13:14)

Serve one another humbly in love. (Gal 5:13)

The greatest example of servanthood was Jesus. On the night of his betrayal and arrest, he began the evening by serving his disciples.

Before the Passover Festival, Jesus knew that his hour had come to depart from this world to the Father. Having loved his own who were in the world, he loved them to the end. . . . So he got up from supper, laid aside his outer clothing, took a towel, and tied it around himself. Next, he poured water into a basin and began to wash his disciples' feet and to dry them with the towel tied around him. (John 13:1, 4–5)

As the goal of spiritual formation is to become like Jesus, it makes sense that a spiritual discipline that helps us become more like Jesus is servanthood.

When we make the often-difficult choice to be a servant, we grow into the image of Jesus.

When he washed his disciples' feet during the Last Supper, Jesus displayed six aspects of servanthood.

Servants express their love. John stated that "Having loved his own who were in the world, he loved them to the end" (John 13:1). Jesus expressed his love for his disciples through his service to his disciples. True servants do not serve out of obligation but out of love.

Servants take action. By its very nature, service is active. Jesus did not just sit around saying, "I love you." He showed it by his actions. He *got up* from the meal, *took off* his outer clothing, and *wrapped* a towel around his waist. After that, he *poured* water into a basin and began to *wash* his disciples' feet, *drying* them with the towel (John 13:4–5). Real love is always active.

Servants have nothing to lose. Jesus laid aside his rabbi robe in order to be a servant (John 13:4). In those days a rabbi held a position of great esteem, especially over his disciples. You would never expect him to take the role of servant and wash feet. Yet, even though Jesus was certainly one of the most famous rabbis of that day, he let go of that in order to serve.

He had already given up all the glories of heaven in order to come to earth and be a man. He became poor in order to make us rich (2 Cor 8:9). He laid aside his divine privilege and took the role of servant (Phil 2:5–7). He had already given up much and knew that he would soon give up even more. He had come to die.

Jesus lived as a man who had nothing to lose. He was not worried about his reputation or recognition or appreciation. He was simply worried about doing what needed to be done. These men needed their feet washed so he got up and washed them. It didn't matter that he was the esteemed Rabbi, their Master. It only mattered that he loved them, and they needed their feet washed.

Servants have nothing to prove. "Jesus knew that the Father had given everything into his hands, that he had come from God, and that he was going back to God. So he got up from supper, laid aside his outer clothing, [and] took a towel" (John 13:3–4).

When Jesus got up to serve:

- He did not have to prove himself. He knew who he was and whose he was. (John 13:3)
- He did not feel the need to announce his service. He just did it.
- He did not play the game of positioning, promotion, authority, and climbing higher in the pecking order. As you recall, earlier when he

caught his disciples playing the positioning game, he set them straight using himself as the example.

> Whoever wants to become great among you will be your servant, and whoever wants to be first among you will be a slave to all. For even the Son of Man did not come to be served, but to serve, and to give his life as a ransom for many. (Mark 10:43–45)

Servants have nothing to hide. Jesus was the man of integrity. There was nothing embarrassing in his closet. He had no dirty laundry. He could serve greatly because he lived rightly. He had nothing to hide, nothing to lose, and nothing to prove. He had all the attitudes of a loving servant.

I find that I often hamstring my ability to serve by a selfish attitude. Selfishness leads me to hide, to try to prove something, to hang on when I need to be letting go and serving.

Servants humble themselves. Jesus not only dropped his rabbi's robe, but he took up the towel of the servant. Jesus humbled himself in order to serve his disciples. Humility is not thinking negatively about yourself. Rather it is thinking accurately about yourself and mostly about others. When Jesus washed his disciples' feet, he was not thinking about himself. This is remarkable considering that in just a few hours he was going to sweat blood in Gethsemane, be arrested, and be shoved down the agonizing path to Golgotha. Being consumed with thoughts about his own needs would have been easy.

I find that my greatest obstacle in being a loving servant is . . . me. *I* am always in the way. *I* am too busy. *I* am too tired. *I* am too focused on *me* and *my* situation to see the needs of others, especially those closest to me. Jesus showed us something most of us need to see—the art of unselfish living. Servants are willing to brush self aside in order to see what someone else needs and act to meet that need.

Jesus loved others by serving others. If I hope to be like Jesus, I will do the same.

3. Forgive One Another

> . . . forgiving one another if anyone has a grievance against another. Just as the Lord has forgiven you, so you are also to forgive. (Col 3:13)

Paul argues that since the Lord has forgiven us, we are to forgive others. Spiritual formation is being changed into his image, and often nothing is more challenging than the spiritual discipline of forgiveness.

Forgiveness Is . . .

Forgiveness is necessary. Whenever you put two people together, you have the potential for conflict. Two opinions, two agendas, two personalities, and two backgrounds add up to a breeding ground for offense and hurt. Therefore, forgiveness is vital for healthy Christian community.

Forgiveness is cancelling the debt. When someone hurts us, they owe us. Forgiveness recognizes the debt they owe and chooses to release them from it.

Forgiveness is setting yourself free. People who hold grudges find that soon the grudge holds them. Forgiveness frees from resentment.

Forgiveness is giving up the right to get even. We tend to keep score of hurts. Forgiveness is choosing to not keep score, to not pay back, to not get even. Forgiveness is suspending the law of revenge.

Forgiveness is looking past the hurt to the person. Hurting people usually hurt people. Bitterness can see only your own hurt. Forgiveness sees the loneliness, brokenness, weakness, self-centeredness, or blind spot of the one who hurt you. Paul advised the Ephesians to put off bitterness by putting on sensitivity.

> Let all bitterness, anger and wrath, shouting and slander be removed from you, along with all malice. And be kind and compassionate to one another, forgiving one another, just as God also forgave you in Christ. (Eph 4:31–32)

Forgiveness is making four promises. Ken Sande teaches that real forgiveness may be described as a decision to make four promises:

1. I will not dwell on this incident.
2. I will not bring up this incident again and use it against you.
3. I will not talk to others about this incident.
4. I will not let this incident stand between us or hinder our personal relationship.[1]

Forgiveness is ultimately wishing the other person well. It is reaching a place where you no longer wish the worst for those who hurt you. You hope good things for them.

Forgiveness is something that usually takes some time. When the person was trusted, when the hurt went deep, and when the act was unfair, forgiveness takes time. You will not wish them well right away. Be patient with yourself. Make the first step. It will get you going, and once on the way, you will never want to go back.

Forgiveness is walking in step with God. Paul told the Colossians that they were to be "bearing with one another and forgiving one another if anyone has a grievance against another. Just *as the Lord has forgiven you,* so you are also to forgive" (Col 3:13, emphasis added). The challenge of forgiveness is learning to treat others as God has treated us.

— Quote to Consider —

"Every human being carries a sticker from God: Made in my image; worth the life of my Son. My prized possession whose value is beyond calculation."

—JOHN ORTBERG[2]

— Questions to Ponder —

1. Which three of the thirty-two "one another" commands do you find most challenging to obey?
2. When it comes to honoring others, how would you rate yourself on a scale of 1 to 3, with 1 being low and 3 being high?
3. Which aspect of servanthood do you find most challenging?
4. Who do you need to forgive?

Notes

1. Adapted from Ken Sande, *The Peacemaker: A Biblical Guide to Resolving Personal Conflict,* updated ed. (Grand Rapids: Baker Books, 2003), 207.
2. John Ortberg, *Everybody's Normal Till You Get to Know Them* (Grand Rapids: Zondervan, 2003), 165.

21 Accountability

Rod Dempsey

The first small group I attended was in college. We met in our dorm room once a week to study the Bible and pray for one another. It was a powerful force in my spiritual formation. The community and concern we had for one another was a powerful catalyst in encouraging us to develop the habits and disciplines that promote spiritual formation. It was a glorious time of growth and development.

Through the years I have either participated in or led hundreds of small-group meetings in homes. For the most part, these groups have been devoted to studying the Bible, praying for one another, and praying and planning for opportunities to share the gospel with people who do not know Christ. Overall such meetings are helpful, but they can devolve into spiritual navel gazing. If they do not have purpose, balance, and outreach, they will invariably be reduced to "us four and no more." Recently, I have added another dimension to small-group gatherings: to set aside some time for the men and the women to meet separately. When they meet separately, they discuss important matters related to their own personal spiritual journeys.

This is not a new development. Through the centuries, it has been a discipline practiced by many groups and churches. For example, Methodist founder John Wesley established "class meetings," "groups of 12 people grouped according to where the members lived, with one of them being appointed as the leader."[1] As Wesley explained: "The particular design of the classes is: to know who continue as members of the Society; to inspect their outward walking; to inquire into their inward state; to learn what are their trials; and how they fall by or conquer them; to instruct the ignorant in the principles of religion; if need be, to repeat, to explain, or enforce, what has been said in public preaching."[2]

Notice again that one aspect of the class meeting was "to inquire into their inward state." Historian David Werner noted, "Wesley's answer to the question of how to foster spiritual growth among a body of believers was mutual accountability to obedience to the will of God."[3]

Further, one purpose of the meeting was to reinforce what had been said in public preaching. This catalyzed spiritual formation for members of the class meeting.

The other element of the class meeting was experiential learning. Historian Michael Henderson explained, "Wesley believed that learning comes through experience. Methodism was an experiential system. . . . The difference between the meetings of the Methodists and other religious groups of their day was that many church leaders were telling people what they *ought* to do, but the Methodists were telling each other what they *were* doing."[4]

This approach, as has been mentioned, was not a new discovery. Richard Baxter had a similar method 100 years prior to Wesley and noticed that for his preaching to be fruitful, he had to follow it up with direct conversation with every family. He observed that he could have a greater impact on a person's life in thirty minutes of "personal work" than he could through ten years of public preaching."[5] The "personal work" was teaching the head of the house how to lead the family in devotions.

> [Baxter's] pastoral strategy focused on the family. He met with 16 families a week to instruct them in the catechism. This rigorous schedule allowed him to contact personally all members of all the 800 families in Kidderminster each year. He led the menfolk to set up family worship in their homes where they themselves could communicate the Christian faith to their families and to others.[6]

This type of personal work led to revival in the community.

Jacob Spener, a contemporary of Baxter, wrote *Pious Desires* and recommended six concrete measures to foster church renewal:

1. A more serious attempt to spread the Word of God. Pastors should preach from the entire Bible and Christians should meet in small groups to study the Bible.
2. The Lutheran doctrine of the priesthood of all believers should receive a new emphasis. The differences between the laity and clergy should be minimized. The clergy in particular should recognize that

their calling involves Bible study, teaching, reproving and consoling and a personal, holy life.

3. More attention should be given to the cultivation of individual spiritual life. Love for God and man should take priority over theological disputes. Knowledge is secondary to practice.

4. Truth is not established in disputes but through repentance and a holy life.

5. Candidates for the ministry should be "true Christians." Their training should include small groups for devotional life and personal Bible study.

6. Sermons should not show the preacher's erudition, but attempt to edify believers and produce the effects of faith.[7]

Notice the third principle for church revitalization: "More attention should be given to the cultivation of individual spiritual life. Love for God and man should take priority over theological disputes. Knowledge is secondary to practice." Both Baxter and Spener were calling for more personal attention and more personal spiritual formation of individual church members. This was taken to another level under the teaching and influence of John Wesley. Wesley eventually codified some "General Rules" to guide spiritual formation for adherents of the Methodist system:

The General Rules

It is therefore expected of all who continue therein that they should continue to evidence their desire of salvation,

First, by doing no harm, by avoiding evil in every kind—especially that which is most generally practiced . . .

Secondly, by doing good, by being in every kind merciful after their power, as they have opportunity doing good of every possible sort, and, as far as possible, to all men: To their bodies, of the ability which God giveth, by giving food to the hungry, by clothing the naked, by visiting or helping them that are sick or in prison. To their souls, by instructing, reproving, or exhorting all they have any intercourse with; trampling under foot that enthusiastic doctrine of devils, that "we are not to do good unless *our hearts be free to it.*"

Thirdly, by attending upon all the ordinances of God; such are:

The public worship of God.

The ministry of the Word, either read or expounded.

The Supper of the Lord.

Family and private prayer.
Searching the Scriptures.
Fasting or abstinence.[8]

These guidelines were the backbone of the movement, and inside the classes and bands they added specific accountability questions. Here is a list of some of the personal questions designed to measure a person's personal piety and acts of mercy:

1. Am I consciously or unconsciously creating the impression that I am better than I really am? In other words, am I a hypocrite?
2. Am I honest in all my acts and words, or do I exaggerate?
3. Do I confidentially pass on to others what has been said to me in confidence?
4. Can I be trusted?
5. Am I a slave to dress, friends, work, or habits?
6. Am I self-conscious, self-pitying, or self-justifying?
7. Did the Bible live in me today?
8. Do I give the Bible time to speak to me every day?
9. Am I enjoying prayer?
10. When did I last speak to someone else of my faith?
11. Do I pray about the money I spend?
12. Do I get to bed on time and get up on time?
13. Do I disobey God in anything?
14. Do I insist upon doing something about which my conscience is uneasy?
15. Am I defeated in any part of my life?
16. Am I jealous, impure, critical, irritable, touchy, or distrustful?
17. How do I spend my spare time?
18. Am I proud?
19. Do I thank God that I am not as other people, especially as the Pharisees who despised the publican?
20. Is there anyone who I fear, dislike, disown, criticize, hold a resentment toward, or disregard? If so, what am I doing about it?
21. Do I grumble or complain constantly?
22. Is Christ real to me?[9]

These questions were used effectively for more than 100 years. Look over the list again and note one or two that really speak to you. The Methodists developed another set of questions to be used every week:

- What known sins have you committed since our last meeting?
- What temptations have you met with?
- How were you delivered?
- What have you thought, said, or done which you're not sure was a sin or not?
- Is there anything you want to keep secret?[10]

To simplify the Methodist model, I have developed something called a "growth group" and have used this tool many times in the groups I lead and the classes I teach. In this tool, we have seven questions for each section. Loving God (upward) has seven questions. Loving one another (inward) has seven questions. And loving your neighbor (outward) has seven questions. First, let me explain how the growth group works.

Spiritual Formation Simplified and Illustrated

In Ephesians 1, the apostle Paul is declaring to the church that God has exalted Jesus and placed "everything under his feet and appointed him as head over everything for the church, *which is his body,* the fullness of the one who fills all things in every way" (Eph 1:22–23, emphasis added). In this passage we see terms like *feet, head,* and *body.* These terms indicate that the church is not like a body, but the church *is* Christ's body, and he is the head of the body. Paul elaborates on this in letters written to the churches at Rome (Romans 12) and Corinth (1 Corinthians 12). In these passages, it is clear that Jesus is the head of the body, believers are members of the body, and the body, when formed, becomes the hands and feet of Jesus to the world. Since the church is the body of Christ, our goal is to connect individual members to the Head (upward), connect all the members to the body (inward), and connect the functioning body to the mission (outward). To effectively implement and monitor the growth and development of an individual, a church will need to develop small groups where members can be voluntarily held accountable for habits and disciplines that will stoke their love for God, their love for one another, and their love for their neighbors. These are gender-specific growth groups for the purpose of spiritual formation.

What Is a Growth Group?

A growth group is a group of three or four persons of the same sex who gather weekly to encourage one another to make progress in their walks with Christ. This group is usually a subgroup of a larger, mixed-gender group. *The purpose of a growth group is for members to grow in relationship to Christ, to one another, and to his mission.* This plan is meant to be simple, relational, and reproducible. The plan for each group meeting relates to the three dimensions of spiritual formation.

1. *Upward*—Time in God's Word and time in God's presence through prayer. Reading and reflecting on Scripture and recording prayer requests and insights.
2. *Inward*—Connected to the other parts of the body in a small group, confession of sins, and using your spiritual gift(s) to build one another up in the Lord.
3. *Outward*—Connecting the body to the mission of Christ. The group regularly prays for others and uses their spiritual gifts to create opportunities to share Christ.

The goal of the growth group would be that all participants grow in their love for God, their love for other members of the body, and their love for their neighbors. You can change or personalize any set of questions group members choose. Can you imagine the health of a small group where all members are dedicated to growing and developing in their love for God, one another, and their neighbors? Now imagine if every member of the church was connected to a growth group and growing in these important areas. Healthy members in healthy groups are where the body of Christ then becomes the visible hands and feet of Jesus serving and loving a community.

Upward (Loving God)

Jesus told his disciples in John 15 that we should "abide" in him. Abiding in Christ means that we spend time in his Word and in his presence through prayer and meditation. We practice a simple form of prayer like ACTS (adoration, confession, thanksgiving, and supplication). Alternatively, we can use the Lord's Prayer as an outline. We also agree to read twenty-five chapters of

Scripture per week (equal to reading through the Bible in one year), and we record insights from God's Word as the Holy Spirit leads.

Questions

1. How is your reading going this week?
2. What is God saying to you through his Word? Are you writing it down? Memorizing?
3. Are you spending time in prayer every day? Explain your prayer practice.
4. What is God saying to you through your time in prayer? Are you writing it down?
5. What is the Holy Spirit revealing to you?
6. What are you attempting only with the Spirit's enabling?
7. Are you fasting for or about anything?

Inward (Loving One Another)

The apostle Paul stated in Ephesians 4 that gifted leaders are given to the body to equip, empower, and release the saints to do "the work of ministry, to build up the body of Christ." We should use the gifts Christ has given to us to encourage and edify the other parts of the body of Christ. In addition to our service to one another, we speak the truth to one another. James 5:16 says, "Therefore, confess your sins to one another and pray for one another, so that you may be healed."

Questions

1. Are you in a small group of believers?
2. How are you serving others in the family of God? (Are you using your gifts?)
3. What sins (lust of the flesh, lust of the eyes, or pride of life) are tempting you this week?
4. Are you holding ill will toward anyone?
5. Have you looked at anything sexually explicit or had lustful thoughts?
6. Are you guilty of falsehood or stealing?
7. Are you guilty of covetousness or envy?

Outward (Loving Our Neighbor)

Jesus said in John 20:21, "As the Father has sent me, I also send you." Jesus came to us on a mission, and now he sends us to the world on his mission. We are to take the gospel to the world and make disciples of Jesus. The challenge is that many disciples are not praying and are not taking the gospel to their world. In this section, we take time to pray by name for two or three people who need a relationship with Christ.

Questions

1. Are you making yourself available for those who are seeking Christ?
2. Have you been praying for those you know are lost? Who?
3. Are you serving people outside your comfort zone to share the gospel? How?
4. Have you actively listened to others who are seeking God? Example?
5. Have you shown and told the gospel in day-to-day life? Are you eating with seekers?
6. To which receptive "person of peace" is the Lord directing you? How is it going?
7. Are you praying for laborers? (Luke 10:2)

Spiritual formation requires personal attention, disciplined focus, and helpful, Christ-honoring accountability. As members of the body of Christ, we are exhorted to "confess our sins one to another" (Jas 5:16) and "speak the truth in love" to one another (Eph 4:15). This requires some sort of accountability to a group of believers who are pursuing Christ. The goal is a spiritual transformation impacting the individual, the church, and the community as a whole. Growth groups are a great way to sharpen the focus of the individual member of the body of Christ so that the body can become healthy.

— Quote to Consider —

"Growing churches have developed a system of small groups where individual Christians can find intimate community, practical help and intensive spiritual interaction."
—CHRISTIAN A. SCHWARZ[11]

— Questions to Ponder —

1. Are you in a gender-specific accountability group? Why or why not?
2. Look over the list of questions for the three directions and select one question from each area that you need to work on.
3. Who can you ask to hold you accountable to "walk in a manner worthy of your calling"?

Notes

1. John Wesley, "Nature, Design, and General Rules," in *Works* 9:69–70.

2. John Wesley, *Zion's Herald*, November 30, 1825, 1.

3. David Werner, "John Wesley's Question: 'How Is Your Doing?'" *Asbury Journal* 65/2 (2010): 74.

4. D. Michael Henderson, *John Wesley's Class Meeting: A Model for Making Disciples* (Nappanee, IN: Evangel Publishing House, 1997), 131.

5. Timothy Beougher and J. I. Packer, "'Go Fetch Baxter': This Feisty Puritan Spent His Life Quieting the Controversies He Started," *Christianity Today*, December 16, 1991, 26–28.

6. Beougher and Packer.

7. "The *Pia Desideria* (Pious Desires)," Christianity Today, accessed February 26, 2018, http://www.christianitytoday.com/history/issues/issue-10/from-archives -pia-desideria-pious-desires.html.

8. The General Rules of the Methodist Church, UMC.org, accessed January 6, 2018, http://www.umc.org/what-we-believe/the-general-rules-of-the-methodist -church.

9. Jake Hanson, *Crossing the Divide: John Wesley, the Fearless Evangelist* (Uhrichsville, OH: Shiloh Run Press, 2016), 30.

10. Bill Hull, "John Wesley, Disciple-Maker," The Bonhoeffer Project Website, accessed January 6, 2018, http://www.thebonhoefferproject.com/john-wesley -disciple-maker.

11. Christian A. Schwarz, *The ABC's of Natural Church Development* (Bloomington: Churchsmart Resources, 2001), 6.

22 Practiced at Home

Rod Dempsey

I grew up in a large family. My twin sister and I were numbers five and six in the birth order in our family, and through a family tragedy my mom and dad took in two of my mother's sisters for a number of years. At one time, we had ten people in our house with one bathroom. Now, I am not going to start talking about how we walked to school (which we did) in the snow (which we did) uphill both ways (well, it was uphill coming home). I am sharing the makeup of our family to talk about the importance of spiritual formation in the family. My mother and father did not come to know Christ personally until they were in their midthirties. As a result, attending church did not occur in our house until the children were older and in school. Some of us were even approaching graduation from high school.

The church we attended growing up was a small rural church with about 150 people present on a good Sunday. The pastor was bi-vocational, and he did a good job preaching the gospel and visiting the sick in the hospital along with other pastoral duties. But spiritual formation was not part of the church's structure. We were expected to attend church "every time the doors are open," but we were not instructed in how to develop the spiritual disciplines that promote personal holiness. Even further removed was instruction regarding how a man could lead his family in spiritual matters. Further complicating the situation was that my father did not have a full education. My father's father died when my father was twelve years old, and he had to go to work in the coal mines to help provide for the family. His job was to remove the impurities from coal racing up a conveyer belt before it dropped into the rail car. School was not the priority; as a result, his reading skills were not great. Therefore, leading the family in Bible reading or reading spiritual devotional books was a source of frustration for my father. By default, spiritual formation in our family, although my mother is a praying saint, was not a priority.

We went to church, we listened, we were faithful, we served, but we were not instructed at home in spiritual matters. Outside of "don't drink, don't curse, and don't date girls who do," we had no real spiritual instruction at home. I fear this is the case in many churches and denominations across the nation. In contrast, family spiritual formation is clearly presented throughout the Bible, and the family should be the primary place where our faith is passed on to future generations of Christ followers. Chap Bettis observes:

> What better discipleship unit than the family? What better model, teacher, and shepherd over a little one than a parent? God's desire for your family is to be a Trinity-displaying, God-glorifying, disciple-making unit. God gives us little children so that we can influence them to become fully devoted followers of Jesus Christ who love Him and love others. It is messy and inefficient, rewarding and frustrating, and ultimately, profoundly glorious work.[1]

Joel 1:3 says, "Tell your children about it, and let your children tell their children, and their children the next generation."

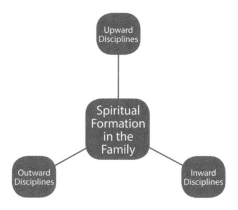

To understand the importance of spiritual formation inside the family, consider the following passages that clearly communicate the priority, the means, the methods, the habits, and the disciplines for spiritually forming our families to reflect the image of God.

- "Honor your father and your mother so that you may have a long life in the land that the LORD your God is giving you" (Exod 20:12).
- "Listen, Israel: The LORD our God, the LORD is one. Love the LORD your God with all your heart, with all your soul, and with all your strength. These words that I am giving you today are to be in your heart. Repeat them to your children. Talk about them when you sit in your house and when you walk along the road, when you lie down and when you get up. Bind them as a sign on your hand and let them be a symbol on your forehead. Write them on the doorposts of your house and on your city gates" (Deut 6:4–9).
- "Therefore, fear the LORD and worship him in sincerity and truth. Get rid of the gods your fathers worshiped beyond the Euphrates River and in Egypt, and worship the LORD. But, if it doesn't please you to worship the LORD, choose for yourselves today: Which will you worship—the gods your fathers worshiped beyond the Euphrates River or the gods of the Amorites in whose land you are living? As for me and my family, we will worship the LORD" (Josh 24:14–15).
- "Sons are indeed a heritage from the LORD, offspring, a reward. Like arrows in the hand of a warrior are the sons born in one's youth. Happy is the man who has filled his quiver with them. They will never be put to shame when they speak with their enemies at the city gate" (Ps 127:3–5).
- "Children, obey your parents in the Lord, because this is right. Honor your father and mother, which is the first commandment with a promise, so that it may go well with you and that you may have a long life in the land. Fathers, don't stir up anger in your children, but bring them up in the training and instruction of the Lord" (Eph 6:1–4).
- "Children, obey your parents in everything, for this pleases the Lord. Fathers, do not exasperate your children, so that they won't become discouraged" (Col 3:20–21).
- Paul, speaking of Timothy's family heritage, wrote, "Remembering your tears, I long to see you so that I may be filled with joy. I recall your sincere faith that first lived in your grandmother Lois and in your mother Eunice and now, I am convinced, is in you also" (2 Tim 1:4–5).
- "Although he was God's Son, he learned obedience from what he suffered. After he was perfected, he became the source of eternal salvation for all who obey him, and he was declared by God a high priest according to the order of Melchizedek" (Heb 5:8–10).

Spiritual Formation Principles from the Passages

From these passages we can learn many things about spiritual formation inside the family unit.

- The first principle we can see from the Ten Commandments is the priority of teaching children obedience. Obedience to parents is the training ground for obedience to our heavenly Father. That is why there are so many injunctions in the wisdom literature on disciplining your children and warnings of what will happen if there is no discipline.
- A correlating principle is shown in that Jesus *learned* obedience to his Father. The passage in Hebrews teaches that obedience in the home leads to obedience to the Father.
- Another foundational passage is Deuteronomy 6. This passage is referred to as the Shema, and it is foundational to following the Lord. The training and instructing of children to love the only Lord God should be done in the home and should be a continual discipline. Listen again to Moses: "These words that I am giving you today are to be in your heart. Repeat them to your children. Talk about them when you sit in your house and when you walk along the road, when you lie down and when you get up" (Deut 6:6–7). Jonathan Williams commented on this type of family spiritual formation: "This is a family saturated with the Word of God. This is a family who invests in the spiritual growth and health of their home in the morning, afternoon, and evening. This is a family that grows daily."[2]

Parents are to be the primary agents of spiritual formation for their children. What I am about to say next may be difficult to hear, but here goes: Mom and Dad, it is your responsibility to talk to your children about the King of kings and Lord of lords. Do not simply delegate this to others. Spiritual formation is not just about words either; they need to see your good example of following Christ. "Who else is in position to talk to our children as the Shema commands—at home, on a journey, when lying down, and when getting up? The answer is not the church. The answer is the family. Yet, how frequently do we miss or squander these opportunities?"[3] The home is the locus of spiritual formation for the family.

- It requires intentionality. When I first started dating my wife, I remember visiting her home for the first time. Above the fireplace was, "As for me and my house, we will serve the Lord." That is writing it on your walls so everyone can know your intention. My wife's mom and dad had family devotions almost every night and personally led their children to know Christ. My wife prayed to receive Christ after family devotions. Both of our sons prayed to receive and follow Christ at home. That is spiritual formation in the home.

- From Psalm 127, we see that children are like sharp arrows in the hands of a warrior. The arrows are to be used in service of God's kingdom—arrows that are going forth, advancing the good news of the gospel, and holding back the kingdom of darkness. That will only happen if they are being spiritually formed and sharpened for the Master's use. The place where they are sharpened and developed is at home.

- From Paul we learn that children are to obey their parents and to honor them "so that it may go well with you and that you may have a long life in the land" (Eph 6:3). This is a promise given to the children and a veiled warning as well. If you want to have a blessed life and a long life, obey and honor your parents! If you do not obey and honor your parents, it may not go so well. Also from this passage is the instruction to fathers not to "stir up anger in your children" (Eph 6:4). To summarize John Piper: Fathers should avoid yelling, excessive discipline, boundaries that are too narrow, harping, bossiness, etc. . . . These things cause anger, and anger is the real cannibal emotion that eats all the others. It is the real killer of a child's soul.[4] Fathers, do not treat your children so harshly that you plant a seed of anger in their souls. Discipline is needed to stop behaving in a harsh or spiteful manner toward your children. Discipline is also needed to "bring them up in the training and instruction of the Lord" (Eph 6:4) and follow the Shema's admonition to "repeat [God's words] to your children. Talk about them when you sit in your house and when you walk along the road, when you lie down and when you get up."

- From the Timothy passage we discover that being spiritually formed is a generational blessing. In Timothy's life, Paul can trace the good news of the gospel all the way back to Timothy's grandmother Lois and to his mother Eunice. The gospel travels along relational lines, and one of the closest relationships is parent to child. This is the most natural path for spiritual formation, and we should be investing spiritual energy and discipline toward the spiritual formation inside our homes. Do not leave it to others. Again, others can help, but it is obvious from the Scriptures that God's plan from the beginning is for moms and dads to be the primary spiritual trainers in the family.

Suggested Spiritual Disciplines for the Family

For the first ten years of my marriage, I did not have a clue as to what I should be doing in terms of family discipleship. I was an inattentive husband, and my parenting skills were lacking. I came to a place of desperation and cried out to the Lord for his wisdom and help, and he granted them. In my daily discipline of reading his Word, I discovered 1 John 5:14–15, "This is the confidence we have before him: If we ask anything according to his will, he hears us. And if we know that he hears whatever we ask, we know that we have what we have asked of him." I began to pray that the Lord would make me a better husband and a better father, and the Lord was gracious to give wisdom and help. With the Lord's help, I started anew. I began researching, reading, and going to conferences. Slowly and systematically I developed new habits and disciplines. Training children requires having a plan and being disciplined. Here are some suggestions for developing spiritual habits in the family that reflect his priorities:

1. *Upward—Love God.* Create a family mission statement that exalts Christ. Attend church together every week. Discuss the pastor's message as a family. Pray together every day.
2. *Inward—Love one another.* Eat at least one meal together every day. Make sure the family is serving the body of Christ. Help your children discover and use their spiritual gifts.
3. *Outward—Love your neighbors.* Go on a family mission trip together. Open your home and show hospitality to your neighbors. Help your children serve your neighbors.

The goal of spiritual formation is obedience to Christ. His Word gives us specific instructions related to the development of families for the kingdom and the glory of God. We must be disciplined in all areas of our lives but especially in the area of spiritual formation in our homes.

⌐ Quote to Consider ⌐

*"First, let us begin by emphatically declaring it is parents
(fathers in particular) and not the church who are given
the primary responsibility for calling the next generation
to hope in God. The church serves a supplementary role,
reinforcing the biblical nurture that is occurring in the home."*

—CHARLES SPURGEON[5]

⌐ Questions to Ponder ⌐

1. Who bears primary responsibility for the spiritual formation of children? Support your answer with Scripture.
2. What is your family spiritual development like?
3. Of the three areas for spiritual formation (upward, inward, outward), which needs the most attention in your family?
4. What is your plan for improvement?

Notes

1. Chap Bettis, *The Disciple-Making Parent: A Comprehensive Guidebook for Raising Your Children to Love and Follow Jesus Christ* (Shelton, WA: Diamond Hill Publishing, 2016), 4–5. Kindle Edition.

2. Jonathan Williams, *Gospel Family: Cultivating Family Discipleship, Family Worship, & Family Missions* (Magnolia, TX: Lucid Books, 2015), 13. Kindle Edition.

3. Mark J. Musser, *The Christ-Centered Home: Turning Your Kids into Christ-Centered Disciples* (CreateSpace, 2015), 42. Kindle Edition.

4. John Piper, "More Thoughts on Fathers from Ephesians 6:4," Desiring God, accessed February 26, 2018, http://www.desiringgod.org/articles/more-thoughts-for-fathers-on-ephesians-64.

5. Charles Spurgeon, "Family Worship," accessed March 16, 2018, http://www.sbts.edu/family/2009/10/28/family-worship/.

The Outward Disciplines—
Love Your Neighbor

23 Praying for Your Neighbors

Dave Earley

As we stated earlier, effective, biblical spiritual formation stretches us in three directions: upward, as we love God; inward, as we love one another; and outward, as we love our neighbors.

Most discussions of spiritual disciplines focus on individual practices such as Bible reading, meditation, fasting, and journaling. But Jesus also put a great deal of emphasis on loving our neighbors and missional living. Since the only command of Jesus that is repeated in all four Gospels and the book of Acts is the Great Commission (Matt 28:18–20; Mark 16:15; Luke 24:44–47; John 20:21; Acts 1:8), Jesus obviously included missional living in the spiritual formation of his followers.

The first spiritual discipline associated with loving our neighbors is praying for them.

Spiritually Receptive People

In June 2011, my wife, Cathy, and I accepted the call to plant a new church in urban Las Vegas. From June 1, 2011, until June 2012, we prayed daily for our future neighbors in Las Vegas. We prayed for "people of peace," people who would be spiritually receptive and ultimately influential (Luke 10:6).

At the same time, on the other side of the country, Randy and his wife, Mickael, were looking for career advancement. During that year, Randy got a job offer to move to Las Vegas. Eventually they decided on a home located at 2834 Via Stella Street.

During that year Cathy and I made several trips to Las Vegas and eventually settled on a home. We chose 2836 Via Stella Street.

A few weeks before we got to Las Vegas, Randy moved in to start his new job. His wife, Mickael, and daughter, Kyla, were still in the San Francisco Bay area until school let out for the summer. Our first night there, May 27, 2012, we were outside in the street playing with the neighbor kids. Soon the street was flooded with kids and their parents. I had been in Vegas a little over an hour, and I was introducing my neighbors to one another. Randy heard the noise and came out to see what was going on. Cathy found out he was alone for a few more weeks and invited him to dinner the next night. He did not hesitate and agreed to come.

We tried to be good listeners, and Randy loves to talk. Cathy is a great cook, and Randy loves to eat. So he enjoyed being at the meal. During dinner he told us he was an atheist, but he did "not dislike Christians." We invited him to come back the next week, and he quickly agreed.

Monday night he came to dinner. We listened and he talked. Cathy cooked and he ate. Then he told us he was going to California on Saturday to load up his family and his furniture. They planned to come back to Vegas on Sunday afternoon. We asked if he needed help unloading. He said no. He told us that he grew up in Las Vegas and was confident that his family and friends had him covered. I gave him my phone number just in case.

Late Sunday afternoon, I got a call. No one showed up to help Randy unload his truck. Our church planting team had several stout young men. They had Randy's truck unloaded and all the furniture put in place in twenty-five minutes.

Randy was delighted. "I will do anything you want. Even come to your church." Randy said excitedly. "Where does it meet?"

"Randy," I said, "you know that we have only been here three weeks." Then I pointed. "For now, our church meets next door in our house."

On Sunday, Randy and Mickael came to the door. "I am a man of my word," Randy said as they walked in. There were about thirty people gathered in our living room.

Randy and Mickael loved it. We invited them to join us for dinner on Monday night. They talked eagerly about the church gathering the previous day. So I asked if they would come back on Sunday. "Absolutely," Randy said.

God honored over a year of intercessory prayer for spiritually receptive people. In a few weeks, Randy was converted. The next week Mickael was converted.

We continued to have dinner with them every Monday night for the next four months. During those months, we read through the Gospels together.

Spiritually Influential People

For the first few months after they were converted, Randy and Mickael got highly involved in our church plant. When we began to meet in a school on Sundays for worship, Randy was a greeter and Mickael helped with setup and the tech crew. They both loved helping us with our large park outreach events.

After we had finished reading through the Gospels, Randy wanted more discipleship. So he and I continued to meet every Monday night. One week his assignment was to share his testimony. He shared it with the ten people who worked on his sales team. The next week the assignment was to share the Romans Road. He shared it with the ten people who worked on his sales team.

Within a few months, Randy had started a small Bible study group in his home with people from his sales team and some of his atheist friends. Over the next couple of years, Randy held prayer, evangelism, and discipleship seminars in small churches all over Las Vegas. He studied hard and received a Bible institute certificate. Currently Randy and Mickael are planting a church. And it all began with persistent prayer by my wife and me for our neighbors.

The Discipline of Prayer Evangelism Is . . .

Prayer evangelism is a spiritual discipline whereby we love our neighbors by sincerely and consistently asking God to work in their lives and draw them to himself. As Dick Eastman said, it is "love on its knees."[1] It is asking God for opportunities to minister and to strategically leverage those opportunities to their fullest.

Prayer Evangelism Because . . .

Jesus Practiced Prayer Evangelism

Jesus was and is an evangelistic intercessor (John 17:20; Rom 8:34; Heb 7:25). He lamented, "Jerusalem, Jerusalem . . . How often I wanted to gather your children together, as a hen gathers her chicks under her wings, but you were not willing!" (Luke 13:34). His heart was broken, and he wept in prayer for the lost: "As he approached [Jerusalem] and saw the city, he wept for it" (Luke 19:41).

When he looked out over the crowds, his heart broke. So confused and aimless they were, like sheep with no shepherd. (Matt 9:36 MSG)

The First Church Practiced Prayer Evangelism

The first church in history got off to a tremendous start. Three thousand people were saved and baptized the first day (Acts 2)! It immediately became a healthy, dynamic, missional, evangelistic church on fire. They experienced effective evangelism, discipleship, community, generosity, power ministry, and praise, ushering in even more explosive evangelism (Acts 2:42–47).

The first church in the world experienced incredible growth and impact. "Scholars estimate that over the thirty year span of the book of Acts, the Christian movement grew from 120 to 100,000 among the Jews alone."[2]

The spiritual discipline that set up the amazing start and development of the first church was prayer.

They went to the room upstairs where they were staying. . . . They all were continually united in prayer, along with the women, including Mary the mother of Jesus, and his brothers. . . . the number of people who were together was about a hundred and twenty. (Acts 1:13–15).

Before the first church in history was ready to experience tremendous evangelism, growth, and impact, it first practiced tremendous prayer.

Two leaders of the first church, Peter and John, were dragged before the authorities and told to stop preaching the gospel of Jesus. What was the church's response? They prayed for more boldness to keep on preaching (Acts 4:24–31)! They not only practiced evangelistic prayers for lost souls, but they also focused on praying for themselves that they would be fearless to share the gospel with the lost people they were praying for.

Paul Practiced Prayer Evangelism

Paul had a broken heart for his fellow Jews who were lost.

I speak the truth in Christ—I am not lying; my conscience testifies to me through the Holy Spirit—that I have great sorrow and unceasing anguish in my heart. For I could wish that I myself were cursed and cut off from Christ for the benefit of my brothers and sisters, my own flesh and blood. (Rom 9:1–3)

Paul turned his passion into prayer, stating, "My heart's desire and prayer to God concerning them is for their salvation" (Rom 10:1).

Paul Told Timothy to Practice Prayer Evangelism

> First of all, then, I urge that petitions, prayers, intercessions, and thanks-givings be made for everyone. . . . God our Savior, who wants everyone to be saved and to come to the knowledge of the truth. . . . Christ Jesus, who gave himself as a ransom for all. (1 Tim 2:1, 3–6)

Evangelistic prayer for all people is rooted in the fact that God wants all people to be saved and that Jesus died for all people. New Testament scholar William Barclay writes of 1 Timothy 2, "Few passages in the New Testament so stress the universality of the gospel. Prayer is to be made for *all* men; God is the Savior who wishes *all* men to be saved; Jesus gave his life a ransom for *all*."[3]

Paul wanted Timothy to know that for the gospel to spread prayer was needed. The church must follow his command. The book of Revelation shows that the gospel not only spread through Ephesus but also to the towns surrounding it—Smyrna, Pergamum, Thyatira, Sardis, Philadelphia, and Laodicea (Revelation 2–3).

Sally Practiced Prayer Evangelism

Sally was an ordinary lady who made an extraordinary impact. She and her husband, Jim, bought one of the first homes in a new subdivision near our church building. Once or twice a day, she prayer-walked her neighborhood, interceding for the salvation of each family that moved in. She also served her neighbors and took an interest in their children. As a result, she spiritually impacted her neighbors.

One day she asked me if she could use one of the large classrooms at the church after the next week's worship service. When I asked why, she said, "Nearly a dozen of my neighbors and their children are being baptized here next week. We wanted to throw a party in their honor."

John Practiced Prayer Evangelism

John Edmiston is an Australian missionary who has been in full-time Christian ministry for more than thirty years. He has served in Australia, Papua New Guinea, and the Philippines. In an article titled "Practical Prayer Evangelism," he gives this testimony.

> In 1993, I led a Bible study series with a group of twenty or so rather boisterous university students who asked to be taught about prayer. In the process we had a book for the prayer points with three columns, Request, Date Entered, and Date Answered.

They started praying for their friends' salvation, and within a couple of weeks the converts started rolling in, two or three a week, and often ending up at the Bible study. Every person "put in the book" for prayer came to Christ, and naturally enough the prayer journal became known as the "book of life."

If memory serves me correctly about 25 people came to Christ, through prayer alone, that semester. Prayer worked, even with inexperienced believers, who hated witnessing, and people were saved.[4]

Neil Practiced Prayer Evangelism

Neil Cole is an organic church planter, author, and the founder and executive director of Church Multiplication Associates. In his book *Search and Rescue*, Cole tells of training a group of new disciple makers. He writes, "I remember a holy moment in my life when the potent power of simply praying daily for people's souls struck me in a new way."[5] He then told of getting goose bumps all over as he realized that these new Christians, who were now making disciples of their own, were people whose names were checked off a "Praying for the Lost" card he carried in his Bible. He said, "I was struck . . . with how powerful the simple idea of prayer is." He concludes, "Of course, we are not praying for souls so that we can check off names on our list and feel good about ourselves. But there is no greater joy than to watch a life born again into the kingdom of God. To that end we pray, God answers, and we rejoice."[6]

Dee and His Church Practiced Prayer Evangelism

Dee Dukes was discouraged, worn out, and on the verge of resigning. But during a four-day pastors' prayer summit, Pastor Dukes realized he had tried everything but prayer.

He determined to go home and preach on prayer for three months, practice personal prayer for one hour a day, pray with one person one hour a day, and lead his church to pray for their lost neighbors.

Later he said, "The more we prayed, the more God put it on our hearts to reach the lost. We experienced a growing sense of urgency to reach our neighbors and the world. We grew in creative ways to reach out to the lost. Almost everyone in the church began praying for lost friends, work associates, family members, mission efforts, and countries around the world."[7]

When Dukes got serious about prayer, the church grew from fewer than 200 to an average Sunday morning attendance of 1,400 people in a town of 2,200. It has dozens of prayer times that take place each week. They also pray around the clock for lost people the ten days before Easter and have twenty-four hours of fasting and prayer the day before Easter. They pray for every single person within twenty miles of their church by name. Every morning their high school students prayer-walk around the school track, praying for their fellow students.

Spurgeon and His Church Practiced Prayer Evangelism

Charles Spurgeon was a giant as a spiritual leader. He grew one of the first modern-day megachurches in London in the nineteenth century. He has been lauded as a great preacher, author, leader, and spiritual entrepreneur. Under his leadership, his church started a Bible college, trained and sent missionaries, planted churches, and created an orphanage and widows' homes. They took Sunday school to the poor. But most importantly, people came to Christ in that church every week for more than thirty years.

Spurgeon frequently commented that this evangelistic success was the direct result of his congregation's faithful prayers. When visitors came to Spurgeon's church, he took them to the basement prayer room where people were always on their knees interceding. Then Spurgeon declared, "Here is the powerhouse of this church."[8]

Every Monday night, a large portion of Spurgeon's huge sanctuary was filled with 1,000 to 1,200 earnest and fervent intercessors. His biographer noted, "In Spurgeon's eyes the prayer-meeting was the most important meeting of the week."[9]

In his autobiography, Spurgeon described the power of his praying church, saying, "We had prayer meetings that moved our very souls, each one appeared determined to storm the Celestial City by the might of intercession."[10]

How to Pray for Your Neighbors

1. Get to know their names. Pray for them by name.
2. Get to know their needs. Pray for their needs.
3. Be consistent. Practice prayer evangelism as a discipline, even when you don't seem to be seeing any progress.
4. Ask the Lord to increase the activity of the Holy Spirit in their lives. Ask him to orchestrate situations and circumstances to get their attention. Ask him to put people around them that can play a part in their coming to him.
5. Ask the Lord to convict them of their sin, lack of righteousness, and deserved judgment (John 16:8).
6. Ask the Lord to open their spiritual eyes to see the beauty of the gospel (2 Cor 4:4).

7. Ask the Lord to draw them to himself (John 6:44, 65).

8. Ask the Lord for opportunities to build a relationship with them and share the gospel with them.

9. Ask the Lord to prevent Satan from stealing his Word from their heart (Matt 12:19).

⸻ Quote to Consider ⸻

"It is possible to move men, through God, by prayer alone."
—HUDSON TAYLOR[11]

⸻ Questions to Ponder ⸻

1. Do you know your neighbors' names? Do you know their needs?

2. Do you have a system of prayer for them?

3. What can you do to better implement the discipline of prayer evangelism?

Notes

1. Dick Eastman, *No Easy Road* (Grand Rapids: Baker Books, 1971), 58.

2. C. Peter Wagner, *Acts of the Holy Spirit* (Ventura, CA: Regal, 1994), 16.

3. William Barclay, *1 Timothy* (Louisville: John Knox Press, 1975), 55.

4. John Edmiston, "Practical Prayer Evangelism," *Lausanne World Pulse Archives*, May 2006, accessed January 6, 2018, https://www.lausanneworldpulse .com/themedarticles-php/326/05-2006.

5. Neil Cole, *Search and Rescue* (Grand Rapids: Baker, 2008), 174.

6. Cole, 174.

7. Dee Dukes, quoted in Daniel Henderson and Elmer Towns, *Churches That Pray Together* (Colorado Springs: NavPress, 2009), 19.

8. Charles Haddon Spurgeon, quoted in Arnold Dallimore, *Spurgeon: A New Biography* (Carlisle, PA: Banner of Truth, 1985), 125.

9. Dallimore, 126.

10. Charles Haddon Spurgeon, *C. H. Spurgeon's Autobiography,* compiled by Susannah Spurgeon and Joseph Harrald (1897; reprt., Toronto, ON: University of Toronto Libraries, 2011), 77.

11. Hudson Taylor, quoted in J. O. Sanders, *Spiritual Leadership* (Chicago: Moody, 1974), 82.

24 Being Light to Your Neighbors

Rod Dempsey

Spiritual formation requires surrendering every area of our lives to the rule and reign of Christ. As we surrender control and allow the Holy Spirit to fill and lead us, we become the visible, tangible witness of the coming King and kingdom. I remember the first time I earned a paycheck and put money into an offering plate at the church I was attending. It was a statement that what I had earned was not mine. The Lord had entrusted a blessing to me. I felt a rush of joy flowing into my heart. To be able to give back to the Lord who loved me enough to die on the cross for me and to give me "everything required for life and godliness" (2 Pet 1:3) was a turning point in my spiritual formation. As I stopped spending recklessly on things I wanted and began to grow in the "grace of giving" (2 Cor 8:7 NIV), I discovered other areas of my life that needed to be brought under the rule and reign of Christ too and that there is a stewardship in all of life. I felt the same way when, for the first time, I began to plan a budget and prayerfully exercise the discipline of sticking to the management of God's resources.

I had the same experience when I discovered that God has specific instructions related to relationships, whether with a friend or an enemy. Obeying those instructions requires that we exercise spiritual discipline and develop spiritual habits to reflect our ownership by Christ. As we submit to Christ in every area of our lives, we become salt and light shining in a dark world. We are to be living witnesses of the resurrection power of Jesus to change us and to make us different from the world. Jesus said in the Sermon on the Mount,

You are the salt of the earth. But if the salt should lose its taste, how can it be made salty? It's no longer good for anything but to be thrown out and trampled under people's feet. You are the light of the world. A city situated on a hill cannot be hidden. No one lights a lamp and puts it under a basket, but rather on a lampstand, and it gives light for all who are in the house. In the same way, let your light shine before others, so that they may see your good works and give glory to your Father in heaven. (Matt 5:13–16)

Becoming salt and light to our neighbors means examining every area of our lives and showing the world that Christ living in us makes a positive difference. If we are not submitting to Christ and if our lives are not considerably different, our witness of the gospel will be seriously hindered. We should be managing every area of our lives to show the lordship of Jesus. Consider Paul's instructions to the church at Corinth: "A person should think of us in this way: as servants of Christ and managers of the mysteries of God. In this regard, *it is required that managers* be found faithful" (1 Cor 4:1–2, emphasis added). This management should extend to every detail and every nook and cranny of our existence. We should live our lives as a statement that Jesus is King of kings and Lord of lords. He is above everything and every area of our lives. Every area of our lives has been redeemed, and God expects us to be the visible representation of the kingdom of Christ. Listen to Paul's description of the universality of the rule and reign of Jesus.

He exercised this power in Christ by raising him from the dead and seating him at his right hand in the heavens—far above every ruler and authority, power and dominion, and every title given, not only in this age but also in the one to come. *And he subjected everything under his feet* and appointed him *as head over everything* for the church, which is his body, the fullness of the one who fills all things in every way. (Eph 1:20–23, emphasis added)

Because of the resurrection of Jesus, every area of our lives should be completely submitted to his management, correction, and oversight. Abraham Kuyper observed, "There is not a square inch in the whole domain of our human existence over which Christ, who is Sovereign over all, does not cry, 'Mine!'"[1] Christ is Lord over all the areas of our lives! We show our love for God by giving back to him things that are important or precious to us. We worship God by offering up our whole world and all the individual pieces of it back to him. As we worship God wholeheartedly, the world can see the visible rule and reign of Jesus in our lives. Let us look at some areas that need to be under Christ's dominion, areas that require spiritual discipline and formation.

The Time We Have

Consider what Paul says to the church at Ephesus regarding the use of time, "Pay careful attention, then, to how you live—not as unwise people but as wise—making the most of the time, because the days are evil. So don't be foolish, but understand what the Lord's will is" (Eph 5:15–17). God's will is that we would "make the most of the time." How does a person make the most of the time? We must carefully consider the building blocks of time the Lord has entrusted to us. Seconds, minutes, hours, weeks, months, years, and decades are the elements we need to examine. We have 86,440 seconds in one day, 1,440 minutes in one day, 24 hours in one day, and 168 hours in one week. We are to manage all of those seconds, minutes, hours, and days carefully for the King. I am not saying you need to go around with a stopwatch and an alarm, but I am saying you do need to be aware that each day is a gift given to us by the Lord.

So, how do we redeem the time? How do we create structure and add discipline to our management of time? First, you need to do something like a time analysis of your weekly schedule. How much time do you spend sleeping? How much time is devoted to work? How much time do you allot for eating and personal grooming? What about relationships? How much time do you spend watching television or movies or sports or on social media? As a professor in graduate school, over the years I have done thousands of time-analysis inventories, and this is what I have discovered almost on a universal scale: Every person spends at least two to three hours a day devoted to personal pursuits. Take out sleep, work, eating, etc. Almost every person (fully 95 percent of the people surveyed) has two to three hours a day that they can use as discretionary. Sometimes a person will protest and say, "Not me." However, upon closer examination, we can find some areas that are not being well managed.

This two to three hours a day in particular is the time we must be "making the most of." This two to three hours is the time that needs to be honed and developed for use in the kingdom. Imagine if every believer was investing fourteen to twenty-one hours a week in kingdom pursuits. Put another way, what if every believer made a commitment to tithe not only their income but to tithe their time to the Lord as well? What do you think would happen to their personal lives, and beyond that, what would happen to the church? Revival is not meant to be utterly mysterious. Revival is about realigning your priorities to reflect his priorities. Revival will happen in our lives if we get serious about obeying the revealed will of God.

The Finances Entrusted to Us

Another way to show our love for God is by not having sticky fingers when it comes to the handling of money. If we are not careful, the love of money can turn our hearts away from trusting Christ. Just listen to a few principles from the Word of God:

- "The one who profits dishonestly troubles his household, but the one who hates bribes will live"— Solomon (Prov 15:27).
- "Place no trust in oppression, or false hope in robbery. If wealth increases, don't set your heart on it"— David (Ps 62:10).
- "In the same way, therefore, every one of you who does not renounce all his possessions cannot be my disciple"— Jesus (Luke 14:33).
- "You still lack one thing: Sell all you have and distribute it to the poor, and you will have treasure in heaven. Then come, follow me"— Jesus to the rich young ruler (Luke 18:22).
- "Don't store up for yourselves treasures on earth, where moth and rust destroy and where thieves break in and steal. But store up for yourselves treasures in heaven, where neither moth nor rust destroys, and where thieves don't break in and steal. *For where your treasure is, there your heart will be also*"— Jesus (Matt 6:19–21, emphasis added).
- "But those who want to be rich fall into temptation, a trap, and many foolish and harmful desires, which plunge people into ruin and destruction. For the love of money is a root of all kinds of evil, and by craving it, some have wandered away from the faith and pierced themselves with many griefs"— Paul (1 Tim 6:9–10).

These passages and more make abundantly clear that we have some clear choices regarding our treatment of money. Some obvious habits we need to develop are:

1. Develop a budget and stick to it.[2]
2. Begin giving to your local church to the point of tithing, and then go beyond the tithe.
3. Pray about big financial decisions before you purchase.
4. Start a savings account (three to six months of your expenses).
5. Pay off all debt but your house.

Now this plan has just five simple habits. What if every believer made a commitment to practice these five disciplines? What do you think the result would be? Let us show our love for God by being salt and light to those around us, especially in the area of finances.

Our Physical Bodies

As I have gotten older, I have realized increasingly that the body I have needs to be "managed" and maintained to the best of my ability. This is what Paul is explaining to the church of Corinth when he says, "Don't you know that your body is a temple of the Holy Spirit who is in you, whom you have from God? You are not your own, for you were bought at a price. *So glorify God with your body*" (1 Cor 6:19–20, emphasis added). The apostle Paul had much to say about the importance of offering our bodies back to Christ and exercising discipline in our physical lives. In Romans, Paul explains that we are to offer all the parts of our body to God:

- "Therefore do not let sin reign in your mortal body, so that you obey its desires. And do not offer any parts of it to sin as weapons for unrighteousness. But as those who are alive from the dead, *offer yourselves to God, and all the parts of yourselves to God as weapons for righteousness*" (Rom 6:12–13, emphasis added).
- "Therefore, brothers and sisters, in view of the mercies of God, I urge you to *present your bodies as a living sacrifice, holy and pleasing to God*; this is your true worship. Do not be conformed to this age, but be transformed by the renewing of your mind, so that you may discern what is the good, pleasing, and perfect will of God" (Rom 12:1–2, emphasis added).

Romans 6:13 says we are to offer all the parts of ourselves to God, and they are to be used as weapons for righteousness. That is a positive principle with a positive impact. The members of our body can be used as weapons for righteousness. Just think what would happen if all believers, to show our love for God, offered all the parts of our bodies to Christ. To make a 100 percent presentation of our eyes, our hands, our feet, our tongues, our ears, and our minds to Christ—what a difference that would make in our churches!

- Our eyes can and should watch good things.
- Our hands can and should be used to bless others as we labor.
- Our feet can and should take us to places where Christ is exalted and where we can serve Christ.

- Our tongues can and should be used to praise God and bless others.
- Our ears can and should be focusing on things that are pure and Christ honoring.
- Our minds can and should be used to think about Christ-honoring themes and be trained to help others think good things about Christ.

Spiritual formation is about offering all the parts of our lives back to Christ to love and worship him. Consider Rom 12:2 again, "Therefore, brothers and sisters, in view of the mercies of God, I urge you to *present your bodies as a living sacrifice, holy and pleasing to God*; this is your true worship" (emphasis added). This is your spiritual worship. This is a primary way we show we love God.

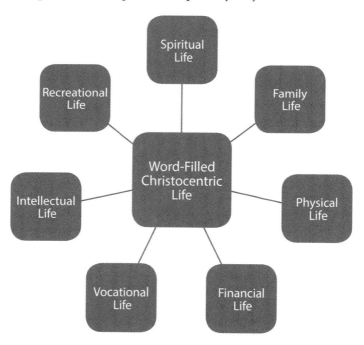

In short, all the areas of our lives should be yielded to Christ so he can rule and reign over us, and as a result we can show that Christ is our Lord. When we are not living disciplined lives, we will negatively affect the community of believers. When we are intentionally submitting every area to the rule and reign of Christ, our witness to his transforming grace shines like a light to our neighbors. Further, we need to surrender to Christ our spiritual gifts, our talents, and our abilities to serve him. We need to give our relationships to Christ. Our jobs and vocation can be a powerful witness to the rule and reign of Christ. Paul again says it this way, "So, whether you eat or drink, or *whatever you do*, do everything for the glory of God" (1 Cor 10:31, emphasis added). Whatever you do should be done for the kingdom and glory of Christ.

— Quote to Consider —

"If God was the owner, I was the manager. I needed to adopt a steward's mentality toward the assets He had entrusted— not given—to me. A steward manages assets for the owner's benefit. The steward carries no sense of entitlement to the assets he manages. It's his job to find out what the owner wants done with his assets, then carry out his will."

—RANDY ALCORN[3]

— Questions to Ponder —

1. Is every area of your life submitted to the rule and reign of Christ?
2. What is the area you struggle with the most to submit to Christ?
3. How can the supremacy of Christ be a witness to the unbelieving world?

Notes

1. James D. Bratt, ed., *Abraham Kuyper: A Centennial Reader* (Grand Rapids: Eerdmans, 1998), 488.

2. If necessary, use an envelope system. For more information see: "The Envelope System Explained," Dave Ramsey, accessed February 26, 2018, https://www.daveramsey.com/blog/envelope-system-explained.

3. Randy Alcorn, *The Treasure Principle: Unlocking the Secret of Joyful Giving*, rev. ed. (Colorado Springs: Multnomah, 2017), 26.

25 Sharing the Good News with Your Neighbors

Dave Earley

Before Jesus ascended into glory, he gave his disciples important instructions. His last words were and still are of supreme significance for several reasons.

The Great Commission

Called the Great Commission, these words are, first and foremost, the last words Jesus said to his followers. As such, they eloquently express his greatest passion and top priority.

Second, in these words, Jesus was essentially saying, "This is the culmination and climax of all I have been teaching you the last three years. If you don't remember anything else I said, remember this!"

Third, these final instructions were repeated on three separate occasions and are the only commands of Jesus that are recorded in all four Gospels *and* the book of Acts (Matt 28:18–20; Mark 16:15; Luke 24:46–47; John 20:21; Acts 1:8). It is as if he was telling them, "Look, I keep repeating this one thing because it is the main thing. If you don't do anything else, be sure to do this!"

Fourth, the final words of Jesus were given to be obeyed. Today we call the final statement the Great Commission. Theologians call it the Great *Commission* because the word *commission* is a military term meaning "an authoritative order, charge, or direction." It is used for a document conferring authority issued by the president of the U.S. to officers in the army, navy, and other military services. With an authoritative order, obedience is not optional. It is expected. To disobey would be considered an act worthy of severe punishment.

It is foolish for people to call themselves followers of Jesus and refuse to fulfill his final wishes and obey his supreme orders. Since this order to evangelize the world by making disciples was clearly and repeatedly given, it must be obeyed. Since we see both the apostles and other believers obeying it (e.g., Acts 8:1, 4), we know it was given to all of us.

Time to Speak Up

Christians are to love our neighbors. To do so, we must display the gospel. But we must also declare it. A point comes in the process of evangelizing our neighbors that we must cross over from prayers and deeds to speaking words. We have to share the gospel.

Paul made the need for gospel proclamation clear in his letter to the Romans.

> For everyone who calls on the name of the Lord will be saved. How, then, can they call on him they have not believed in? And how can they believe without hearing about him? And *how can they hear without a preacher?* And how can they preach unless they are sent? As it is written: How beautiful are the feet of those who bring good news. (Rom 10:13–15, emphasis added)

Notice the various steps in the salvation process. The lost person is saved when they *call* on the name of the Lord *after* they *believe in* him. But they can't be expected to believe until *after* they *hear* of him. But they only hear of him *after* they have been *told* the good news. The gospel must be proclaimed to be effective.

Previously in the letter to the Romans, Paul spoke of the gospel. He could be bold because the gospel is the power of God for salvation. But this power is not released until the gospel has been proclaimed.

> So I am eager to preach the gospel to you also who are in Rome. For I am not ashamed of the gospel, because it is the power of God for salvation to everyone who believes. (Rom 1:15–16)

The Spiritual Discipline of Sharing the Gospel

The discipline of sharing the gospel is a commitment to tell others the good news of the death, burial, and resurrection of Jesus Christ for our sins (1 Cor 15:3–40). It is clearly outlining the facts of the gospel and calling for a response.

As such, proclaiming the gospel becomes the ultimate act of loving our neighbors as we help lead them to become our brothers and sisters in Jesus Christ.

Sharing the Gospel Was Jesus's Mission

The first recorded message by Jesus in Luke's Gospel occurred in the synagogue at Nazareth. When the time came to read the Scripture, he read the messianic prophecy found in Isa 61:1–2:

> The Spirit of the Lord is on me, because he has anointed me to preach good news to the poor. (Luke 4:18; Isa 61:1)

When he did this, Jesus was both declaring that he was the Messiah and giving his ministry mission statement: "to preach the good news to the poor." Sharing the good news was what Jesus did almost continually for the next three and a half years. Therefore, if we hope to be like him, we must do what he did—proclaim the gospel. So we will practice the spiritual discipline of evangelism.

Sharing the Gospel Is Telling Good News

A literal translation of the word *gospel* (*euangelos*) is "good message" or "good news." The word most often translated *preach* or *proclaim* in the New Testament comes from the same root and literally means "to communicate good news."

The fact that Jesus died to pay for our sins and open the way for us to get to God is good news. In fact, it's the best news! But that news does others no good unless, or until, we share it. We have to preach the good news.

The word *preach* sounds formal, like some man in suit and tie in church on a Sunday standing behind a pulpit pointing his bony finger in your face. That is one way to preach but certainly not the only way. Anytime we tell another person the good news of Jesus's death, burial, and resurrection for our sins, we are preaching the gospel. It could be over coffee at Starbucks, or across the fence with a neighbor, or during bedtime prayers with your kids, or over the phone with a loved one in another state, or over the internet, or in a children's Sunday school class. The issue is not *how* we preach but *that* we preach.

"One Beggar Telling Another Beggar Where to Find Bread"

D. T. Niles has said, "Evangelism is one beggar telling another beggar where to find bread."[1] I love that! Evangelism is a positive opportunity to help someone else. It is not talking down to someone as if you are better—you aren't better. It's not looking down a self-righteous nose and saying, "Sinner, repent!" It's realizing that spiritually we are all beggars in need of living bread. It is saying,

"We have found that Jesus is the living bread." Evangelism is telling someone how to meet the living bread, the Lord Jesus Christ.

> This is the bread that comes down from heaven so that anyone may eat of it and not die. I am the living bread that came down from heaven. If anyone eats of this bread he will live forever. (John 6:50–51)

Sharing the Gospel Is a Moral Obligation

Imagine I have a neighbor who is blind and, therefore, he does not realize that after a big rain a huge crevice has opened up in his backyard. I may pray for him, serve him, have him over for dinner, and live an exemplary life in front of him. But if I really love my neighbor, I will be sure to tell him about the danger lurking in his backyard.

Of course, no one wants to hear there is a gaping, deadly hole just outside the door. So he may not want to hear about the death pit. But if I love him, I will do what it takes to convince him to stay away.

Or, imagine I am a medical doctor and one of my patients has life-threatening cancer, and without a painful surgery he will die. Of course no one wants to hear a diagnosis of cancer, especially the deadly kind. But if I am a good person and a good doctor, I will tell him what is wrong with him and how it can be fixed.

Imagine a deadly plague is wiping out entire cities in a matter of days. Let's also imagine I have found the cure for the devastating influenza. Let's also say I do not like my neighbors. They are rude and arrogant. It does not matter. I still have a moral obligation to share the cure with my neighbors and everyone else for that matter.

We live in a world where people are spiritually starving to death. Therefore, sharing the gospel is a moral obligation.

In many ways, we are like the poor Samaritan lepers after they fled the starving city and discovered the treasure left by the vanished enemy army. For them to fail to tell the others where to get food would be morally wrong. Therefore, they said:

> We're not doing what is right. Today is a day of good news. If we are silent and wait until morning light, our punishment will catch up with us. So let's go tell the king's household. (2 Kgs 7:9)

Sharing the Gospel Is the Expected Result of Spiritual Formation

Henry Martyn was a missionary to India and Persia (present-day Iran). Tremendously industrious, in a few short years he had started five schools for children and had translated the New Testament into Hindi, Urdu, and Persian. He was often heard to pray, "Let me burn out for God."

Henry was what was called a "one-way missionary." At the turn of the twentieth century, when a "one-way missionary" left home for the mission field, he packed all of his belongings in a coffin and bought a one-way ticket to the mission field. This was because he did not plan to return home alive. This proved prophetic as Martyn died on the mission field at the young age of thirty-one.

Martyn understood something we must not forget: authentic spiritual formation will result in missional living. Martyn said it well, "The spirit of Christ is the spirit of missions. The nearer we get to Him, the more intensely missionary we become."[2]

Share the Gospel by . . .

Sharing Your Story

For many of us, the hardest part of evangelism is building a bridge so we can get into telling the gospel in a nonoffensive way. One of the easiest ways to do so is by sharing your testimony. When we speak of sharing your story or telling your testimony, we are talking about proclaiming to others how you came to Christ. You are giving a witness. "In a courtroom, a witness isn't expected to argue the case, prove the truth, or press for a verdict; that is the job of attorneys. Witnesses simply report what happened to them or what they saw."[3]

Every believer has a testimony. If you have been saved, you have a salvation story. Granted, some may be more dramatic than others, yet people need to hear *your* story. No one else's story is exactly like yours, so you need to share it, or it will be lost forever.

In my evangelism training courses, I have students practice sharing their stories in a minute—three twenty-second sections. We also have them write their testimonies on paper. They can do it in fewer than a thousand words. Many love this project because in writing their testimony they realize what God has done for them. They realize they do have a story, and after writing it down, they feel much more confident in sharing it.

The three sections of a salvation testimony are:

1. *What my life was like before Christ.* This is where you use a few adjectives to describe your life prior to Jesus. In one sentence mine is: *I was lonely and depressed. I was drinking too much and got scared when I began to have suicidal thoughts.* Your story may deal with

the fact that you were religious but lost or that you started dating a Christian and saw something you needed.

2. *How I met Christ as Savior.* This is where you share the gospel by telling about the Lord drawing you to himself for salvation. My story is: *I had a few Christian friends who clearly had something I needed. They kept inviting me to a young adult Bible study. One night after the study, I went home, locked myself in my room, got down on my knees, and asked the Lord to forgive me. I knew Jesus's death on the cross for me was real. I told the Lord that if he wanted my life, he could have it, all of it.*

3. *How Christ changed my life.* This is where you tell about post-conversion blessings. My story is: *When I woke up the next morning after giving my life to Christ, I felt the weight of my sin gone. I had so much joy I found myself smiling all the time. People wanted to know what drug I was taking to be so happy. For the first time, I felt deeply loved and that I had a reason to live.*

Sharing your salvation story builds a relationship bridge of understanding that Jesus can walk across, into the heart of a lost person. It can be a convenient and effective way to bypass intellectual defenses. It is difficult to argue with the evidence of a changed life. Plus, a story well told often holds the interest of the hearer longer than would happen otherwise. People will listen to you because instead of being a "professional salesman," you are a "satisfied customer."

Sharing the Facts of the Gospel

People need enough information about Jesus to believe in him and commit their lives to him. Salvation is the result of believing certain truths. These truths include:

1. There is a God.
2. I am responsible to God.
3. I have erred in my responsibility. I have sinned.
4. Sin has some negative consequences—death/separation from God.
5. Jesus never sinned.
6. Jesus died to pay for my sin.
7. His righteousness is good enough.
8. We receive his gift of eternal life by committed belief in him.
9. Our belief is evident through our repentance and conversion.

Helping Them Cross the Bridge of Faith

Loving our neighbors and praying for them is not enough. We need to do more than serve them and even share the good news with them. A point comes when we need to help them cross the bridge of faith and be saved.

When you sense the Lord is speaking to your neighbor and that your neighbor is ready to trust Christ and be born again, take these simple actions:

1. Review the key aspects of the gospel as mentioned above.
2. Ask if they believe the key aspects of the gospel.
3. Ask them if they are willing to put their faith in Jesus as their Savior and confess Jesus as Lord.
4. Offer to lead them in prayer. You can say a sentence of prayer, and they can repeat it after you. It can include these elements:

Father in heaven,
I admit that I have sinned.
I believe that Jesus is the Son of God and died to pay for my sin.
I believe that Jesus rose from the dead to give me eternal life.
Right now I call on the name of the Lord Jesus to save me.
I turn from my sin and want to start a new life following Jesus.
Please forgive my sin and save me.
Please help me live for you every day for the rest of my life.

⭶ Quote to Consider ⭸

"For I am not ashamed of the gospel, because it is the
power of God for salvation to everyone who believes."

—PAUL IN ROM 1:16

⭶ Questions to Ponder ⭸

1. Have you neglected the spiritual discipline of sharing the gospel?
2. What makes this discipline difficult for you to apply?
3. Have you ever helped anyone across the bridge of faith? Who? When?

Notes

1. D. T. Niles, *That They May Have Life* (New York: Harper and Brothers, 1951), 96.

2. Henry Martyn, *Journal and Letters of Henry Martyn* (London, Forgotten Books, 1865), 300.

3. Warren, *The Purpose-Driven Life*, 290 (see chap. 3, n.1). For additional practical information about evangelism and discipleship, I suggest that you read two other books in this series: Dave Earley and David Wheeler, *Evangelism Is . . .* (Nashville: B&H Academic, 2010), and Dave Earley and Rod Dempsey, *Disciple Making Is . . .* (Nashville: B&H Academic, 2013).

26 Loving the Least of These

Dave Earley

Jesus's practice was to seek out hurting, broken, cast-off, disregarded nobodies and make them feel like somebodies. He let them know that he accepted them even though he did not approve of their behavior. Even though he was a popular rabbi, not to mention the holy Son of God, even infamous sinners felt welcomed by him and comfortable in his presence. It changed many of their lives.

Lepers were the untouchable outcasts of the first century. They were considered unclean. They had to live apart from everyone else. Their disease was considered so physically contagious and so religiously abhorrent, it was viewed as dangerous, reckless, and offensive to even touch them. Yet Jesus loved and healed them (Mark 1:40–47; Luke 17:11–19).

Jesus gave morally compromised women forgiveness and hope (Luke 7:47; John 8:1–11). Jesus ate with hated tax collectors and those viewed as especially wicked sinners (Matt 9:10). He brought light and deliverance to the demonized (Matt 12:22; 17:14; Mark 1:21–25; 5:1–20).

The self-righteous Pharisees hated him for it (Luke 15:1–2). But Jesus could not help it. Loving the least was part of who he was. If we hope to be like him, we must do the same.

The Spiritual Discipline of Loving the Least

The spiritual discipline of loving the least includes intentionally stretching to provide food and/or clothes to someone in need. It is giving your time, energy, money, and heart to those who can never give back. It is treating the poor and broken as Jesus in disguise. It is seeing and treating the least as worthy and valuable gifts from God. It giving to the unloved and doing it with Jesus, for Jesus, to Jesus—and then doing it over again.

Loving the Least Because . . .

We cannot honestly read the Bible without being confronted with God's heart toward the helpless and hopeless. Because he loves the least, as we are spiritually transformed into his image, we will do the same. Even though we may not find such actions easy or comfortable, loving the least is an essential discipline for those who are serious about being like Jesus.

The Bible offers at least ten compelling reasons to adopt the spiritual discipline of loving the least. The Scriptures are clear. Read and ponder them slowly.

1. God actively loves the least.

> The helpless one entrusts himself to you; you are a helper of the fatherless. . . . Lord, you have heard the desire of the humble; you will strengthen their hearts. You will listen carefully, doing justice for the fatherless and the oppressed. (Ps 10:14, 17–18)

> I know that the Lord upholds the just cause of the poor, justice for the needy. (Ps 140:12)

> For you have been a stronghold for the poor person, a stronghold for the needy in his distress. (Isa 25:4)

2. God the Father equates how we treat the poor with how we treat him.

> The one who oppresses the poor person insults his Maker, but one who is kind to the needy honors him. (Prov 14:31)

> Kindness to the poor is a loan to the Lord, and he will give a reward to the lender. (Prov 19:17)

3. God blesses those who care for the poor.

> A generous person will be blessed, for he shares his food with the poor. (Prov 22:9)

> Give to him [your poor brother], and don't have a stingy heart when you give, and because of this the Lord your God will bless you in all your work and in everything you do. (Deut 15:10)

He also said to the one who had invited him, "When you give a lunch or a dinner, don't invite your friends, your brothers or sisters, your relatives, or your rich neighbors, because they might invite you back, and you would be repaid. On the contrary, when you host a banquet, invite those who are poor, maimed, lame, or blind. And you will be blessed, because they cannot repay you; for you will be repaid at the resurrection of the righteous." (Luke 14:12–14)

4. God curses those who refuse to care for the poor.

Now this was the iniquity of your sister Sodom: She and her daughters had pride, plenty of food, and comfortable security, but didn't support the poor and needy. (Ezek 16:49)

Woe to those enacting crooked statutes and writing oppressive laws to keep the poor from getting a fair trial and to deprive the needy among my people of justice, so that widows can be their spoil and they can plunder the fatherless. What will you do on the day of punishment when devastation comes from far away? Who will you run to for help? Where will you leave your wealth? (Isa 10:1–3)

He has toppled the mighty from their thrones and exalted the lowly. He has satisfied the hungry with good things and sent the rich away empty. (Luke 1:52–53)

5. God expects his people to care for the poor.

The godly care about the rights of the poor; the wicked don't care at all. (Prov 29:7 NLT)

If anyone has this world's goods and sees a fellow believer in need but withholds compassion from him—how does God's love reside in him? (1 John 3:17)

6. Jesus stated that his mission was to serve the poor and broken.

He came to Nazareth, where he had been brought up. As usual, he entered the synagogue on the Sabbath day and stood up to read. . . . "The Spirit of the LORD is on me, because he has anointed me to preach good news to the poor. He has sent me to proclaim release to the captives and recovery of sight to the blind, to set free the oppressed, to proclaim the year of the Lord's favor [Isa 61:1–2] . . . . Today as you listen, this Scripture has been fulfilled." (Luke 4:16–21)

7. Jesus equates how we treat the poor with how we treat him.

> When the Son of Man comes in his glory, and all the angels with him, then he will sit on his glorious throne. All the nations will be gathered before him, and he will separate them one from another, just as a shepherd separates the sheep from the goats. He will put the sheep on his right and the goats on the left. Then the King will say to those on his right, "Come, you who are blessed by my Father, inherit the kingdom prepared for you from the foundation of the world.

> For I was hungry and you gave me something to eat; I was thirsty and you gave me something to drink; I was a stranger and you took me in; I was naked and you clothed me; I was sick and you took care of me; I was in prison and you visited me."

> Then the righteous will answer him, "Lord, when did we see you hungry and feed you, or thirsty and give you something to drink? When did we see you a stranger and take you in, or without clothes and clothe you? When did we see you sick, or in prison, and visit you?"

> And the King will answer them, "Truly I tell you, whatever you did for one of the least of these brothers and sisters of mine, you did for me." (Matt 25:31–40)

8. Jesus will judge us according to how we have treated the poor.

> Then he will also say to those on the left, "Depart from me, you who are cursed, into the eternal fire prepared for the devil and his angels! For I was hungry and you gave me nothing to eat; I was thirsty and you gave me nothing to drink; I was a stranger and you didn't take me in; I was naked and you didn't clothe me, sick and in prison and you didn't take care of me."

> Then they too will answer, "Lord, when did we see you hungry, or thirsty, or a stranger, or without clothes, or sick, or in prison, and not help you?"

> Then he will answer them, "I tell you, whatever you did not do for one of the least of these, you did not do for me."

And they will go away into eternal punishment, but the righteous into eternal life. (Matt 25:41–46)

9. Jesus was poor.

For you are becoming progressively acquainted with and recognizing more strongly and clearly the grace of our Lord Jesus Christ (His kindness, His gracious generosity, His undeserved favor and spiritual blessing), [in] that though He was [so very] rich, yet for your sakes He became [so very] poor, in order that by His poverty you might become enriched (abundantly supplied). (2 Cor 8:9 AMPC)

10. For a season of his life, Jesus was homeless.

As they were traveling on the road someone said to him, "I will follow you wherever you go." Jesus told him, "Foxes have dens, and birds of the sky have nests, but the Son of Man has no place to lay his head." (Luke 9:57–58)

Loving the Least Demands Action

Too often I have not done much for the poor. A few years ago, after reading the aforementioned Scriptures, I was determined to change that. I do not want to stand before Jesus and hear him say, "Whatever you did not do for one of the least of these, you did not do for me" (Matt 25:45).

Several years ago, we moved to the heart of Las Vegas to follow the mission statement of Jesus: "To preach good news to the poor . . . to proclaim release to the captives and recovery of sight to the blind, to set free the oppressed, to proclaim the year of the Lord's favor" (Luke 4:18–19). As a result, we started a church service in a middle school. We also started a ministry on the campus of UNLV. We also found ourselves helping street kids in one of the least reached areas of Las Vegas. The 89119 zip code had more than 48,000 people. It contained only a handful of small evangelical churches. But it was full of the least—the poor, the homeless, the addicted, the abused, the outcast, the violent, and the broken.

We held many large outreach events in a park in the neighborhood. When we started, six gangs operated out of that park. The only people in the park in the evenings were the homeless, the drug addicts, the prostitutes, and gang members.

But God loves the poor, and he changed the atmosphere at that park. Soon children began to come and play on the neglected swings and slides.

My son started a weeknight Bible study in that park. Soon more than 100 people showed up. Time and again, at the Bible study gathering, God seemed to preserve the food supernaturally to feed every last person all they wanted.

At the prompting of my son, I made a bad business decision but a great kingdom decision. I began to raise money to start an outreach center where we could give people a place to find hope, love, food, and clothes seven days a week. We wanted to create a place of acceptance that gave people a hand up and not merely a hand out.

It was tough. The day after we signed the lease, our primary donor backed out. But God has a big heart for the poor. If we truly love God, we will love *what* he loves—poor people—and love *like* he does—with active effort and faith. Within hours, God prompted another donor to step up and provide twice what we hoped. But then a seemingly corrupt, dishonest landlord bungled the renovation of the property so badly the city threatened to shut down operations. But God has a big heart for the poor. So after a lot of hard work, prayer, more fund-raising, and patience, the center opened four months behind schedule. From the first day, people began coming in and finding hope, love, help, and best of all, Jesus!

But the evil one was constantly attacking. Equipment was stolen. Key people got painfully sick. Marriages were attacked. It was hard.

Soon we started a midweek Bible study and a Sunday night worship service in that location. Many of the people who had been helped at the center became the primary teachers at the midweek gathering.

I must confess, operating the center was a struggle all the way. It was hard to keep raising the money and gathering the necessary food products. With limited resources, finding the necessary staff was difficult. Following up with the people we reached was challenging. Working with the landlord was infuriating. But we were especially heartbroken when someone came in, got help, got saved, got off drugs, got a job, got a paycheck, and then forgot us and God.

But week after week, we felt the smile of God on that little outreach center and worshipping community. People were saved by the power of the gospel. Addicts were delivered. The abused were healed. Lives were given meaning and purpose.

I learned not to treat poor people as projects but as friends and brothers and sisters. And I learned to do it *with* Jesus and *for* Jesus. The spiritual discipline of loving the least changed my life.

By the way, at the writing of this book, the center in Vegas has grown and is reaching more people than ever.

Ways to Love the Least

1. *Make friends with the poor.* Treat them with dignity and respect. Never treat them as projects to relieve your guilt.
2. *Move into the neighborhood.* Don't just parachute in once a year. Become part of the fabric of the community.

> The Word became flesh and blood, and moved into the neighborhood. (John 1:14 MSG)

3. *Fast each week and set aside the unused food money to feed the poor.*

> Isn't this the fast I choose: To break the chains of wickedness, to untie the ropes of the yoke, to set the oppressed free, and to tear off every yoke? Is it not to share your bread with the hungry, to bring the poor and homeless into your house, to clothe the naked when you see him, and not to ignore your own flesh and blood? (Isa 58:6–7)

4. *Consistently volunteer at a ministry that serves the down and out.*
5. *Financially adopt orphans and/or widows in an underdeveloped part of the world, and be personally involved in their lives.*
6. *Take a homeless person to eat lunch with you in a restaurant.*

— Quote to Consider —

"We try to pray through our work by doing it with Jesus, for Jesus, to Jesus. That helps us to put our whole heart and soul into doing it. The dying, the cripple, the mental, the unwanted, the unloved—they are Jesus in disguise."

—MOTHER TERESA[1]

— Questions to Ponder —

1. How does it make you feel when you read Matt 25:31–46?
2. How are you practicing the discipline of loving the least?
3. What will you do differently in regard to practicing this discipline?

Note

1. Mother Teresa, from an interview conducted by Edward W. Desmond in 1989 for *Time* magazine. Excerpts from the interview appeared in *Time* magazine, and the full text of the interview appeared in *The National Catholic Register*, accessed February 24, 2018, http://www.ncregister.com/daily-news /mother-teresa-seeing-and-loving-jesus-in-the-poor.

27 Loving Your Enemies

Rod Dempsey

Joseph had eleven brothers, and they hated him. Probably a better description is that they despised who he was, what he said, and how he behaved. On top of this, their father loved Joseph more than he loved any of them. Ouch. We see the seeds of the problem as we pick up this story of love, loathing, hatred, jealousy, and forgiveness in Genesis 37.

> Now Israel loved Joseph more than his other sons because Joseph was a son born to him in his old age, and he made a robe of many colors for him. When his brothers saw that their father loved him more than all his brothers, they hated him and could not bring themselves to speak peaceably to him. (vv. 3–4)

Joseph did not help the situation when he told his brothers about a dream he had. The story continues,

> Then Joseph had a dream. When he told it to his brothers, they hated him even more. He said to them, "Listen to this dream I had: There we were, binding sheaves of grain in the field. Suddenly my sheaf stood up, and your sheaves gathered around it and bowed down to my sheaf." "Are you really going to reign over us?" his brothers asked him. "Are you really going to rule us?" So they hated him even more because of his dream and what he had said. (vv. 5–8)

This situation brewed for a number of years until one day the brothers saw their chance, and they acted upon their hatred for their spoiled-rotten little brother.

One day Israel (Jacob) sent Joseph out into the country to find his brothers, and this is what happened next:

> So Joseph set out after his brothers and found them at Dothan. They saw
> him in the distance, and before he had reached them, they plotted to kill
> him. They said to one another, "Oh look, here comes that dream expert!
> So now, come on, let's kill him and throw him into one of the pits. We
> can say that a vicious animal ate him. Then we'll see what becomes of his
> dreams!" (vv. 17–20)

The rest of the story is that they did not kill him, but instead they sold him into slavery. Nice brothers! Joseph spent the next thirteen years in prison and it was a total of twenty-four years before he was reunited with his brothers and father in Egypt. While Joseph was in prison, he encountered many challenges and obstacles. Eventually he was all but forgotten and languished in prison until the king of Egypt had a dream. None of the pharaoh's magicians or soothsayers could interpret the dream, and so Joseph, the dreamer, was summoned, and he revealed the dream to Pharaoh. Joseph was exalted to the highest position of power in the kingdom, second only to Pharaoh.

Pharaoh's dream was about seven years of prosperity and seven years of famine. When the famine hit, all the surrounding territories and countries had to come to Egypt for grain, which had been stored under Joseph's direction during the years of prosperity. As the famine intensified, Joseph's brothers and father relocated to Egypt. In a tearful and dramatic reunion, Joseph revealed himself to his brothers and eventually to his father. Years later Joseph's father died in Egypt. After he died, the brothers became fearful that Joseph would have his revenge. "When Joseph's brothers saw that their father was dead, they said to one another, 'If Joseph is holding a grudge against us, he will certainly repay us for all the suffering we caused him'" (Gen 50:15). The brothers sent a message to Joseph,

> "Before he died your father gave a command: 'Say this to Joseph: Please
> forgive your brothers' transgression and their sin—the suffering they
> caused you.' Therefore, please forgive the transgression of the servants of
> the God of your father." Joseph wept when their message came to him.
> His brothers also came to him, bowed down before him, and said, "We
> are your slaves!"
>   *But Joseph said to them, "Don't be afraid. Am I in the place of God?
> You planned evil against me; God planned it for good to bring about the
> present result—the survival of many people.* Therefore don't be afraid. I
> will take care of you and your children." And he comforted them and
> spoke kindly to them. (Gen 50:16–21, emphasis added)

Joseph forgave his brothers! These are the same brothers who threw him into a pit and planned to kill him. The brothers who sold him into slavery. The brothers who told his father he was dead. The brothers who now needed help from Joseph, and if they did not receive help, they would die, and the entire family of Israel would die. Ironic? Yes. God's plan? Yes. You see, forgiveness of enemies is part of God's redemptive plan.

The principles from this story are numerous and varied, from "Do not be a brat" and "Do not show favoritism to your children" to "Be faithful wherever you find yourself" and "Do not give up on God's dreams for your life." However, the greatest principle to learn from this story is forgiveness. Joseph could have easily exacted revenge on his brothers, and no one would have blinked an eye. Except God. God's entire plan for humanity revolves around love and forgiveness. This story from the Old Testament holds up Joseph as a person who understood that God's plans and God's ways are not our ways. Joseph understood that he was not God. He realized that even though his brothers planned "evil against [him]; God planned it for good to bring about the present result—the survival of many people." What wisdom, what understanding, and what faith! Joseph could forgive his onetime enemies, who planned to kill him, because of the wisdom God gave him. We need this type of wisdom to love our enemies.

Love as Christ Loved

Spiritual formation is about love. It is the process of becoming more like Christ, who is the personification of love. "Therefore, be imitators of God, as dearly loved children, and walk in love, as Christ also loved us and gave himself for us, a sacrificial and fragrant offering to God" (Eph 5:1–2). The goal of spiritual formation is that we would love as Christ loved—that we would love God with all of our heart, soul, and mind like Jesus did; that we would love another and serve our brothers and sisters like Jesus; and that we would love our neighbors to the point of willingness to take their punishment like Jesus. Hear Paul's love for the Jewish people: "For I could wish that I myself were cursed and cut off from Christ for the benefit of my brothers and sisters, my own flesh and blood" (Rom 9:3).

The love God wants to create in us enables us to love like Christ. It makes us willing to love our enemies as God has loved us. "But God proves his own love for us in that while we were still sinners, Christ died for us" (Rom 5:8). To understand God's love, we look to the cross, and we understand that God loved us when we were his enemies. In addition, Jesus, from the cross, said, "Father, forgive them, because they do not know what they are doing" (Luke 23:34). The world rarely sees this type of love, and when it catches glimpses of this love, it is in awe. This type of love is not of this earth. This type of love is most clearly seen in the plan of God and the mission of Jesus. Earlier Jesus had said, "No one has greater love than this: to lay down his life for his friends. You are my friends if you do what I command you" (John 15:13–14). Jesus laid down his life for us when we were in rebellion against his kingdom. Jesus,

> who, existing in the form of God,
> did not consider equality with God
> as something to be exploited.
> Instead he emptied himself
> by assuming the form of a servant,
> taking on the likeness of humanity.
> And when he had come as a man,
> he humbled himself by becoming obedient
> to the point of death—
> even to death on a cross. (Phil 2:6–8)

Jesus is our example of how to love. Joseph is a type of Jesus. He became a slave to save his people from death. Jesus became a slave to save humanity. Joseph forgave his brothers who were his enemies. Jesus forgave us "while we were still sinners." Loving and forgiving our enemies has redemptive power. If someone is your enemy, can you lay down your emotions and begin to love them as Christ loves them? Being spiritually formed means we will walk in the power of the Spirit of Christ, and the Spirit will enable us to do things humanly impossible like loving our enemies. Don't try to love your enemies without the power of Christ flowing in and through your life.

Where does this otherworldly love start? It starts with believing in God's love for us.

> For God loved the world in this way: He gave his one and only Son, so that everyone who believes in him will not perish but have eternal life. For God did not send his Son into the world to condemn the world, but to save the world through him. Anyone who believes in him is not condemned, but anyone who does not believe is already condemned, because he has not believed in the name of the one and only Son of God. (John 3:16–18)

Our ability to love enemies grows as we grow in love. Listen to Paul again, "Now the goal of our instruction is love that comes from a pure heart, a good conscience, and a sincere faith" (1 Tim 1:5). And Paul told the Corinthians,

Love is patient, love is kind.
Love does not envy,
is not boastful, is not arrogant,
is not rude,
is not self-seeking, is not irritable,
and does not keep a record of wrongs.
Love finds no joy in unrighteousness
but rejoices in the truth.
It bears all things, believes all things,
hopes all things, endures all things. (1 Cor 13:4–7)

Controlled and Empowered by the Spirit

When we grow in Christ, we are controlled by the Spirit of God, and the fruit of the Spirit begins to shine through. "But the fruit of the Spirit is love, joy, peace, patience, kindness, goodness, faithfulness, gentleness, and self-control. The law is not against such things. Now those who belong to Christ Jesus have crucified the flesh with its passions and desires. If we live by the Spirit, let us also keep in step with the Spirit" (Gal 5:22–25). When we are Spirit controlled, we will love everyone as Christ loves us (see chapter 9). When the Spirit does not control us, we have this type of fruit: "hatreds, strife, jealousy, outbursts of anger, selfish ambitions, dissensions, factions, envy" (Gal 5:20–21). Notice that it says "hatreds," plural. The old flesh keeps and holds grudges. Look around and notice that where there is strife and jealousy, there also are outbursts of anger. And where selfish ambitions, dissensions, and factions rule, envy is also present. Walking in the way of Christ is walking in and through the power of the Spirit. We cannot love our enemies in the power of our old flesh. Consider John Piper on this matter:

> Our only hope for loving our enemy is to be a new creation in Christ. And our only hope for being a new creation in Christ is to be reconciled to God through the death of his Son. "If anyone is in Christ, he is a *new creation*. The old has passed away; behold, the new has come. All this is from God, who through Christ *reconciled* us to himself" (2 Cor 5:17–18).
>
> The only hope that we might love our enemy is that God loved us when we were his enemy. "If while we were enemies we were reconciled to God by the death of his Son, much more, now that we are reconciled, shall we be saved by his life" (Rom 5:10). This is the great root of the good tree we are becoming: "Forgive one another, *as God in Christ forgave you*" (Eph 4:32).[1]

Spiritual formation is following the life and teachings of Jesus in the power of the Spirit. Listen to the words of Jesus concerning the spiritual challenge of loving our enemies from the Sermon on the Mount:

> You have heard that it was said, Love your neighbor and hate your enemy. But I tell you, love your enemies and pray for those who persecute you, so that you may be children of your Father in heaven. For he causes his sun to rise on the evil and the good, and sends rain on the righteous and the unrighteous. For if you love those who love you, what reward will you have? Don't even the tax collectors do the same? And if you greet only your brothers and sisters, what are you doing out of the ordinary? Don't even the Gentiles do the same? Be perfect, therefore, as your heavenly Father is perfect. (Matt 5:43–48)

Love your enemies! Pray for those who persecute you! Loving others, including our enemies, is proof that we are sons and daughters of our Father in heaven. These are radical concepts from a radical way of love. Paul instructed the church at Rome in these matters:

> Do not repay anyone evil for evil. Give careful thought to do what is honorable in everyone's eyes. If possible, as far as it depends on you, live at peace with everyone. Friends, do not avenge yourselves; instead, leave room for God's wrath, because it is written, Vengeance belongs to me; I will repay, says the Lord. But if your enemy is hungry, feed him. If he is thirsty, give him something to drink. For in so doing you will be heaping fiery coals on his head. Do not be conquered by evil, but conquer evil with good. (Rom 12:17–21)

Paul had already given the foundation for obeying Christ and becoming sons of God: "So then, brothers and sisters, we are not obligated to the flesh to live according to the flesh, because if you live according to the flesh, you are going to die. But if by the Spirit you put to death the deeds of the body, you will live. For all those led by God's Spirit are God's sons" (Rom 8:12–14). If we follow the desires of the flesh, we will not and cannot love our enemies. However, if we walk in the power of God's Spirit, the Spirit of Christ, we will really live. Loving our enemies is proof positive that we are sons of God. As we love our enemies through the power of the Spirit of Christ, someone may see Christ and want to know more about this God of love. Follow the example of Joseph and the example of Jesus and love your enemies. Let them experience the love of Christ.

⎯ Quotes to Consider ⎯

*"If you take the 'love your enemy' out of Christianity,
you've 'unChristianed' the Christian faith."*

—Miroslav Volf[2]

*"You never so touch the ocean of God's love as
when you forgive and love your enemies."*

—Corrie ten Boom[3]

⎯ Questions to Ponder ⎯

1. Are you holding a grudge against anyone?
2. Based on the example of Joseph and the teachings of Christ, what is the Holy Spirit prompting you to do?
3. How could loving our enemies help lead others to faith in Christ?

Notes

1. John Piper, "Love Your Enemies," Desiring God, accessed February 28, 2018, https://document.desiringgod.org/love-your-enemies-en.pdf?ts=1446647825, emphasis in the original.

2. Miroslav Volf, "Inspiring Quotes," accessed March 16, 2018, https://www.inspiringquotes.us/author/9910-miroslav-volf/page:2.

3. Martin H. Manser, ed., *The Westminster Collection of Christian Quotations* (Louisville: Westminster John Knox Press, 2001), 90.

Conclusion

In this book, Rod and I have told how the process of spiritual formation has worked in our lives. But please understand that the principles and practices shared in this book have also helped many others.

Let me tell you about my friend Scott. When I met him six years ago, he was busy, yet bored, working as a security guard at a casino in Las Vegas. By his own admission, he was going nowhere spiritually.

But after getting involved in the church we started in Las Vegas, his spiritual passion was ignited. He started to take spiritual formation seriously. Over the next couple of years, I saw Scott practice all the disciplines and apply all the principles we have discussed in this book. The change in him was evident and contagious.

His wife, Krystal, caught his fire and became a bright light on her job. Their three daughters were saved and became shining witnesses in their school.

Soon, Scott and Krystal were leading a life group that was making a huge difference in the lives of a dozen adults. Then Scott started an after-school Good News Club that was impacting spiritually lost children with the gospel. Next he led a youth group that reached many radically unchurched teenagers.

We not only put him on our staff, but we also ordained him for the ministry. The reason was his practical wisdom and Christlike character. Today the five members of the family are serving the Lord in South Africa as missionaries.

Humanly speaking, none of this would have happened if Scott had not committed himself to spiritual formation.

Your Turn

We want to congratulate you for making it to the end of this book. You have completed an overview of spiritual formation and have learned the primary principles, philosophy, and practices that will help you enjoy a lifetime of spiritual health and growth. You have been stretched in your thinking regarding your relationship with God, your relationship with other followers of Jesus, and outwardly to those who do not yet know Jesus.

We would like to ask you to do one more thing:

Apply what you have learned.

Pastor James was adamant about the importance of application.

> But be doers of the word and not hearers only, deceiving yourselves. Because if anyone is a hearer of the word and not a doer, he is like someone looking at his own face in a mirror. For he looks at himself, goes away, and immediately forgets what kind of person he was. But the one who looks intently into the perfect law of freedom and perseveres in it, and is not a forgetful hearer but a doer who works—this person will be blessed in what he does. (Jas 1:22–25)

Jesus was also serious about his hearers applying what they had learned.

> Not everyone who says to me, "Lord, Lord," will enter the kingdom of heaven, but only the one who does the will of my Father in heaven. (Matt 7:21)

— Final Questions —

1. What area of your spiritual life needs the most work?
2. What spiritual principles and practices will you apply to see transformation in this area?

Appendix:
Spiritual Formation and Growth Group Assessments

Rod Dempsey

We hope you are following the suggestion in the introduction and are just starting this book. You are willing to grow in your love for God, for other believers, and for your neighbors. Go ahead and take the assessments, and identify some areas that need attention. Then begin the book.

Spiritual formation is the process of becoming more and more like Jesus in word, thought, attitude, and action. We become more like Jesus as we love God with our whole heart, love our brothers and sisters in the faith, and sacrificially love our neighbors. Jesus is the picture of supreme love. When we love God, love one another, and love our neighbors, we are following Jesus. This is the reason Paul told Timothy that "the goal of our instruction is love that comes from a pure heart, a good conscience, and a sincere faith" (1 Tim 1:5). As we grow in our love for God, for one another, and for our neighbor, the body of Christ becomes the visible witness of love to an unbelieving world. This book is about being spiritually formed to love like Christ.

This is a process God initiates at salvation and continues as we continue to walk in the ways of Christ. God has the primary role of acting and prompting us to act. We respond by obeying the Spirit and daily putting on the new man and daily putting off the old man. Every morning, the process starts over. The goal of this daily process is that we would love like Jesus: love God with our whole heart, like Jesus; love one another with our whole heart, like Jesus; and love our neighbor with our whole heart, like Jesus.

To aid in the process, we have developed two assessments. The first assessment is to measure an individual's progress as it relates to spiritual formation. The second assessment is to measure a church's or a group's progress as it relates to spiritual formation. The assessments are designed to measure the love level in the three primary areas: love for God, love for one another, and love for neighbor.

We encourage a person or a group to take the assessment and identify their weakest area first. Then identify the weakest sub-point in the weak area. Then put on some new habits or "put off" some old habits related to that facet of the weak area. We encourage a church or larger group to take a similar course of action. The goal would be to diagnose first and then prescribe some specific steps with accountability to make improvements in the weak area. Then continue on to the next-weakest area and so on and so on until the person or the group is making significant progress toward "work[ing] out [their] own salvation with fear and trembling" (Phil 2:12). When this happens, the individual, the group, and the church will see the invisible body of Christ becoming visible to a community, county, city, region, etc. When this is not happening, then the body of Christ is invisible to the world. We become the head, heart, and hands of Jesus as we love God, love one another, and love our neighbors.

Personal Spiritual Growth Assessment

On the left side of each statement, rate yourself on a scale from 1 to 10 (low to high).

Love for God (Up)

_____ 1. I am daily reading God's Word.

_____ 2. I am systematically memorizing God's Word.

_____ 3. I am writing out key passages and meditating on God's Word for application.

_____ 4. I have a daily prayer time and plan.

_____ 5. I have a dated prayer request list for people and requests.

_____ 6. I pray daily to be filled with the Holy Spirit.

_____ 7. I keep a journal and record how the Lord is at work in my life and around me.

_____ 8. I regularly practice fasting from food and other areas for my spiritual development.

_____ 9. I regularly disconnect from the world (including all media) and in solitude connect to Jesus.

_____ 10. I try daily to listen and follow the still small voice of Jesus.

Add up the section _____ and divide by 10 = _____

Love for One Another (In)

_____ 1. I meet weekly in a small group with other believers.

_____ 2. I have discovered my spiritual gift.

_____ 3. I am using my spiritual gift to build up others in the body of Christ.

_____ 4. I am daily praying for other believers.

_____ 5. I am guarding against the lust of the flesh, the lust of the eyes, and the pride of life.

_____ 6. I am confessing my faults, sins, and shortcomings to other believers.

_____ 7. I am not involved in gossip against other believers.

_____ 8. I am not holding a grudge or offense toward any person.

_____ 9. I regularly clear up/resolve hurts and offenses toward other believers.

_____ 10. I am daily praying with my family or for my family.

Add up the section _____ and divide by 10 = _____

Love for Our Neighbors (Out)

_____ 1. I have a prayer list for people who do not know Christ.

_____ 2. I am praying specific requests for their salvation.

_____ 3. I am seeking friendships and relationships with people who do not know Christ.

_____ 4. I am listening first to what they have to say.

_____ 5. I am planning for opportunities to eat with people who don't know Christ.

_____ 6. I am seeking to use my spiritual gift to serve others outside the body of Christ.

_____ 7. I am praying for opportunities to show and share the good news of the gospel.

_____ 8. I have prepared a simple explanation of the gospel to share with others as God opens the door.

_____ 9. I am seeking to become a blessing and serve the poor and under-resourced in my community.

_____ 10. I am seeking to build bridges with people who have hurt me and to love them like Christ.

Add up the section _____ and divide by 10 = _____

Overall Score

Add up the three sections _____ and divide by 3 for an overall score = _____

- Discuss: What is your strongest area?
- Discuss: What is your weakest area?
- Discuss: Plans for improvement?

Group Spiritual Growth Assessment

On the left side of each statement, rate your group score on a scale from 1 to 10 (low to high).

Love for God (Up)

____ 1. Allegiance to Christ is the priority in our group.

____ 2. Going, baptizing, and teaching people to obey Christ is our goal.

____ 3. New believers in our group are growing in their ability to surrender and sacrifice for the kingdom.

____ 4. The "whole counsel of God" (grand narrative) is being explained and illustrated in our group.

____ 5. A majority of the saints have daily quiet times. What is the percentage? _____

____ 6. A majority of the saints are praying and listening daily for the voice of Christ. What is the percentage? _____

____ 7. Believers are consistently seeking to be controlled by the Holy Spirit.

____ 8. The Spirit of God is leading the church through the members and leaders of the body.

____ 9. Believers are eager and willingly investing their financial resources in the kingdom of God.

____ 10. Worship occurs at the individual level, and it is powerfully manifested when the body gathers together.

Add up the section _____ and divide by 10 = _____

Love for One Another (In)

_____ 1. New believers are intentionally and individually nurtured and developed.

_____ 2. The saints are growing in maturity in community (i.e., connecting to Jesus through the disciplines).

_____ 3. The saints are growing in unity and love for one another.

_____ 4. The saints are encouraged to discover their spiritual gifts in community and use their gifts.

_____ 5. A majority of the saints spend time with one another outside the official group meetings. What is the percentage? _____

_____ 6. A majority of the saints are using their gifts properly (according to God's design). What is the percentage? _____

_____ 7. Leaders see their role as equipping and empowering the saints.

_____ 8. Leaders are being developed through the discipleship process.

_____ 9. Families are being discipled by fathers and mothers in the body.

_____ 10. Restoration of other believers is done with grace and truth (church discipline is practiced).

Add up the section _____ and divide by 10 = _____

Love for Our Neighbors (Out)

_____ 1. Passionate prayer is continually being offered up for the lost and for laborers.

_____ 2. A majority of the group members have developed a mission field and strategy. What is the percentage? _____

_____ 3. The group is creating partnerships with other like-minded groups/agencies.

_____ 4. The gospel is being proclaimed in word and action by the members of the body.

_____ 5. The poor and "least of these" are intentionally being served and helped through the members of the body of Christ.

_____ 6. Areas of the city are being intentionally occupied by ambassadors of Christ.

_____ 7. The body of Christ (hands and feet of Jesus) is visible to the community.

_____ 8. The group is working with other churches to create a gospel net within a community (connecting the loops).

_____ 9. New churches are emerging in the community in response to the group's work.

_____ 10. The mission of Christ is being accomplished locally, regionally, nationally, and globally by members from within the local body.

   Add up the section _____ and divide by 10 = _____

Overall Score

Add up the three sections _____ and divide by 3 for an overall score = _____

- Discuss: What is your strongest area?
- Discuss: What is your weakest area?
- Discuss: Plans for improvement?

Scripture Index